LISBOA · 25 DE MAIO DE · 1967 · CELTIC 2-1 INTER · 50° CELTIC FC · ANIVERSARIO

50th ANNIVERSARY *of* LISBON
C E L T I C   F O O T B A L L   C L U B

Written by Paul Cuddihy | Foreword by Brendan Rodgers

'WE DID IT BY PLAYING FOOTBALL. PURE, BEAUTIFUL, INVENTIVE FOOTBALL.'
JOCK STEIN

CONTENTS

FOREWORD

FOREWORD

Celtic's European Cup success in Lisbon back in 1967 represents a triumph for a group of players who, against all the odds, shaped the history of a nation and a club. It is why, when I became manager of this football club, one of the first things I said was that the respect these guys should be given is that we fill the Lisbon Lions Stand. That's how much it meant to me that it was one of my first thoughts. From afar, when I was looking at Celtic, I could see that the stand wasn't being filled and, for me, it was something I felt didn't seem right, after everything that these legends had given to this club, that we had a stand named after them and then didn't fill it. So that's what the 1967 success means to me. It means great pride in the fact that this was the first group of players from Britain to win the European Cup, as it was known then, and set a precedent for British football going forward.

The thing that strikes you is that they were all local players, and I'm not sure that will ever be done again in modern football, where a group of players within a 30-mile radius of Celtic Park came together like a boys' club and took on the best in Europe, and won. It gives you great pride to understand their story and what their achievements were.

That success back in 1967 is imprinted on every supporter, absolutely, and especially now, when the modern era is all about the Champions League and who wins it, that star on your shirt – it's a real one, it's not of league titles, it's of being the best team in Europe, and that provides a great source of inspiration to everyone who works at the club. When you walk past the trophy at Celtic Park, or when I see John Clark, who I do most days at Lennoxtown, that gives me huge pride and is another great source of inspiration, because this is a guy who has won the European Cup, so I know I have to be good here because that's the level that these guys have set.

The biggest thing I find with the older generation of players, and especially the best ones, is their humility. I've had the great pleasure of getting to know John Clark, and I got a sense of energy when I met Bobby Lennox, and he still looks so well and bright. I also had the great pleasure at our first home league game of the season against Aberdeen of meeting Billy McNeill, and when you think of Billy picking up that European Cup trophy – my uncles always referred to him as Cesar – it's special, particularly because of everything they've given this club. But the biggest thing is their humility and how they approach their life and how humble they are, and it's a great lesson to us all in modern football.

As for the manager, Jock Stein was a wonderful innovator. When you go back to that era and when you listen and read clips and articles of what Jock and also the likes of Bill Shankly were talking about, these guys were way ahead of their time. Jock was a great innovator of the game and he really put in place the identity and the style which Celtic plays to this very day. So the ethos and philosophy of football he imprinted on the team back then is what served this club, and that was the beginning of Celtic being the club that it is and the style of football it looks to play, and for managers like me coming in, it's a great reference in terms of maintaining that way of working.

The Lisbon Lions are a great source of inspiration and, as a football club, we have to keep pushing on and creating new and great memories for the modern-day supporter, but while doing that, of course, you must never forget your past because the people from that era made this club great and it's our duty as supporters, players, coaches and managers to defend that history – and we defend that culture in the club's history.

The Lisbon Lions give you hope of what you can achieve. In the modern game it is very difficult, but we owe that respect to the players and the families of those who have sadly passed away, and also to the current players, for these guys to be held up as great symbols of what this club is and the qualities that we hold at this club now.

If we look at the three morals and values at this club that we work with the players now – respect, unity and excellence – this was a group of players who demonstrated those qualities and values all the way back then, and to this day we feel it's our duty to maintain that. I think the real quality of that Celtic team was the team – the spirit that they had, which was all cultivated by an inspirational manager.

Coming here, the job is to dominate Scottish football, and also to return and restore Celtic's name and the pride of Celtic back into Europe. And we've been able to do that as a football club, not just as a manager but as a club – supporters, staff, players – and we're really demonstrating the force that Celtic can be.

It's our duty to serve the supporters, to make them proud of their team and make them happy and smile every day because they support Celtic, and for all our fans around the world. So to be able to do that as the manager, to lead the team out in some of the most prestigious arenas in European football, I take great pride in that.

Brendan Rodgers
Manager, Celtic Football Club

September 2016

INTRODUCTION

INTRODUCTION

Where did it all begin? Is there a moment that can be identified as the genesis of Celtic's golden era of the 1960s and '70s under Jock Stein, a single event or decision that supporters can point to and say, 'That was when it started,' or, as is generally the case in football, was it a set of circumstances that, individually, could not have made the impact which, collectively, they did?

The rudiments of the story are remarkable in themselves; a team that finishes eighth in the Scottish league in 1965 is, within two years, the best team in Europe, having also collected five of the six major Scottish honours available in that same period. But how did that extraordinary turnaround in fortunes happen, and within such a short timescale?

Jock Stein's Celtic connections are absolutely vital to the story. It is difficult, if not impossible, to imagine what would have happened to the club and where it would be now if the decision hadn't been taken to engage him as manager to replace Jimmy McGrory in March 1965. That decision, made by chairman Robert Kelly and the Celtic board, is arguably the single best decision in the history of Celtic Football Club. That Kelly also relinquished the influence and control of the team which had previously been his prerogative was a key component in the success which followed, and enabled a group of highly-promising young footballers to fulfil their potential rather than flattering to deceive in the way that great Celts such as Charlie Tully, Bobby Evans, Willie Fernie, Neilly Mochan, Bertie Peacock, Bobby Collins and others did; not that it was their fault, given the way the club and the team was run in the pre-Jock Stein years, but if there had been no change in that aspect of Celtic's modus operandi, it's unlikely that Stein would have made the move from east to west, swapping the green and white shirts of Hibernian for the green and white Hoops of Celtic.

Stein had the advantage of being a former Celtic player, having been there between 1951 and '57, and then working as a reserve coach before moving into management with Dunfermline Athletic, so he knew what was wrong and what needed to change. The decision to bring him back, as a player, to Scotland from Welsh side Llanelli, had proved beneficial in the short-term, as he helped the team win the Coronation Cup in 1953 and the league and Scottish Cup double that subsequent season as captain. However, he would have endured his fair share of frustration at boardroom interference and control over team matters. Injury deprived Celtic of Stein's services from 1957 when he retired – he missed out on the famous 7-1 League Cup final victory over Rangers – and while that, too, was a blow to the player, it pushed him into coaching at the club, allowing him to develop some of the ideas which would later transform Celtic's fortunes, while making initial contact with the talented young players coming through the ranks of the club which, again, would later prove beneficial.

He moved to Dunfermline Athletic in 1960, to the disappointment of his young charges, but he was desperate to forge his own career in management. He did so in spectacular style, steering the Fife club to their first ever Scottish Cup success, ironically against Celtic. That would not have gone unnoticed by the powers-that-be at Celtic Park, though it would be a further four years before they made their move for their former captain. Interestingly, during his time at East End Park, Stein took a trip to Italy in 1963 along with Kilmarnock manager, Willie Waddell, to study the coaching methods of Inter Milan's Argentinian coach, Helenio Herrera, who was on the verge of leading the Italian side to consecutive European Cup triumphs in 1964 and '65. The student would soon out-think and out-smart the teacher.

While Jock Stein was building a reputation at Dunfermline, and subsequently at Hibernian, Celtic continued to languish in a mire of mediocrity, although behind the scenes, assistant manager Sean Fallon was acquiring a number of promising young players for Celtic, something which would later pay the richest of dividends; players such as Tommy Gemmell and Bobby Murdoch came through the ranks, joining the likes of Billy McNeill and John Clark, who'd arrived at Celtic while Jock Stein was still working with the reserves at Celtic Park, while Ronnie Simpson was bought from Hibernian – sold by Stein – and Bertie Auld returned from his sojourn in England. Sean Fallon might have had aspirations of becoming Celtic manager himself, but just as he relinquished the captaincy to Stein back in the 1950s, a decade on he again did what he believed was best for Celtic and accepted the role of assistant to his former team-mate; it was to become as good a managerial partnership as any football had seen before or has seen since.

In season 1964/65, Jock Stein was in charge of Hibernian, while Celtic were enduring another disappointing season. Behind the scenes at Celtic Park, there was an acceptance that things had to change. Whether that was due, in part, to a realisation that they would see an exodus of talent from the club if they didn't act isn't known, but it's highly likely that players such as Billy McNeill, who was being courted by some of England's top teams, would have headed off to pastures new, and where the Celtic captain led, others would undoubtedly have followed. Thankfully, Jock Stein arrived in the nick of time.

It was announced in January 1965 that Stein would be returning to Paradise, though it would be a further two months before he arrived. In that time, he steered Hibernian to the semi-final of the Scottish Cup, knocking out Rangers in the last eight of the competition, but he left the Easter Road club before their semi-final against Dunfermline Athletic, instead taking up his seat in the Celtic dugout to see his new charges beat Motherwell at the second time of asking to set up a final showdown with Dunfermline at Hampden.

By common consensus amongst the Celtic players of that time, the 1965 Scottish Cup triumph was one of the defining moments in that era. It gave the club its first major honour since 1957, and its first success in the competition in eleven years. It transformed a group of underachieving players into winners and reinforced Jock Stein's reputation as a man who won trophies. In that light, Billy McNeill's header with nine minutes of the match remaining, which gave the Hoops a 3-2 victory, has to be seen as one of the most important goals in the club's history. The majority of the 108,800 supporters in the national stadium on April 24 were Celtic supporters, well used by now to seeing the phrase 'long-suffering' put in front of their description. They celebrated the success against a very good Dunfermline side who twice led in the final with joy, relief – even disbelief – and looked forward to the following campaign in the hope that there would be an improvement on the team's league position.

The statistics of that time will be examined again later in this book, but they are so spectacular, it's worth mentioning them at every opportunity because they do, in as much as any statistics can, illustrate the stunning turnaround in Celtic's fortunes in the space of twelve months. There was little that Jock Stein could do to change the fortunes of the 1964/65 season, and in the nine games he was in charge up to the end of the season, the team won three games and lost five as the Hoops finished a lowly eighth in the table, winning a total of sixteen games, drawing five and losing thirteen, scoring seventy-six goals and conceding fifty-seven. The following season Celtic secured their first league title in twelve years, winning twenty-seven of their games, drawing three and losing just four, and in doing so they scored 106 goals and conceded just thirty.

That 1965/66 season the team also reached the semi-final of the Cup-Winners' Cup, losing 2-1 on aggregate to Liverpool. It was Celtic's second European semi-final, having previously reached the last four of the same competition in 1964 where they squandered a 3-0 first leg lead against MTK Budapest to lose 4-3 on aggregate. Both experiences ultimately proved beneficial when it came to the club's inaugural European Cup campaign; six Lions faced MTK in 1964 – Gemmell, Clark, McNeill, Johnstone, Murdoch and Chalmers – while two years later, the six players plus Ronnie Simpson, Bobby Lennox and Bertie Auld played over the two legs against Liverpool.

While the 1966/67 season was to prove the most successful in Celtic's history, it could not have come to pass without the achievements of the previous campaign, in particular winning the league title, because that provided the gateway to the European Cup. The league title was eventually secured on the last day of the season, with Bobby Lennox scoring the only goal of the game to beat Motherwell 1-0. It meant Celtic were champions, finishing two points clear of second-placed Rangers. The Hoops had actually lost the first derby that season, going down 2-1 at Ibrox in the third league game of the season, but the corresponding fixture at Celtic Park on January 3, 1966, proved to be a crucial game. Trailing 1-0 at half-time after losing a goal inside the first couple of minutes, Stein's men produced a stunning second-half display, scoring five goals without reply, including a Stevie Chalmers hat-trick. It was a breathtaking performance and was another clear sign that the balance of power was beginning to shift in Scottish football.

The league trophy duly secured after a tight title race, Celtic could now look forward to retaining that title while also having a first tilt at the European Cup but, before that all-conquering 1966/67 campaign got underway, Jock Stein took his squad to North America for a close season tour between May 12 and June 12. They played games in Bermuda, the United States and Canada – eleven in total – and remained unbeaten through the tour, winning eight of the eleven games, drawing the other three, and scoring a total of forty-seven goals, conceding just six. The opposition varied throughout the tour, ranging from Tottenham Hotspur (three times), Bayern Munich and Bologna, to Bermuda YMCA and New Jersey All-Stars, as well as games against St Louis CYM All-Stars, Atlas, Bermuda and a Hamilton Primo XI. More than the results or number of goals scored, however, was the sense of camaraderie that was fostered during that time away, and which the players subsequently cited as a key factor in their sense of togetherness which stood them in good stead throughout the season. And just to prove that the tour had been beneficial, the Hoops beat Manchester United 4-1 at the start of August in a pre-season friendly at Celtic Park.

Celtic won their first eight league games, scoring thirty-three goals and conceding seven, before they dropped their first points of the season when they drew 1-1 in a match against St Mirren on November 5, though they were without their inspirational captain, Billy McNeill, while Bobby Murdoch was sent off. By that time, the League Cup had already been won, with Celtic winning all ten of their fixtures in the competition, including a 1-0 victory over Rangers in the final at Hampden, courtesy of a Bobby Lennox goal on 19 minutes. Two days after the St Mirren game, Jock Stein's side won the Glasgow Cup with a 4-0 win over Partick Thistle, Lennox hitting a hat-trick and Stevie Chalmers also scoring. Stein's team was acquiring a winning habit.

The European Cup campaign had already kicked off, with FC Zurich (5-0 on aggregate) and Nantes (6-2 on aggregate) both defeated before Christmas. It meant that the Hoops could look forward to a quarter-final clash with Yugoslavian champions, Vojvodina Novi Sad, although they ended 1966 with a 3-2 loss against Dundee United at Tannadice, the team's first defeat of the season. Jim Craig came in at right-back for the following game, and two weeks later, on January 14, 1967, the men who would shortly become known as the Lisbon Lions took to the field as a starting XI for the first time, in front of 19,000 fans at Muirton Park against St Johnstone. They duly won the match 4-0, the goals coming from Stevie Chalmers, Bobby Lennox and a double from Jimmy Johnstone; it was a winning start for what would become a legendary line-up.

By that stage in the campaign, Celtic were having to do without the services of their top goalscorer, Joe McBride, who suffered a knee injury following a 1-1 draw against Aberdeen at Pittodrie on Christmas Eve. The striker wouldn't play another competitive match that season, yet still ended the season with 35 goals to his name. It is one of football's great imponderables as to what Jock Stein would have done had Joe McBride been available for selection up to and including the European Cup final in May. It seems highly likely that McBride would have played, given his potency in front of goal, yet if he had, who would have missed out? We shall never know, of course, and any personnel change would have affected and possibly altered the whole season, not just the European Cup final, so the speculation will be never-ending. The reality was that, even without the prolific McBride, the Hoops continued to sweep all before them, with the exception, somewhat strangely, of Dundee United, who recorded the double over Stein's Celts with another 3-2 league win, this time at Celtic Park at the beginning of May; indeed the only other team they lost to in a competitive match that season was Vojvodina in the first-leg of the quarter-final clash (1-0 in Yugoslavia), while there was also a 1-0 friendly defeat against another Yugoslav team, Dinamo Zagreb.

Two goals from Willie Wallace, who'd arrived at Celtic Park from Hearts at the beginning of December 1966, gave Celtic a 2-0 victory at Hampden over Aberdeen to lift the Scottish Cup, and a 2-2 draw at Ibrox, when Jimmy Johnstone scored both goals in front of the watchful eye of Inter Milan coach, Helenio Herrera, secured a second consecutive title. Having swept all before them in Scotland, Celtic could now focus on the European Cup final, which they'd reached by virtue of a 3-1 aggregate victory over Dukla Prague in the semi-final. It was the first time that a British team had reached this showpiece football final, which represented a major achievement in itself, but Jock Stein and his charges were not just content to go there and make up the numbers. They were going to the Estadio Nacional on May 25, 1967 to win the European Cup.

Given Inter Milan's European pedigree, having won the competition in 1964 and '65, and then knocking out holders, Real Madrid, at the quarter-final stage on their way to the showdown with Celtic, it's no surprise that the Italians were favourites to lift the trophy for a third time in their history, though it could be argued that this helped the Celtic squad, who arrived in the Portuguese capital in a confident but relaxed frame of mind. With the benefit of hindsight, particularly when considering and comparing the two European Cup final appearances of 1967 and '70, the contrasting preparations are often seen as pivotal; the relaxed, almost naïve way the team approached the final in Lisbon is seen in marked contrast to the more cautious build-up to the 1970 final against Feyenoord in the San Siro Stadium, with the former leading to success against Inter Milan while the latter saw the Dutch side triumph.

The fairytale quality of the Celtic story that Billy McNeill often referred to was never more apparent than on May 25, 1967 when a group of young men all born within a 30-mile radius of Celtic Park defeated arguably the best club side in the world at that time to become the champions of Europe. It was a remarkable triumph for those players and their manager, given where the team had been just two years previously. It was an even more remarkable success for a club founded by Irish immigrants to raise money to help alleviate poverty amongst the poor and unemployed in the East End of Glasgow. The club remained rooted in that area of the city, proud of where it had come from and prouder still of where it had journeyed to. Nearly eighty years after the meeting in St Mary's Church hall in the Calton district of Glasgow which formally constituted Celtic Football Club, Brother Walfrid's team were the best in Europe.

The story of that incredible 1966/67 season is familiar to many but it's one that Celtic supporters never tire of re-living; the games, the goals, the glory and the glimpse behind-the-scenes amongst a group of players who became more than a team. They were a band of brothers. It was to be the pinnacle of the golden era under Jock Stein and a benchmark which every subsequent Celtic team and manager has striven to match or surpass.

The underdogs from the East End of Glasgow may have conceded an early goal to the aristocrats of Italian football – a penalty kick converted after just seven minutes by Inter legend, Sandro Mazzola – but it did not deflate or deter them, as their opponents had hoped. Instead, it merely drove them on in search of the victory which seemed to be pre-ordained. That it took until the sixty-second minute to equalise, a thunderous strike from left-back, Tommy Gemmell, did not lessen the belief amongst Jock Stein's side, and if Inter Milan felt they had been trying to stem an irresistible tide of Celtic attacks before that goal, for many of the Italian side, that equalising goal was a sign that they were not going to enjoy a third European Cup success, and while they continued to battle as any top professionals always do, there was an inevitability about Celtic's second, and winning goal, which came from the boot of Stevie Chalmers with just five minutes of the match remaining.

The celebrations in Lisbon's Estadio Nacional when West German referee, Kurt Tschenscher's whistle sounded to bring the game to an end were joyous, thousands of Celtic fans who had made the trip to the Portuguese capital flooding on to the pitch, while around the world, many thousands more celebrated with an equal sense of joy and disbelief; the welcome the team received at Celtic Park the evening after the final another unforgettable occasion. The triumph was, first and foremost, a Celtic one, though it also allowed Scottish football to bask in the glow of the champions' success.

It was also a victory for entertaining, attacking football, which had defeated the cautious, defensive philosophy which Inter Milan embodied. It's no coincidence that the emergence of Feyenoord and, more significantly, Ajax, along with the Netherlands national side in the early 1970s, employing a style of play that became known as 'total football', came in the wake of Celtic's 1967 European Cup triumph.

Where did it all begin? Is there a moment that can be identified as the genesis of Celtic's golden era of the 1960s and '70s under Jock Stein? Perhaps it goes all the way back to November 6, 1887 when the founding fathers declared that 'a football club will be formed for the maintenance of dinner tables for the children and the unemployed.' Those origins, unique in the world of football, set Celtic Football Club on a course that would see them be leaders on and off the field for nearly one hundred and thirty years. That they became the first club from northern Europe to win the European Cup is remarkable, but within the Celtic story, shouldn't be seen as a surprise. And it remains, fifty years later, something to savour and be proud of. It truly is a grand old team to play for and a grand old team to see.

LISBOA
25 DE MAIO DE
1967
CELTIC 2-1 INTER
50° CELTIC FC ANIVERSARIO

FC ZURICH

FC ZURICH

Celtic's first ever opponents in the European Cup might have been a part-time team, but victory over FC Zurich and progression to the second round of the competition was not a foregone conclusion. The Swiss league and cup holders were now under the charge of Barcelona's legendary Hungarian forward, Ladislav Kubala, who had been appointed player/coach in the summer of 1966. It was not their first foray into the European Cup either. Indeed, in the 1963/64 season they had reached the semi-final before losing 8-1 on aggregate to Read Madrid.

Celtic, however, were more experienced in terms of European football, despite this being their first appearance in the continent's premier club competition. Season 1966/67 was their fifth European campaign, a period which had included two semi-final appearances in the Cup-Winners' Cup, although it was only with their first Scottish league championship success in twelve years the previous season that they were granted entry to the elevated company of fellow champions. The draw which paired them with the Swiss champions was also the first time that Celtic played their opening match of a European tournament at home. The club, however, were keen to dampen down the dismissive reaction of many observers in the Scottish media that the tie was a formality, as the *Celtic View* of July 13, 1966 revealed:

'...Celtic directors and manager are most surprised that they have, according to a section of the press, 'an easy match'. They and the players will treat Zurich as they deserve to be treated – as the champions of their country. Indeed, Celtic prefer to think they will have a difficult match … No, Zurich will not be easy – as least not as far as Celtic, who have to play them, are concerned.'

The first leg at Celtic Park was not scheduled until Wednesday, September 28, and in the intervening period, Jock Stein's side played eleven domestic games – three in the league and eight in the League Cup – winning them all, scoring thirty-nine goals and conceding just eight. It meant a place in the semi-final of the League Cup, while it also represented an impressive start to the defence of the title. The three league wins had included a 2-0 derby triumph over Rangers at Celtic Park, the goals coming from Bertie Auld and Bobby Murdoch in a blistering opening four minutes. In the League Cup section, meanwhile, Joe McBride scored thirteen of Celtic's twenty-three goals in their six wins, a portent of the striker's form in the first half of the season.

The club registered a squad of twenty-five players for the first round tie with FC Zurich, which included four goalkeepers. The Celtic squad was: Fallon, Kennedy, Martin, Simpson; Craig, Gemmell, Halpin, McCarron, O'Neill; Brogan, Cattanach, Clark, Cushley, McNeill, Murdoch; Auld, Chalmers, Connelly, Gallagher, Hughes, Johnstone, Lennox, McBride, Quinn, Taylor. Explaining the make-up of the squad in the *Celtic View*, the club stated:

'It will be noted that all four goalkeepers on the staff have been included. This may seem an unnecessary luxury, but the management are taking absolutely no risks. The first of the games with Zurich is more than a month ahead. A lot can happen in that time, especially as in the interval, Celtic will have an average of three matches per week to play (League Cup or league championship or Glasgow Cup, Reserve League Cup, or reserve league, and Combined Reserve League).'

Celtic faced a trip to Dundee on the Saturday before their inaugural European Cup tie, and it was the home side who took the lead just before the half-hour mark. However, Bobby Lennox equalised soon after, and Stevie Chalmers netted the winner with twelve minutes of the match remaining. It was another two points for Stein's side, although the main talking point from that game was the knee injury suffered by McBride, which saw him replaced by Chalmers. Given the former's proficiency in front of goal since the beginning of the season, his absence would represent a blow for Jock Stein ahead of an important European game, although if he wasn't able to call upon McBride's services, there was still an abundance of striking talent in the squad, with Lennox, Chalmers and John Hughes able to lead the line, while the likes of Jimmy Johnstone and Charlie Gallagher could provide creativity, and goals from the flanks. In the event, McBride came through a couple of training sessions unscathed, and so Stein was able to choose from his full complement of strikers.

The Celtic manager's pre-match observations in the *Celtic View*, published on the day of the game, echoed the cautious note that had previously been voiced in the club newspaper. Stein wrote:

'Now it is our first-ever venture in the European Cup. Our visitors from Switzerland come as league champions and cup holders in their own country. Let no-one forget that. We shall treat Zurich as national champions and with the respect they deserve. Contrary to the ideas of some, we shall approach tonight's game in the belief that it could be difficult for us … We look forward to the match and go into it with the aim of building a lead to stand us in good stead for the return game next week.'

Supporters were also reminded that the kick-off for the European Cup tie at Celtic Park was 7.30pm, as opposed to 8pm, which had previously been agreed by Glasgow police and the magistrates, the SFA and Scottish League as the kick-off time for important midweek games. This was due to FC Zurich's wish to travel back to Switzerland immediately after the match, and although they later changed their plans, it was too late to move the kick-off time.

An impressive crowd of 50,000 packed into the stadium under the floodlight pylons which lit up the East End of Glasgow sky as a Celtic starting XI of Simpson, Gemmell, O'Neill, Murdoch, McNeill, Clark, Johnstone, McBride, Chalmers, Auld and Hughes lined up against their Swiss opponents for the club's first ever European Cup tie. Tommy Gemmell, who would make a telling contribution throughout the campaign, culminating in a blistering equaliser in the Estadio Nacional on May 25, 1967, was in the right-back position, while Willie O'Neill occupied the left-back berth. Jock Stein had delayed naming his team ahead of the game, citing numerous factors he had to take into consideration such as the weather, the condition of the pitch and how wet or dry the grass was, but it was undoubtedly another facet of Stein's character as a master tactician and the master of mind games that he wished to keep his cards close to his chest.

Eight of the team that would walk out into the Lisbon sunshine just eight months later to face Inter Milan in the European Cup final took to the field against FC Zurich, though neither they nor any of the Celtic supporters that September night could have imagined such a scenario at the time; only Jim Craig, Bobby Lennox and Willie Wallace, who wouldn't arrive at Celtic Park until the start of December, missed out.

Whatever high hopes might have been held, if not for the whole European campaign, at least for the game against FC Zurich, were almost undone in the opening exchanges when the Swiss side nearly grabbed the opening goal of the tie. They surged forward and their Italian forward, Rosario Martinelli, found himself bearing in on goal. Celtic's goalkeeper, Ronnie Simpson, recalled the incident in his 1967 autobiography, *Sure It's A Grand Old Team To Play For*:

'... I probably had my best save of the European Cup competition in the opening minutes! Zurich's Italian inside-forward Martinelli came through fast and hit a shot at my goal which swerved in flight. I had to change direction as I went for the shot and was fortunate enough to get one hand to the shot and save it.'

It may have given the Celtic players a fright, but what they found more difficult to cope with throughout the ninety minutes was the tactics employed by the Zurich players. Kubala, their manager, had dismissed his own side's chances ahead of the first game, and while some observers saw that as mind games on the part of the Zurich manager, the robust manner in which his team played suggested that he was astute enough to realise that he couldn't beat Stein's Celtic in a straightforward game of football. Their approach was defensive, their challenges often illegal, their incessant time-wasting frustrating, and the evidence of a goal-less first-half suggested that those tactics were bearing fruit.

A Celtic team which had started the season producing free-flowing football and scoring goals for fun, suddenly found it hard to reproduce that style and they couldn't penetrate the Swiss defence. Celtic's cause was hindered, while Zurich's was helped, by the Danish referee, Frede Hansen, whose control of the game remained fragile throughout the ninety minutes, allowing the Swiss players an unacceptable degree of latitude in their tackling, and even in the last breath of the contest, he continued to play a pivotal, and controversial part in proceedings.

Half-time came with the 50,000 crowd still waiting for a goal. The second-half, however, saw an upturn in Celtic's fortunes, and two goals as reward for their efforts. The honour of Celtic's first ever European Cup goal fell to Tommy Gemmell, who picked up a pass from John Clark, strode forward and from over thirty yards out hit a powerful shot which crashed in off the underside the crossbar, leaving Zurich goalkeeper, Otmar Iten, with no chance. The goal galvanised Celtic, who pushed forward in search of a second, roared on by the supporters. Within five minutes, they doubled their lead. Joe McBride, who had missed a couple of chances earlier in the game, fired home a shot from the edge of the box following an interchange of passes with Bertie Auld that saw the midfielder set up his striking team-mate with an impetuous back-heel which fooled the Zurich defenders.

The result could have been even better for Celtic when McBride appeared to score in the dying seconds of the match. The striker headed home a cross from close-range, but it was ruled out by the Danish referee who explained that he'd already blown his whistle for full-time, which could only have happened when the ball was in mid-flight towards the Zurich goal. It capped an incompetent refereeing display while also ensuring that the Swiss champions remained in the tie; the loss of another goal ahead of the return leg would have delivered a fatal blow to their aspirations of a comeback. As it was, they retained a glimmer of hope, feint though that was.

The *Celtic View* was still in its infancy at that time, having only started in August 1965, and was then a four-page newspaper. Even so, there was a surprising lack of information about the 2-0 victory over FC Zurich in the pages of the club publication. Indeed, the most eye-catching article in the *View* of October 5 was a less-than subtle rebuke to those supporters who had ignored the previous warnings regarding the kick-off time.

'Last Wednesday night the kick-off at Celtic Park had to be delayed because several thousands of people were queuing for admission at the advertised time of start, 7.30pm – and this despite the much-publicised request of the club that spectators should try to come earlier to matches.

'It is reckoned that not more than 5,000 of the attendance of 50,000 for the match with Zurich caused the start to be delayed and that 45,000 were inside comfortably before

7.30. As in the past, the great majority of the 'fans' are being put to inconvenience for the sake of a small minority.

'Celtic will have liaison with the police in all matches to come about the advisability of delaying the kick-off, but the club will press for starting at the advertised time except in the most exceptional circumstances. Celtic feel that not only are spectators being made to suffer by latecomers, but that the players and the officials who have to control the match are having unnecessary tension inflicted on them.'

The 2-0 victory – which should have been 3-0 but for the eccentric decision of Mr Hansen to disallow McBride's goal – saw Celtic's European Cup campaign off to a winning start, although work still remained to be done the following week in Switzerland to ensure progress to the next round of the competition. The victory also maintained an impressive Celtic record. It meant that the Hoops remained unbeaten at home in a European tie, while also ensuring a home clean sheet run that stretched all the way back to the club's first ever European tie, against Valencia in the Fairs-Cities Cup in 1962. Indeed, the Spanish side's two goals to secure a 2-2 draw in that game were the only two, to date, that Celtic had conceded at home in European competition, during which time they had scored twenty-six goals without reply.

Jock Stein might have been reticent ahead of the game of appearing over-confident. His comments ahead of the second leg, however, showed the confidence he had in his team, and perhaps also a touch of annoyance at the tactics FC Zurich had opted to employ at Celtic Park. Writing in the *Celtic View* on the day of the game in Switzerland, the Celtic manager stated:

'Many of us will not forget for a long time the first match which the club played in the European Cup. Officials, players and supporters of Celtic are in agreement that the match with Zurich at Celtic Park was played in an atmosphere completely different from that of any other game in which we have taken part. Perhaps the early fright which the team had when they almost lost a first-minute goal, perhaps the fact that for once in a while they did not take an early lead filled the Celtic players with apprehension.

'At any rate, they did not play with the gay abandon of almost all of their games this season. So the supporters did not get the same chance to applaud and cheer. Then, of course, the continual infringing of the rules by the Swiss team and the later retaliatory fouls by Celtic players, spoiled the match as a real football spectacle. No doubt the further we go the more unpleasant experiences we shall have in the European Cup, the most important club tournament in Europe.

'I've always had mixed views about the advantage (so-called) of playing the first game of a double-barrelled tie at home. The game with Zurich has convinced me that a great case can be made out for playing the first match on the opposition's ground – so much so, that we shall give serious consideration to the European rule which says that a club that has had two successive ties at home for the first leg is permitted to ask for the third game to be played first on the opponent's ground. I am sure now that I prefer the first game away and the second to be on our own ground before our own fans.

'Irrespective of how we fare tonight in Zurich, we shall not meet a rougher or more defensively-minded team than the Swiss side. When I saw them some weeks ago play in their own city, their club officials were concerned that the game would be a good sporting one. No-one who was at Celtic Park a week ago saw such a game. The fact is that a team composed of supposed semi-amateurs displayed more of the shady tricks of the game than any other side we've faced.

'Without being boastful, I am quite confident that the goals we scored at Celtic Park will be enough to take us through to the next round. We won't change our style of play much, but if they want to try to reach the next round they will have to do so drastically. Then we shall see our quick-thrusting forwards getting their opportunity to show their real goalscoring ability.'

The second leg of the European Cup first round tie saw Celtic travel to Switzerland for the second time, having previously faced FC Basel in the 1963/64 Cup-Winners' Cup first round. That tie had seen the Hoops win the first leg 5-1 in Switzerland, completing the job in Glasgow with a 5-0 victory. Six of the side who played in Basel back in September 1963 took to the field just over three years later in Zurich – Tommy Gemmell, Billy McNeill, John Clark, Bobby Lennox, Stevie Chalmers and John Hughes – and while the margin of victory might not have been as hefty this time around, Celtic's dominance on the pitch was again comprehensive.

Stein's pre-match confidence was certainly not misplaced and having recorded a 6-1 victory over St Johnstone in a home league match the Saturday prior to the match in Switzerland, with Jimmy Johnstone, Bobby Lennox and Joe McBride all scoring two goals apiece, the confidence of the manager was replicated amongst the players. The only change to the team which dismantled St Johnstone was the inclusion of Stevie Chalmers at the expense of Joe McBride, the Celtic boss hoping that the pace of Lennox and Chalmers would trouble the Zurich defence. In the event, that's exactly what happened, with latter getting on the scoresheet in a comfortable 3-0 victory.

The date of the game, October 5, was also notable for being Jock Stein's 44th birthday, and it was reported that part of his pre-match pep talk included a birthday plea – 'Give me an early goal and I will be happy for the rest of the year!' That early goal came on twenty-two minutes when Tommy Gemmell scored a near replica of his Celtic Park strike, picking up the ball on the halfway line, striding forward and unleashing a powerful shot from thirty yards that, once again, Otmar Iten in the Zurich goal was unable to deal with. Celtic had already scored before then when Jimmy Johnstone fired home from ten yards out, but Stevie Chalmers, who was on the goal-line, was ruled to be interfering with play. Chalmers, however, made up for his inadvertent error when he doubled Celtic's lead with seven minutes of the first-half remaining. A Johnstone corner from the right-hand side caused consternation in the Zurich defence, and Chalmers pounced to make it 2-0.

The second-half proved to be an exhibition of attacking play from Stein's side, particularly when Gemmell made it 3-0 from the penalty spot just three minutes after the break following a foul on Bobby Lennox inside the area. Zurich were a beaten and forlorn side, while Celtic were exuberant and entertained the appreciative home support, whose applause only served to rub salt in the wounds of the Swiss side.

Returning to Scotland, Celtic travelled to Easter Road and Joe McBride marked his return to the starting XI with four of Celtic's five goals in a thrilling 5-3 victory over Hibernian, who even had the temerity to twice take the lead in the game. Writing in the *Celtic View* the following week, Jock Stein reflected on his side's successful start to their inaugural European Cup campaign.

'Celtic have advanced to the next round of the European Cup and we shall know tomorrow (Thursday, October 13, 1966) whom we meet in the first round proper. The result in Zurich was a very good one for the club. But I was more than a little surprised to learn on the eve of the match how many people thought we would have a very hard match. For my own part, I believed that the only danger we could possibly be in was sitting back with our two-goal lead and letting the initiative pass to the Swiss club.

'There was, of course, no chance at all of me allowing any such mental attitude to develop. There is always this to remember, of course – we are basically an attacking team. So it would be unfair to the Celtic players to advise them to change their style considerably, especially when we thought we could win the match – let alone the tie on aggregate.

'We did, however, vary our style of play slightly. Realising that Zurich needed goals badly, we were prepared to let them have more of the ball in midfield than otherwise we would have done. Our style was based on quick counter-thrusts so well achieved by Steve Chalmers and Bobby Lennox. It succeeded beyond all shadow of doubt. I think we can say with certainty that we left behind a very good impression. Any bad feeling caused by the first game had completely vanished before our departure from Switzerland.'

Celtic's reward for their victory over Zurich was a second round tie with French champions, FC Nantes, who had seen off KR Reykjavík in the first round. By any standard, the tie represented a tougher test for Jock Stein's side than the one posed by the Swiss side, but the squad approached the contest full of optimism. Winning their opening European Cup tie by an aggregate victory of 5-0 was an impressive start, and Tommy Gemmell had the honour of scoring the first goal of the campaign. He wasn't to know, of course, that there would be a more important goal to come, but for Gemmell, who lined up at right-back in both legs, it was a good start for him and for the team.

'I scored three goals in two games," he said. "I scored a 35-yarder at Celtic Park and an identical goal over there in Zurich. You would have thought the goalkeeper would have been clued from the first match. The goal in Zurich was from exactly the same distance and exactly the same angles as at Celtic Park, and still he wasn't ready for it. There was nothing flukey about it. Every day in training we worked on hitting the ball from that distance. Everything we did was worked at, every day of the week. We did not play the game off-the-cuff, although you would get off-the-cuff stuff from wee Jinky; we didn't know what he was going to do next. I don't think he knew what he was going to do next, so what chance did we have and what chance did the opposition have? We gave Zurich a going over and that set us up for the next round.'

While Gemmell occupied the right-back role, Willie O'Neill was at left-back, and Jock Stein addressed supporters' concerns as to Jim Craig's future at the club. Craig had made his first-team debut in a Cup-Winners' Cup tie against Go Ahead Deventer back in October 1965, and had played his part in the subsequent championship success that season. However, he had rarely featured since the start of the 1966/67 campaign. Stein wrote in the *Celtic View*: 'Those readers who are anxious to know why Jim Craig has not been playing recently for any Celtic side can be assured that the club continue to have a very high opinion of his talents as a player and that nothing whatsoever is wrong between player and club. The facts of the matter are that Jim has been studying intensively in connection with his final examinations for a dental surgeon's degree and has been under much strain which has, not surprisingly, led to deterioration in his physical condition. As soon as Jim is back in top-class condition he will be wearing a Celtic jersey again with distinction.'

It would be just after the turn of the year before the aspiring dentist returned to the first-team on a regular basis and made the right-back role his own, with Gemmell switching to left-back and Willie O'Neill dropping out, but his team-mates had another European hurdle to negotiate and a first trip for Celtic to France in major European competition, although the Hoops had played Sedan in the Anglo-French-Scottish Friendship Cup back in 1960, drawing the home game 3-3 and losing 3-0 in France.

LISBOA
25 DE MAIO DE
1967
CELTIC 2-1 INTER
CELTIC FC
50° ANIVERSARIO

FC NANTES

FC NANTES

The wait for European football would be a relatively long one for the Celtic supporters following the win over Zurich on October 5. While the draw for the next round of the competition was organised soon after the first-round ties were completed, pitting Celtic against Nantes, the first leg in France wouldn't take place until November 30. It wasn't as though there was a lack of football, however, with Jock Stein's side playing ten games in the interval between the Zurich match and the first meeting with Nantes – eight in the league and two League Cup ties.

In keeping with the extraordinary start to the campaign, Celtic remained unbeaten in this period, winning nine of the ten games, with a 1-1 draw at home against St Mirren the only blot on an otherwise perfect copybook. In the eight league fixtures, Celtic scored thirty-one goals and conceded thirteen. Among the notable games was a 5-3 victory over Hibernian at Easter Road, a 7-3 home win over Stirling Albion and a dramatic 5-4 win against Dunfermline Athletic at East End Park, where the Hoops came back from 4-2 down to take the points, thanks to a last-minute Joe McBride penalty. The final league game before the team travelled out to Nantes was a home game against Hearts and, again, McBride scored from the spot in the last minute, putting the seal on a dominant 3-0 victory.

If the league campaign was near perfection, then the defence of the League Cup proved to be just that. Six victories in the group stage of the tournament was followed by a 9-4 aggregate win over Dunfermline Athletic in the last eight. That set up a semi-final clash at Hampden against Airdrie, a game that Celtic won despite the Lanarkshire side's best endeavours, thanks to second-half goals from Bobby Murdoch and Joe McBride. It was Celtic's third consecutive appearance in the final and, like the previous two finals, the opponents were Rangers.

The final at Hampden, on October 29, also gave Nantes the opportunity to cast their eyes over their opponents and a delegation duly travelled to Glasgow for the game. It put them, albeit temporarily, at an advantage over Celtic because Jock Stein's attempt to go on a scouting mission of his own to see Nantes take on Lille earlier in the month had been scuppered when fog caused the cancellation of his flight from Abbotsinch Airport (now Glasgow International Airport).

A crowd of 94,532, including the Nantes officials, watched the Hoops retain the trophy they'd won the previous year. The only goal of a physical game that did not show Celtic at their free-flowing best came after nineteen minutes when Bobby Lennox fired home a Joe McBride knockdown. It was the first part of what would ultimately prove to be a quintuple success for Celtic in season 1966/67, and nine days after the League Cup success, the Hoops lifted the Glasgow Cup with a 4-0 victory over Partick Thistle at Celtic Park, with Lennox scoring a hat-trick and Stevie Chalmers also on target.

Having been suitably impressed by the spectacle of the League Cup final at Hampden and, in particular, the size of the partisan crowd, the visitors from France then enjoyed the post-match celebrations, having been invited by Celtic to be part of the official victory reception in a Glasgow hotel. It was there, too, that Jock Stein arranged a reciprocal visit to France to watch Nantes take on Nice the following week. The Celtic manager was naturally pleased to see his side retain the League Cup, but there was an added enjoyment, in a strange way, in the fact the team didn't reach the high standards they had been setting for themselves so far that season. Stein hoped that this misleading impression of his side would be one that Nantes would take home with them and perhaps dictate how they approached the tie.

Nantes' home ground – Stade Marcel-Saupin (also known as Stade Malakoff, its original name) – had a considerably lower capacity than Celtic Park. It was around 25,000, and within that number, only five hundred tickets were allocated to the Celtic support, who were invited to apply for a ticket. Those successful in the ballot were flying out to Nantes on the day of the game on one of the five charter planes organised for the fans. Further indication of the difference between the size of both clubs can be seen from the fact that Celtic's league game against Hearts the Saturday prior to the tie in France attracted a crowd of 40,000, whereas 15,464, including those five hundred Celtic fans, watched the match in the Stade Marcel-Saupin.

Stein returned to Glasgow, having witnessed his opponents lose 3-1 to Nice, believing that, while it wouldn't be an easy task, Celtic were more than capable of beating the French side and progressing to the quarter-final of the European Cup. There was obviously still an element of an unknown quantity about Nantes, particularly amongst the Celtic support, deprived of any opportunity to assess the latest continental opponents, although the team's stunning start to the season saw a groundswell of optimistic rise up around Paradise.

Going into the first-leg away to Nantes, Celtic's 1966/67 record in all competitions was extraordinary. They had played twenty-seven games (12 league, 10 League Cup, 3 Glasgow Cup and 2 European Cup), winning twenty-six of the fixtures and drawing the other one, scoring an incredible ninety-seven goals and conceding just twenty-one. There were already two pieces of silverware in the trophy cabinet at Celtic, the League Cup and the Glasgow Cup, and a feeling was beginning to take root amongst the Celtic support that this could turn out to be a very special season, though not even the most optimism or wildly-imaginative fans could have envisaged just how special that would turn out to be.

The *Celtic View* also printed a feature that was originally published in *France Football* entitled, *'Can One Beat Celtic?'* The writer stated: 'The answer is yes. One must play fast, not hold the ball and make the ball do the work in its very widest sense. Celtic's system is simple with a 3-5-2 formation. Their permutations of this formation are, however, unceasing. The Celtic players have got an iron constitution! They play between 70 and 80 matches a season. They fear nobody! Their confidence in themselves is extraordinary! However, their conception of the game is imperfect. Of the five goals scored against Zurich, two were from the back Gemmell, and from far out. Gemmell also scored with a penalty. The fourth was from a corner-kick and only one goal was from a quick counter-attack. Celtic attack with the two backs advancing all the time bombarding lateral balls across the goalmouth. The answer is simple if the forwards are strong enough. At Nantes, one must mount a non-stop attack for Celtic, who know only too well how to attack and attack but do not know as well the art of counter-attack.'

It would have been interesting to get the thoughts of the French journalist who wrote this assessment after the first-leg in France and see how his perception of Celtic had changed because Jock Stein's side would prove to be masters of the attack, and the counter-attack, on the night. Unlike the previous round, which had involved a circuitous journey to Zurich via London, the Celtic party flew direct from Glasgow to Nantes, and while they received a warm enough welcome on arrival, they soon discovered that their opponents were intent on trying disrupt preparations for the game.

That might have been motivated by fear and an acknowledgement that Celtic would be formidable opponents. When Jock Stein and his squad of players turned up at the Stade Marcel-Saupin the night before the game for training, they were informed that they wouldn't be allowed to train in the stadium. This was due to concerns over the state of the pitch, the Nantes officials explained, with the venue having hosted a rugby union match the previous weekend. As a result of that, the groundstaff were still repairing the turf. Sent to a smaller training ground, the Celtic squad discovered that Nantes were still training there, and even after the French side finished their session, they remained to cast their eyes over the Scottish champions. Stein was unperturbed by this attempt to unsettle his side, though, indicating that if circumstances were similar the following week in Glasgow, then the Nantes team could have no complaints at being re-directed to Celtic's Barrowfield training ground about half-a-mile along London Road from Celtic Park.

Around five hundred Celtic supporters made the trip out to Nantes for the tie, and the *Celtic View* offered advice for any of those fans wanting to pay religious observance to St Andrew, patron saint of Scotland, whose feast day was that same Wednesday, November 30, stating: 'This is St Andrew's Day, and the Scots in Nantes today for Celtic's European Cup tie will find a close link with home. Monsignor Ward of St Mary's Church, Abercromby Street, Glasgow, has arranged for a Mass to be said in the Cathedral of St Peter in the French town by one of his curates, Father Holloran. It is hoped that the Mass will begin at 12noon. A number of parishioners of St Mary's have travelled on a charter flight with Father Holloran and Brother Casimir.'

Jock Stein was confident that his side were good enough to see off Nantes and on the Monday before the game had gone so far as to state that, barring injury, he would select the same starting XI as that which had defeated Hearts at the weekend. It was an uncharacteristically bold declaration from the Celtic manager, who was usually loathe to reveal any details of his team selection ahead of telling his players. It may have been a move designed to unsettle his opponents and relax his own players at the same time, and certainly the mood in the Celtic camp was a positive one. There was also the fact that he had a potent trio of strikers to call upon in the shape of Stevie Chalmers, Bobby Lennox and Joe Bride, who had already netted fifty-five goals between them that season, McBride leading the way with an impressive haul of thirty-three. Stein's pre-match assessment of the trio was further indication that Celtic were not going to deploy traditionally defensive away European tactics.

'You have seen them (Chalmers, Lennox, McBride) in action. It is not in their make-up to play deep in their own half of the field. They are so fast, and Chalmers and Lennox so direct, that either they are used in attack or we lose their full value … We are not going to be stupid enough to leave ourselves wide open at any time, and certainly not at the beginning of the game, but I think we can win, both in France and in Scotland.'

It was indeed the same Celtic starting XI from the previous Saturday that took to the field at the Stade Marcel-Saupin, although that nearly wasn't the case as Bobby Lennox explained in his autobiography, *Thirty Miles From Paradise*.

'There was a bit of a glitch before the match – as our coach approached the stadium, Joe McBride realised that he had forgotten to bring his boots. Jock lost the place with him and Joe and Neilly Mochan, our kit man and trainer, had to take a taxi back to the hotel and then return to the ground, where they had to wade through the crowd to get to the dressing-room with minutes to spare before the game began. This was one of the few occasions on which anyone was allowed to make such a 'faux pas' and still play but Joe was our top scorer that season and Jock was always practical in his decision-making.'

Celtic started the game intent on trying to grab an early goal on a wet night in Nantes, which had made for a heavy pitch. Chalmers was denied by goalkeeper, Andre Castel, and then Jimmy Johnstone hit the bar with a fierce shot, but it was the home side who took the lead against the run of play after sixteen minutes through Francis Magny after Celtic had lost possession while launching another attack. However, that lead only lasted for eight minutes before McBride, now suitably booted, latched on to a Lennox pass and scored with what was his first shot of the game. Ronnie Simpson was called into action a couple of times during the rest of the first-half but there was no further scoring.

The second-half illustrated Celtic's strength as they scored two goals without reply to give Jock Stein's side a 3-1 first-leg lead to take back to Glasgow. Bobby Lennox gave the Hoops the lead five minutes after the break, latching on to a precise Bobby Murdoch pass through a gap in the Nantes defence and surging forward to finish with characteristic precision. Then, with just over twenty minutes remaining, Stevie Chalmers scored a third goal for Celtic. Jimmy Johnstone might not have got on the scoresheet that night but he was the tormenter-in-chief, giving left-back Gabriel De Michele a torrid time from first minute 'til last, while Bertie Auld was influential in the middle of the park. The 3-1 first-leg victory put Celtic in the driving seat and the favourites to progress to the quarter-final, the result a vindication of Stein's bold team selection as well his pre-match confidence.

The return leg at Celtic Park would be played the following week, and the day before the game, on December 6, there was a new arrival at the club in the shape of Willie Wallace. The Hearts striker had fallen out with his club, unhappy over his wages to the point where he considering not just quitting Hearts, but actually leaving Scotland for a new life in Australia. Jock Stein was aware of the player's discontent, as well as rumblings that Rangers were also interested in trying to secure his signature, so there was a sense of urgency when the Celtic manager met the board on December 2. The deal was sanctioned, and four days later Wallace had gained his 'freedom' from Tynecastle, with Celtic paying a club record £30,000 fee to get the player.

The presumption was that Stein was planning to pair Wallace and Joe McBride to create a potent strike-force that could shoot Celtic to success both in Scotland and in Europe. It was unfortunate, therefore, when McBride picked up a knee injury after Christmas which effectively ended his season, though even by then he had already scored an impressive thirty-five goals. Wallace, meanwhile, who made his Celtic debut in a league game against Motherwell on December 10, four days after he signed, wouldn't play his first European game for the Hoops until the semi-final first-leg against Dukla Prague in April 1967 due to bureaucratic red tape which meant he wasn't eligible for the quarter-final clash with Yugoslavian champions, Vojvodina Novi Sad.

Regardless of that, Wallace was never going to be available for the return leg against Nantes, given the ink had barely dried on his contract signature, so he had to take his place in the main stand at Celtic Park for the game, which attracted a crowd of 41,000, nearly 10,000 lower than the attendance for the FC Zurich match in the previous round. Those who did stay away may have thought the tie a foregone conclusion after the first-leg win, but the fans who headed to Paradise, drawn inexorably towards the ground on a Wednesday night by the bright floodlights which beamed out across the East End of Glasgow like beacons in the dark December sky, were treated to another Celtic victory.

Nantes arrived in Glasgow knowing they had the proverbial football mountain to climb and Stein, remembering their antics the previous week in France, allowed them to use

Barrowfield as opposed to Celtic Park for their pre-match training session. Celtic, meanwhile, had one concern in the shape of Joe McBride, and a knee injury would ultimately rule him out of the game, with Charlie Gallagher drafted into the side. Jock Stein had displayed great confidence in his side ahead of the trip to France, and the 3-1 victory had only served to reinforce his belief that Celtic were too good for Nantes. However, he preached caution ahead of the return leg.

'Don't imagine Nantes are here merely to be slaughtered. They haven't by any means given up hope of winning the tie. We still must concentrate on reaching the next round – that is all-important. But though we are two goals ahead, we shall not make the mistake of merely trying to hold what we have. Nantes have got to attack right from the start, and we won't meekly let them take the initiative. We'll be going for goals and more goals while taking sensible precautions.'

In the event, Celtic replicated the first-leg scoreline, winning 3-1 on the night to progress to the quarter-final of the European Cup with a 6-2 aggregate victory. This time around, Jimmy Johnstone gave the Hoops the lead after just thirteen minutes, cutting through the Nantes defence and firing home. A difficult task became nigh impossible for the French champions, although they did not capitulate, perhaps realising their European ambitions were all but finished, and the side, wearing the bright yellow shirts that gave them the nickname of 'Canaries', rallied, going so far as to equalise with just under ten minutes of the first-half remaining when Gerard Georgin scored. The goal was the first that Celtic had conceded at home in Europe since their very first European tie back in 1962 against Valencia, and Georgin was denied a second goal on the night just before half-time thanks to a great save from Ronnie Simpson.

Once again, Celtic emphasised their superiority after the break, having initially found Nantes' offside trap a difficult and frustrating hurdle to overcome. Johnstone was at the heart of the move, delivering a cross into the boss for Stevie Chalmers to head home, and with twelve minutes remaining, Bobby Lennox scored Celtic's third on the night, again from a pass supplied by Johnstone, to ensure a place in the last eight.

Nantes' disappointment at their elimination did not, however, temper their admiration for Stein's Celtic side, with midfielder, Jacques Simon, going so far as to suggest that Celtic were good enough to go and win the European Cup that season. Whether the French internationalist wagered a few francs on that outcome or not isn't known, but he certainly proved to an astute analyst of the Hoops' potential. Stein, writing ahead of the December 15 quarter-final draw, emphasised the importance of progression in the tournament, which would always take precedence over any other demands placed upon the team.

'We await tomorrow's draw for the European Cup quarter-finals with interest and a certain amount of excitement. Those who were disappointed with our display in the return match with Nantes should remember that the French team, as I said here last Wednesday, were not merely lambs for a Parkhead slaughter. Celtic are not going to try to show off in these games. The object is first and foremost to win a place in the next round. We shall neither concentrate on trying to score goals nor on attempting to have a defensive shut-out. We shall, I hope, play in a sensible fashion, never losing a chance to play entertaining football but never losing sight of the fact that our job is to win with honour and glory for Celtic.'

European football after Christmas wasn't an unfamiliar prospect for Celtic supporters since the club first began participating in UEFA's competitions in the early 1960s, the team having previously reached the semi-final of the Cup-Winners' Cup in both the 1963/64 and 1965/66 seasons. The first occasion saw the Hoops race into a 3-0 first-leg lead against MTK Budapest, only to capitulate 4-0 in Hungary. Their second semi-final appearance was a closer affair, with Liverpool winning 2-1 on aggregate, although a late Bobby Lennox goal at Anfield was disallowed for offside, erroneously according to most observers. Had that goal stood, Celtic would have progressed to the final on the away goals rule which had been introduced into that particular tournament for the 1965/66 season, to face Borussia Dortmund at Hampden.

However, this was the club's first European Cup campaign, and to reach the last eight of the continent's premier club competition represented an impressive achievement by Jock Stein's young Celtic side. The draw saw Celtic pitted against the winners of the Atletico Madrid versus Vojvodina Novi Sad tie. The first leg had seen the Yugoslavian side win 3-1, while the Spanish side triumphed 2-0 in the return leg. At that time, the away goals rule did not apply to the European Cup – it would be 1969 before it was introduced – and so a play-off match was scheduled, with Atletico apparently handed an advantage with the game being played at their Vincente Calderon Stadium on December 21.

Celtic certainly believed that they would be heading to the Spanish capital in March, the club also announcing that the quarter-final tie at Celtic Park would be an all-ticket affair because 'Atletico would be considered such attractive opposition'. The preferred 'glamour' of the Spanish champions aside, there were also other factors to consider, according to the club, not least more suitable kick-off times in both Glasgow and Madrid.

However, in the event it was the Yugoslavian champions who triumphed on the night to set up a last eight meeting with Celtic. Despite going 2-0 down inside the first five minutes of the play-off, Vojvodina rallied and scored twice – once in the first-half and then an equaliser with just over twenty minutes of the tie remaining – to take the match into extra-time. And a goal from Silvester Takac, his second of the match, was enough to give Vojvodina a dramatic 3-2 victory. Celtic would be heading to the northern Yugoslav city of Novi Sad on March 1, 1967 on the latest stage of their European Cup adventure.

VOJVODINA NOVI SAD

LISBOA
25 DE MAIO DE
1967
CELTIC 2-1 INTER
50° CELTIC FC
ANIVERSARIO

VOJVODINA NOVI SAD

Celtic supporters had nearly three months to anticipate the quarter-final clash with Vojvodina Novi Sad, and their knowledge of the Yugoslavian side wouldn't expand too much in that intervening period, given the absence of any coverage of European football in the media and the lack of available resources to provide information. One supporter did pen a letter to the *Celtic View*, pointing out that Vojvodina's penalty in their 3-1 home leg win over Atletico Madrid in the previous round had been scored by their goalkeeper, Dragan Pantelic, and given that it was a vital spot-kick, the letter-writer surmised that Pantelic must be Vojvodina's regular penalty taker. Quite apart from that piece of information, fans would also have been aware that the previous champions of Yugoslavia, Partizan Belgrade, had reached the 1966 European Cup final, losing 2-1 to Real Madrid who scored with two late goals after Partizan had taken the lead. Indeed, the relative strength of teams like Partizan, Vojvodina and Red Star Belgrade would subsequently see the Yugoslavian national team reach the final of the 1968 European Championships where they lost to Italy.

That, of course, was for the future. The present was the challenge that Vojvodina posed for Jock Stein's side and their bid to reach the semi-final of the European Cup at the first time of asking. That was something which occupied Stein and his assistant, Sean Fallon, during those three intervening months after beating FC Nantes, though the immediate focus for them, and the players, was the league campaign and trying to retain the title they'd won for the first time in twelve years the previous season.

Celtic ended 1966 with an impressive set of statistics for the first half of season 1966/67. They had played thirty-four games, winning thirty, drawing three and just losing one competitive match. That came on the last day of the year when the Hoops travelled through to Tannadice to take on Dundee United. Despite twice taking the lead, through Bobby Lennox and Willie Wallace, Celtic ultimately lost the game 3-2, conceding two goals in the last twenty minutes of the match. The defeat was a disappointing one but couldn't take the gloss off the campaign thus far, with Stein's Celtic side having scored 116 goals and conceded just thirty-one. And normal service was renewed in the first competitive game of 1967 when the Hoops thrashed United's Tayside rivals, Dundee, 5-1 at Celtic Park.

The other festive disappointment came with the knee injury picked up by Joe McBride after the 1-1 draw against Aberdeen at Pittodrie on December 24. The seriousness of the injury wasn't immediately apparent, but it would see the striker ruled out for the rest of the season. What McBride's ultimate goals tally for that campaign would have been had he remained fit will always be open to conjecture, though he would, in all probability, have come close to Jimmy McGrory's record of fifty-seven goals that the Celtic legend scored in season 1926/27. McBride's tally of thirty-five by the turn of the year would only be bettered come the end of the campaign by Stevie Chalmers, who netted thirty-six, the goal which saw him overtake McBride being, of course, the winner in the European Cup final.

At the turn of the year, Jock Stein stated his priorities for the remainder of the 1966/67 season, declaring that: 'Winning the League championship and maintaining our position as the leading club in Scotland is still our No.1 priority. Second is improving our reputation in Europe. The players and I believe we can do both.' Certainly, Celtic's form up to the European Cup quarter-final first leg against Vojvodina in Novi Sad on March 1 was near enough faultless. The Hoops played nine games – seven in the league and two Scottish Cup ties. They won eight of those matches, scoring thirty-five goals and conceding just three. The only blemish in an otherwise perfect record came the weekend before the team flew out to Yugoslavia when they drew 1-1 way to Stirling Albion. Billy McNeill actually thought he'd headed home a late winner at Annfield, but it was disallowed when the referee awarded a free-kick to the home side.

Most history books only record competitive matches, and the statistics for season 1966/67 are extraordinary by anyone's interpretation. It also means that the friendly match that Stein organised for his side early in February as preparation for the forthcoming European challenge from Eastern Europe has, to all intents and purposes, been forgotten. That game, on Tuesday, February 7, saw Dinamo Zagreb, one of Vojvodina's rivals in the Yugoslav league, travel to Glasgow for a friendly match. The choice of opposition made perfect sense for Celtic, while Stein also announced in the lead-up to the game that he was going to try a different formation and game-plan, something, he explained, that the team had been working diligently on at the Barrowfield training ground.

The Hoops duly lined up in a 3-4-3 formation, as opposed to the 3-5-2 shape that had proved so productive already, with Stein deploying three centre-backs – Davie Cattanach, Billy McNeill and John Clark – Tommy Gemmell and John Hughes were wide midfielders while Bobby Murdoch and Bertie Auld were in central midfield. Up front was the trio of Stevie Chalmers, Willie Wallace and Bobby Lennox. It might only have been a friendly match but an impressive crowd of 46,000 gathered at Celtic Park, no doubt infused by enthusiasm for European football, given the team's success thus far in the season.

Celtic had played Dinamo Zagreb back in the 1963/64 Cup-Winners' Cup campaign, winning the home leg 3-0 and losing 2-1 in Yugoslavia, and it was one of the players from that earlier meeting, Slaven Zambata, who scored the only goal of the game with two minutes remaining. Despite the defeat, the Hoops played well in their new formation, and but for uncharacteristic profligacy in front of goal from both Chalmers and Lennox, the result could have been different. It may be that Stein was trying out something different that could be used again when the competitive European football resumed although, given the fact that the minutiae of the game would be reported back to Vojvodina by their fellow countrymen, it could well have been another deliberate move by the Celtic manager to sow seeds of doubt into his opponents' heads as to what they might expect come March 1.

While events on the park were continuing at an impressive pace, off the field the club announced through the *Celtic View* the launch of a new commercial product – Celtic Cigarettes. The club newspaper told fans: 'The eagerly awaited launching of Celtic Cigarettes took place last Saturday. This is no gimmick of a production. The tobacco has been specially selected and blended to distinguish it from other brands. Indeed it is exclusive to Celtic Cigarettes. The reproduction of the packet in the advertisement on page 4 of this issue of the 'View' shows the thought that has been given to the presentation in harmonising the club colours and official emblem.'

Some fifty years on and it is beyond comprehension that a football club would not only endorse a tobacco product but would actually have their own brand, given the breadth of knowledge regarding the major health risks involved in smoking. One or two astute readers of the *Celtic View* were dismayed at the time, however, as the *Letters' Page* of the newspaper reveal:

> '*Sir, with the name of Celtic now revered at home and in Europe as a club unparalleled in play and policy, what a pity the upward direction of the graph should take a sudden downward plunge. This is not only in my estimation, but that of all who hold sport and physical fitness as a means to a healthy mind and body. The reason for this downward plunge is the introduction of 'Celtic' cigarettes – more so the fact that the club applauds their introduction. In the light of recent medical evidence connecting smoking with lung cancer, surely this is a retrograde step for any organisation connected with health and fitness – and who is closer than Celtic? – to append the name of such an illustrious institution to such an unworthy product.*
>
> *Yours, etc., James Burns*
>
> '*Sir, my dad is not in favour of Celtic having a cigarette named after them. He thinks it encourages young 'fans' like myself to smoke too soon. He said we might be having some 'fly puffs on the quiet' just for the sake of having smoked a Celtic cigarette. Dad says I will never be able to play for Celtic if I start smoking cigarettes.*
>
> *Yours, etc., Andrew Allan (age 10)*

On football-related matters, the club through the *Celtic View* continued to update supporters on the progress of Joe McBride, given his importance to the team and popularity on the terraces. By the middle of February it appeared that he was well on the road to recovery, playing in a reserve game against Dundee on February 21. He scored in the 2-2 draw, but that game did not herald his return to action. Instead, he would end up having a cartilage operation on March 10 which, although it didn't save his season, did end up saving his career.

While Jock Stein would have to do without the services of his top goalscorer, he was also unable to select Willie Wallace, a player he had acquired in order to supplement the already potent attacking options at his disposal. Wallace, who had signed for the club on December 6, 1966, was not eligible for the quarter-final ties. The explanation for this was given to supporters via the *Celtic View*:

'Willie Wallace, who was transferred from Hearts to Celtic on December 6 of last year, cannot take part in the European Cup quarter-final because he has not been a Celtic player long enough.

Article 10 of the regulations for the European Cup reads: 'Only players who have been qualified for their club by August 15 may take part in the first two rounds of the competition. Only players who have been qualified of their club three months prior to the date fixed for the beginning of each of the following rounds (quarter-finals, semi-finals and final) may take part in the matches of these rounds. The date fixed for the beginning of the quarter-finals was December 16. The date fixed for the beginning of the semi-finals is March 21, so if Celtic get through to the semi-finals, Wallace will be eligible to play.

(Note: 'Qualified for' is the equivalent of 'signed by'.)

It meant that Stein would have to rely on the attacking pace of Stevie Chalmers and Bobby Lennox and the goalscoring instincts of John 'Yogi' Hughes, who would play in both legs against Vojvodina. Perhaps it was with this in mind that the Celtic manager had selected Hughes for the six games prior to the first leg in Yugoslavia, with Hughes netting three goals in that period. Indeed, even when Wallace was able to play his part in the European campaign, tellingly in the semi-final first leg against Dukla Prague, Hughes was still in the team that night.

Apart from focusing on how he would line up his team on the night in the Vojvodina Stadium (now known as the Karadorde Stadium), Jock Stein also had to contend with other, related issues, such as what strips the sides would be wearing. Vojvodina had declared, in advance of the tie, that they intended to wear an all-white kit in both legs. This would, inevitably, lead to a clash of colours with Celtic who, although wearing green and white hooped shirts, had a preponderance of white on their whole kit. Stein was in no mood for any nonsense from his opponents, reminding them of the competition rules which stated that, in the event of a clash of colours, it was the home side who had to wear an alternative kit. The Celtic boss even went so far as to reveal that his side would wear their all-green strip when the sides met at Celtic Park in the second leg. Stein also knew that Vojvodina, in whatever kit they ended up wearing, would prove to be very difficult opponents, renowned as they were for being a tough and combative side, and he was keen for his side to avoid getting drawn into a physical confrontation with them.

'I would warn our supporters not to expect a lot of attacking heroics from our team," he said. "Our job is to make certain that we win this tie on aggregate and qualify for the semi-final. Vojvodina must, of course, go for goals, so we shall have no 'Iron Curtain' defence to contend with. I never attempt to forecast a score. I much prefer to tell our supporters that I am reasonably confident that we shall return to Glasgow in the knowledge that Celtic Park a week hence will be a place to enjoy success.'

Some 5,000 Vojvodina supporters had gathered the night before the match to get their first glimpse of Celtic, watching as the players were put through their paces, and many more gathered the following evening – over 25,000 – for the game itself. The pitch was illuminated by two giant floodlights placed at either end of the stadium. At first glance it looked as though there wouldn't be enough light to cover the pitch but, in the event, the Celtic players were impressed with the quality of the floodlights. Bobby Lennox, in his autobiography, recalled a noisy crowd, set against dull weather and a drab setting, and the welcome when the teams walked out on to the pitch ahead of kick-off, which involved Scottish folk singer Donovan's song, *Mellow Yellow*, being played over the tannoy system. Vojvodina still wore white shirts, though with a red sash sliced across it. Celtic, as Stein had stated, were in the Hoops.

By that time, too, the Celtic players would have been aware of the European Cup holders, Real Madrid's elimination from the competition the previous night, beaten 3-0 on aggregate by Inter Milan, although their focus was solely on the ninety minutes ahead of them. What challenges that the Italians might pose, and given that they had eliminated Read Madrid, those would be many, they were for another day if, or when, Celtic saw off Vojvodina. The Yugoslav side were unable to field what they considered their strongest side for the match against the Scottish champions. Both Dobrivoje Trivic and Pusibric were suspended following their sendings-off in the previous round against Atletico Madrid, while Savic was ruled out through injury. Silvester Takac, meanwhile, whose goal had set up the quarter-final clash with Celtic, moved to France following the decisive game against Atletico, so it was a Vojvodina side denied of their main attacking threats who took on Celtic.

However, Jock Stein's side, so used to dominating possession and taking the game to the opposition, were forced on to the defensive as the Yugoslav side looked to establish a first-leg lead, but the Hoops were resolute in their defending, restricting their hosts mainly to long-range shots, with Ronnie Simpson barely troubled throughout the first half. Having weathered the Vojvodina storm in the opening forty-five minutes, Celtic showed more attacking intent after the break and came close to opening the scoring five minutes into the second-half when Bertie Auld set up Bobby Lennox, but his shot was well-saved by goalkeeper, Dragan Pantelic. John Hughes had a couple of chances, including one created by Billy McNeill, while Tommy Gemmell was denied by another good save from Pantelic. At this point, the Hoops were in control of the game but an uncharacteristic mistake from Gemmell, whose pass to John Clark was intercepted by Milan Stanic, saw the Vojvodina winger fire home what would prove to be the only goal of the game. It was a disappointing result for a Celtic side that had deserved a draw at least from their endeavours, but it did set the scene for a tense and dramatic night at Celtic Park when the sides met a week later. Ronnie Simpson was suitably impressed by the Yugoslav side, as he later noted in his autobiography.

'They were a disciplined side with a lot of talent and well-groomed by Vujadin Boskov, a former international left-half of world class. I thought we paced the game in Novi Sad to perfection and did everything right. Then, just as we had the Yugoslav champions on the retreat, we lost a goal – and a daft one at that… At the banquet in the Petrovaridan fortress, overlooking the Danube, where Tito apparently has a private suite, the Vojvodina 'keeper, Illja Pantelic, who is the No.1 in Yugoslavia, sought me out. He told me he was amazed I was still playing in goal at the age of 36. He said: 'If I'm still playing at 30 or 31, I'll consider myself lucky.' He made me feel like an old man!'

Vojvodina's manager, Vujadin Boskov, was delighted with the first-leg victory, and was bullish in his post-match comments: 'It is the best possible result for us. After all, we were a weakened team and we'll be much stronger in Glasgow. I think actually we will win at Parkhead as well.' He wouldn't get a chance to experience Celtic Park before the actual semi-final second leg clash, however, since the Celtic manager declared that the pitch was too soft following days of heavy rain and the Yugoslav team would only be able to train at Barrowfield.

Celtic had faced an away game against St Mirren at Love Street on the Saturday sandwiched in between the two Vojvodina games, and it was an emphatic 5-0 victory for the Hoops, although only one of those goals – the first of a double from Willie Wallace – came in the first-half. Jock Stein would be denied the services of the striker when the team took on the Yugoslav champions for a place in the semi-final of the European Cup, but it didn't stop the manager from selecting Wallace for the league game. The one worry from the game in Paisley was the injury picked up late in the game by Bertie Auld. He was replaced on the day by Jimmy Johnstone and while

Stein remained confident in his public pronouncements, when it came to the match, the combative midfielder was missing from the starting XI, his place taken by Charlie Gallagher, a selection that would prove highly significant.

Celtic's record for season 1966/67, going into the match against Vojvodina on Wednesday, March 8, continued to make impressive reading. Of forty-five competitive games played, which included three Glasgow Cup ties, they had won thirty-nine and lost just two, scoring an incredible 157 goals and conceding just thirty-five. The team, and its supporters were infused with a confidence that was backed up by the evidence, though the fact that Vojvodina were only the second team to inflict a defeat on the Hoops that season was reason enough to remain cautious, as was the realisation the club were now in uncharted waters. They may have enjoyed two appearances in the semi-final of the Cup-Winners' Cup, but this was different. This was the European Cup, the competition of champions, and Celtic, making their bow in the tournament, were just ninety minutes away from a place in the last four. Ahead of the game, Jock Stein issued a rallying cry in the pages of the *Celtic View*.

'This can be Celtic supporters' – as well as players' – finest hour-and-a-half this season. We are a goal down to Vojvodina in the European Cup quarter-final, but though I do not visualise an easy task, I am much more than hopeful that Celtic will win the tie and qualify for the semi-finals.

'We have had wonderful support throughout the season but I am calling for a special effort tonight from our faithful following. There is no good of thinking one thing and saying another. Celtic had far from a warm welcome from the Yugoslav crowd last Wednesday night and I want our supporters to show Vojvodina how we can welcome a team from overseas. But once that first whistle blows, I want every Celtic supporter to join with the team in defeating the opposition. There need be no bounds to the measures adopted to beat Vojvodina so long as they are fair.

'So far as the Celtic players are concerned, they have had drummed into them that their professionalism, their common-sense, will be severely tested tonight. They understand that they have a duty not only to the club and themselves but also to the supporters. On this night more than most I shall not stand for anyone not giving of his best for the club; I may excuse mistakes but I shall never pardon lack of enthusiasm or of real Celtic effort. Since we returned from Yugoslavia we have been thinking out ways and means of winning this match. I want the supporters to realise that our immediate aim is to remain in the competition. To do that we have to score only one goal so long as we do not lose one. By so doing we would be able to have a third go on neutral ground.

'So though we shall try for a quick goal at the start, there will be no ram-stam, desperate attacking. We intend to probe for possible defects in the Vojvodina defence but we mean to do so methodically. If we do not get a quick goal, the players and I shall not be terribly disappointed. We shall be patient, though no less determined to win this tie – and, of course, this match. So the supporters should copy the players in the knowledge that it will not be the end of the world if we do not score...

'We have had rehearsals of moves that Vojvodina never saw from us at Novi Sad. Without giving any of our plans away, I can say that I shall be looking for the trickiness of Jimmy Johnstone, the strength of John Hughes, the speed of Steve Chalmers and special backing from behind being trump cards for us. I am also hoping that we shall have much fairer refereeing than we had in Novi Sad and, accordingly, a great deal less of the blatant obstruction and much worse that several of our players had to suffer there. In this connection I must compliment the Celtic players on their conduct in the first match. They deserve great credit – and I mention Steve Chalmers in particular – for not losing their tempers. After all, there is a breaking point in every player – even the most disciplined one. My final words today must be that it is my sincere wish that all of us have something well worth celebrating tonight.'

A crowd of 75,000 packed into Celtic Park on a cold March evening in the East End of Glasgow, ready to play their part in ensuring their team's progress to the last four of the European Cup. The first-half of the match, however, did not go entirely to script in that Celtic, wearing their all-green change strip, didn't score to level the tie, although it did prove just how difficult the team from Yugoslavia were. Indeed, when it came to later reflections on the historic 1966/67 European Cup triumph, the mantra from the Celtic players was that 'Vojvodina were the best team we played in the tournament.'

The Yugoslav side began the game intent on trying to grab a vital away goal and squandered an early opportunity when Pusibric, back in the team following his suspension, fired wide from only six yards out. It was a let-off for the Hoops, but the first forty-five minutes were frustrating, particularly as the Yugoslavs employed the time-wasting tactic of passing back to their goalkeeper, Pantelic, to great effect, which raised the ire of the Celtic players and supporters alike. There would have been extra jubilation, therefore, when Celtic scored in the fifty-eighth minute through Stevie Chalmers to level the tie, given that it was an error from the Vojvodina goalkeeper which led directly to the goal. John Clark had played the ball out to Tommy Gemmell racing down the left wing. He fired a cross into the box which Pantelic attempted to gather, but instead he fumbled the ball, allowing it to drop in front of Chalmers who slotted the ball home.

Galvanised by the goal and with 75,000 supporters roaring them on, Celtic launched attack after attack on the Vojvodina goal, looking for the strike which would win the match and the tie, but they found that Pantelic, despite his earlier error, remained a tough barrier to breech. He denied Chalmers, Johnstone and Hughes, while a Gemmell effort which went narrowly over the bar had Celtic trainer Neilly Mochan on his feet and throwing a towel in the air, thinking it was a goal.

Time was ticking away from Celtic, and they were faced with the prospect of a play-off game in Rotterdam; extra-time was only employed in play-off games at that time. With less than a minute of the match remaining, the Hoops won another corner. Charlie Gallagher went over to take the set-piece and initially looked as though he was going to take a short corner involving Jimmy Johnstone. However, he changed his mind and, as Stevie Chalmers moved out of the box, dragging a number of defenders in his wake, Billy McNeill appeared in the area and met Gallagher's pinpoint cross with a powerful header that directed the ball beyond Pantelic and into the net. Paradise erupted, the Celtic players celebrated wildly, scenes mirrored on the touchline with the Celtic bench. Vojvodina barely had time to re-start the match before the Swedish referee blew for full-time. Celtic were in the semi-final of the European Cup.

Charlie Gallagher's delivery for the winning goal was a moment of precision and perfect, and would be remembered fondly by Celtic fans in the intervening years, in much the same way that his corner-kick in the 1965 Scottish Cup final, which was also met by the head of Billy McNeill, had also become a pivotal moment in the golden years under Jock Stein's managerial reign. Gallagher made 171 appearances for the Hoops between 1958 and 1970, scoring thirty-two goals for the club. A cousin of Pat Crerand, Gallagher was an important part of the Celtic squad during that period, and his exploits for club also saw him recognised for his country – in this case, the Republic of Ireland, with Gallagher's appearance against Turkey in Ankara on February 22, 1967 securing his place in Irish football history, given that he was the first Scots-born player to represent the Republic of Ireland, being able to do so by virtue of his parents being from Donegal. There is much to admire in Gallagher's career at Celtic, yet reflection always returns to those corner-kicks. Speaking to the *Celtic View* about his European highlights, Gallagher said:

'I was always proud of the Vojvodina game in 1967 and that's one that sticks out in my mind. Everybody knew the game was finishing, and when big Billy headed that ball into the net and put us through it was the best feeling ever. When I go out now to a supporters' event, it's always the thing that comes up. I remember saying to my wife that I played a lot of half-decent games for Celtic but all I'm remembered for is two corner kicks, but she said, 'At least you are remembered for something'. Everyone remembers who took the corner kicks and who scored the goals. So I contributed something.'

There wasn't much time for Gallagher and his team-mates to reflect on the triumph, however, given that there was a Scottish Cup quarter-final that Saturday, against

Queen's Park at Celtic Park. Tommy Gemmell scored an own goal inside the first minute of the match, and although the Hoops bounced back to score four goals in the first-half, their amateur opponents refused to lie down, and scored two further goals to reduce the deficit. It was only when Bobby Lennox scored with six minutes of the match remaining to make it 5-3 could the 34,000 crowd relax and look forward to a Scottish Cup semi-final, as well as a European Cup one as well. It's unlikely that Jock Stein would have enjoyed the luxury of relaxing that the supporters did, but there's no doubt that the Celtic manager was delighted at his side's progress in the European Cup as he displayed in his *Celtic View* column: 'Last week was a great cup-tie week for Celtic with entry to the semi-final of the European Cup and the Scottish Cup as the immediate reward for the players' efforts. I suppose every game leaves a memory for someone, but there can be few Celtic supporters who will not include Billy McNeill's winning goal against Vojvodina among the real treasures of their memories. It was, indeed, a golden moment in which all the frustration and the anxiety of the previous 89 minutes and some seconds vanished. I myself can remember other glorious last-minute goals, especially when they were winning ones for Celtic. We are constantly reminded of the great goals headed by Jimmy Quinn and Jimmy McGrory, but Billy McNeill's will surely rank with any of them.

'I do not believe too much can be said about the way in which our supporters encouraged the players and helped them to regain confidence for the renewed effort in the second-half to break down the Yugoslavs' strong, efficient defence. The players went out for the second-half believing that they could win this match, let alone the tie, and they were further confident when they heard the crowd willing them to victory. Let us all pay tribute to Tommy Gemmell for his great run which led to Stevie Chalmers scoring and taking the strain off all of us. It more than compensated for the mistake Tommy make in Novi Sad which gave Vojvodina their goal – a mistake which Tommy bitterly regretted. All of us at Celtic Park should remember at least one lesson of this match – that there are games in which nothing is lost or won until time runs out.'

Celtic's victory saw them join Inter Milan, Dukla Prague and CSKA Sofia in the semi-final draw, and while there would have been delight at reaching this stage of the competition, it's likely that the feelings in Glasgow, Prague and Sofia would have been much the same – they all wanted to avoid Inter Milan. Quite apart from the fact that the Italian champions had eliminated the European Cup holders, Real Madrid, in the quarter-finals, Inter could also boast of being one of only four clubs to have won the trophy since the tournament's inception in the 1955/56 season; they had done so on two occasions, beating Real Madrid in 1964 and repeating their success the following year, this time with a victory over Benfica in the final. They were the favourites to succeed again in 1967, and that feeling certainly manifested itself within the blue and black half of the San Siro.

Dukla Prague had seen off Ajax in the quarter-finals, while CSKA Sofia had disposed of Linfield, both sides winning by a 3-2 aggregate scoreline. It meant that three out of the four teams in the draw were making their first appearance at the semi-final stage of the competition, and it was the champions of the former Czechoslovakia who would provide the last barrier for Jock Stein's side in their aim of reaching the final of the competition, to be played at the Estadio Nacional in Lisbon on May 25.

DUKLA PRAGUE

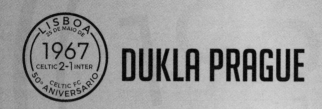

DUKLA PRAGUE

It might have been expected that the only topics of discussion amongst Celtic supporters in the wake of their cup triumphs both in Scotland and on the European stage would have been the impending semi-final fixtures. With two trophies already safely secured in the Celtic Park trophy cabinet – the League Cup and the Glasgow Cup – the prospect of adding to that haul had taken a significant step closer, allied to the fact that Jock Stein's side led the Scottish First Division. However, it was Stein's decision to act as judge, jury and executioner in respect of one of his own players which divided opinion amongst a support that in most other respects were united behind the manager and his team.

The topic of debate and division was Stein's decision to suspend Jimmy Johnstone for seven days following what was deemed to have been 'bad behaviour' towards the end of Celtic's Scottish Cup quarter-final clash with Queen's Park. The amateur side had proved to be surprisingly stubborn opponents, and while they were eventually defeated 5-3, it wasn't an easy afternoon for a Celtic side that had become accustomed to sweeping all before them that season. Frustration eventually got the better of Jimmy Johnstone, who had endured typically physical and robust challenges from his opponents throughout the ninety minutes, and as he got to his feet following yet another bad challenge, moved towards his opponent as if he was going to butt him; the officials didn't see the incident but Jock Stein did. It was, in his view, unacceptable behaviour, and the club took the decision to suspend the player. There was little detail on the incident or decision to placate or even illuminate supporters, though Stein did state, 'Suffice it to say that we hope the step that has been taken will make a better player for Celtic. We are, first and foremost, interested in the future of the club, but we are also very interested in the future of each individual player connected with us.'

Johnstone accepted the punishment without protest – he had no other choice – and while he still trained with his team-mates, he missed out on the following Saturday's home league game against Dunfermline Athletic, a match that Celtic won 3-2, though he did return to the starting XI two days later when Stein's side beat Falkirk 5-0 in another home league match. The suspension had no impact on the club's European campaign – Johnstone had already played his part in the defeat of Vojvodina to book a place in the semi-final – but it was a timely reminder, both to the player and the rest of the Celtic squad as to who was the boss and what was expected in terms of discipline on the park. Johnstone mentioned the incident in his autobiography, *Fire In My Boots*, published a couple of years later:

'Apart from one or two very minor incidents, I had a fairly clean record for the next two years. Then, in March 1967, I learned how determined Celtic can be to impose their own discipline, irrespective of what action the referee or the SFA might take. We were playing against the amateurs, Queen's Park, at Hampden in the quarter-final of the Scottish Cup. We weren't making much of it and I was getting annoyed with myself that opposition like this was stopping a team which was within a few weeks of competing in the European Cup final. I was battling to get things going when this Queen's Park player, sticking to me closer than a magnet, finally whipped the feet from me. I picked myself up and in a moment of blind fury, made to butt him with my head. The referee didn't see it, but Mr Stein did and I was hauled before him and promptly suspended by the club for seven days.'

The letters' page of the *Celtic View* in the wake of the announcement of Johnstone's suspension reflected the divided mood amongst supporters. Some praised the manager for his principled stand while other expressed varying degrees of disappointment, disagreement or disgust.

Patrick Reilly asked, 'Where is the justice in punishing a whole team ... for the offence of one player?', arguing also that the supporters could suffer if a weakened Celtic team lost. Thomas A. Feeley, meanwhile, believed that Johnstone had reached breaking point against Queen's Park. 'Time after time this season I have seen Johnstone being crudely buffeted and fouled by inferior opponents who had no other means at their disposal to stop him.' T. Gray agreed with Stein's decision to suspend the player, although he argued that 'I think that this was the referee's job and not the Celtic manager's,' while T. Cassells wrote, 'To Jimmy Johnstone I would say – accept the club's decision like the true Celt we know you to be, and try hard to erase this human but sad failing which despoils an otherwise brilliant and entertaining player.'

As the club and its supporters waited for the official European Cup semi-final draw, they were already making contingency plans for how they would approach, not the last-four clash, but the final itself. If the draw kept Celtic and Inter Milan apart, the Hoops were keen to arrange a friendly match against Uruguayan side, Penarol. The reigning world club champions, who had claimed the title by defeating Real Madrid the previous year, were on a European tour and the plan was to try and organise a game, although because of building work set to be undertaken at Celtic Park, an alternative venue would have to be found. In the event, the sides would play in 1967 at Celtic Park, though it wasn't until in September of that year, by which time Celtic were the European champions and the game was part of their preparations for their forthcoming world club championship clashes with Racing Club of Argentina; Celtic beat Penarol 2-1 with the Lisbon Lions starting the game, but whatever football experiences they might have gained against South American opposition didn't really prepare Stein's side for what they ultimately faced against the Argentinians later in the year.

When the identity of Celtic's European Cup semi-final opponents was revealed as Czechoslovakian champions, Dukla Prague, along with the dates of both ties – the first leg was to be at Celtic Park on Wednesday, April 12 – details of the ticket sale were quickly announced. Over 50,000 tickets went on sale on Sunday, April 2 at Celtic Park, starting at 12noon. Supporters were allowed to buy a maximum of two enclosure tickets (10 shillings [50p] per ticket) and five ground tickets (6 shillings [30p] each), while Stand season ticket holders could purchase one stand seat ticket (£1 10s, or £1).

The day before tickets for the Dukla Prague game went on sale, Celtic were in Scottish Cup semi-final action, facing Clyde at Hampden in front of a crowd of nearly 57,000. Only Bobby Murdoch from the side who would eventually line up in Lisbon was missing from the game at Hampden, with John Hughes in the starting XI. It was a disappointing game, with Celtic perhaps showing the effects of having played four league games in nine days – all of which they won, incidentally – although they did have a late penalty claim denied which would have given them the opportunity of a late winner. As it was, a replay was set for the following Wednesday. Another impressive crowd of just over 55,000 gathered at Hampden, the majority of them Celtic fans, and they saw the Hoops open the scoring after just two minutes through Bobby Lennox. Bertie Auld doubled Celtic's lead on twenty-four minutes and a place in the Scottish Cup final was duly secured, where they would face an Aberdeen side who had beaten Dundee United in the other semi-final.

The victory over Clyde was Celtic's forty-sixth of the season out of fifty-three competitive games played thus far – twenty-nine league, ten League Cup, six European Cup, five Scottish Cup and three Glasgow Cup – while the two goals scored brought their cumulative total to a staggering 181, while only forty-one had been conceded. It was a level of consistency that had barely seemed imaginable just two years previously, when Jock Stein first arrived at the club from Hibernian. It also ensured that Dukla Prague would approach both legs of the tie well aware of the threat they faced from the team in green and white Hoops.

While the demand for European Cup semi-final tickets was uppermost in supporters' minds, one optimistic travel company, Holiday Enterprises, placed an advert in the *Celtic View* of March 29, which stated *'If you are going to LISBON or just thinking about it, do nothing until you've had a word with Jim McGinley of Holiday Enterprises'*. Indeed, it was estimated that as many as 3,000 Celtic fans were intending to make the trip to the Portuguese capital for the European Cup final on May 25 regardless of whether the team made it. Considerably more were planning to in the event of a successful semi-final outcome.

Celtic had one more domestic fixture to complete before facing the champions of Czechoslovakia, and that was an away trip to Fir Park to take on Motherwell. Second-half goals from Willie Wallace and Tommy Gemmell from the penalty spot gave the Hoops a 2-0 victory and maintained their position at the top of the Scottish First Division table. Now, attention could turn to Dukla Prague and the first-leg of the European Cup semi-final.

Jock Stein took the squad down to their Ayrshire base at Seamill to prepare for the game, with some of the players knowing that they would also be facing an important international match the following Saturday. Five Celts – Ronnie Simpson, Bobby Lennox, Tommy Gemmell and Willie Wallace – had been selected for Scotland's game against England at Wembley on April 15, three days after Celtic's clash with Dukla Prague. It was the first meeting between the two countries since England's 1966 World Cup triumph, and Bobby Lennox was told by Stein at Seamill that he would be in the starting line-up for the Auld Enemy clash at the weekend. In his autobiography, Lennox also revealed:

'Later that day, Jock had a less welcome piece of news for me when he announced the Celtic team to play Dukla and I wasn't included. The disappointment was enormous but it's not in my nature to mope about something like that. If there's nothing you can do to improve a certain situation, there is no point in worrying about it. It was of some compensation to know that I was playing for Scotland on the Saturday but, given the choice between the two, I would rather have been playing for Celtic against Dukla Prague.'

Bobby Lennox's disappointment at missing out on Celtic's biggest game of the season to date had to be tempered as he was still part of the pre-match preparations at Seamill, and the consolation for him, though he wasn't to know it at the time, would be that, when he returned to the Celtic side for their next game after the European Cup semi-final – a home league match against Aberdeen – it would be a run in the side that would take him all the way to the end of the campaign and Lisbon's Estadio Nacional.

The day of the Dukla Prague game saw Jock Stein's reflections in the *Celtic View*, declaring the tie as 'probably the most important Celtic have ever had to play.'

'Tonight we shall try to sow some seeds, the harvest of which we hope to reap in the return match in Prague. This is the night on which the Celtic players will be asked for 100 per cent concentration on victory for the entire 90 minutes of the match. Everybody simply has to be on their toes – the players on the field, the staff behind the scenes, and, not least important, the supporters. I want a lead tonight sufficient to see us through in Prague without such strain as might damage our prospects in the Scottish Cup final, which has to be played only four days after our match in Czechoslovakia. The better we do tonight, the better will be our chance of success later on in all the competitions in which we are engaged ... Although, as I have said, the first match with Dukla could be considered the most important in the history of Celtic, it must not be allowed to distract us from another primary objective – the retaining of the league championship and the consequent certainty of taking part in the main European competition next season.

'Sympathy has been extended to the club in having so many commitments at this vital stage of the season. We could moan about the heavy fixture list and the risk of being asked to do too much in a short space of time. But I prefer to count our blessings and be thankful that we are so much in the limelight. I realise that for a club to do itself full justice in Europe, greater breathing space must be permitted. On the other hand, I appreciate that the Scottish football authorities have to legislate for the unsuccessful as well as the successful…

'Dukla will be very solid, difficult opposition. Remember that they knocked out Anderlecht and Ajax in earlier rounds and remember, too, that they, like Celtic, are trying to be the first club from their country to reach the European Cup final. But they will know they've been playing tonight right from the first blast of the referee's whistle.'

For the second European home game in a row, Celtic Park was packed to the rafters as a sell-out crowd of 75,000 turned the stadium into a cauldron of noise, giving the team what they hoped would be the requisite backing to establish a commanding first-leg lead to take to Prague. There were nerves too, and plenty of them, as Dukla produced, in spells during the ninety minutes, the sort of form that had seen off Esbjerg, Anderlecht and Ajax to reach the last four of the competition. Indeed, it was the Czech side who started off more strongly, and the Hoops had Ronnie Simpson to thank for producing a couple of early saves which prevented the visitors taking the lead. While Celtic had been in the middle of a heavy programme of fixtures since defeating Vojvodina, their Czech opponents had enjoyed a 10-day hiatus to prepare for the game, and they certainly looked the fresher of the two sides in the early exchanges.

Having weathered the early fright, Celtic muscled their way into the match, inspired by the genius of Jimmy Johnstone, now restored to the side and with all memory of his recent suspension now forgotten. Stevie Chalmers headed home a Johnstone cross for what looked like the opening goal of the night, only for it to be ruled out when Johnstone was penalised for a high boot in the build-up to the goal, much to the annoyance of the Celtic supporters. The home side were not to be denied, however, and it was Celtic's inspirational No.7 who scored on twenty-seven minutes. Willie Wallace, making his European debut for the Hoops, hit a shot from twenty yards which deflected off a Dukla defender and into the path of the inrushing Johnstone who coolly controlled the ball with his chest before lobbing it over Ivo Viktor in the Dukla goal. The visitors were stunned, Celtic Park was jubilant and the players buoyant as they pushed to extend their lead.

However, disaster struck just a minute before half-time. Dukla's talismanic midfielder, Josef Masopust threaded the ball through to Josef Nedorost. Celtic failed to clear the ball, which seemed to get tangled up on the edge of the box amongst a number of defenders, and Stanislav Strunc was the first to react, dragging the ball into the area before slotting it beyond Ronnie Simpson. It was a real blow to the team and the fans, but the half-time break allowed Stein to settle his team and encourage them to keep attacking a Czech side he was sure would tire the longer the game progressed.

The second-half saw Celtic push forward in search of a second goal which would restore their lead, with Jimmy Johnstone continuing to torment the Dukla defence, and Bobby Murdoch came close to scoring when his left-footed shot from just inside the box flashed narrowly wide of the post. If Celtic were producing some impressive, flowing football, it was a straightforward ball over the top which eventually created another goal. Tommy Gemmell's intervention was as much a clearance as it was a pass from the halfway line, and when it was misjudged by the Dukla players, Willie Wallace pounced on the ball, flicking it beyond Viktor from the edge of the six-yard box with the outside of his right foot. It was Wallace's first European goal in Celtic colours, and it was quickly followed by his second and Celtic's third just six minutes later.

This time, the goal owed much to the impudent genius of Bertie Auld. Celtic had been awarded a free-kick about twenty-three yards from goal after Jan Zlocha had stopped a through ball from Murdoch with his hand. With the Dukla wall lined up to their goalkeeper's satisfaction, Auld stepped forward as if to take the kick and then stopped and crouched down, looking as though he was going to re-place the ball. Instead, he slid the ball to his right, rendering the wall useless and unable to do anything to prevent Wallace smashing a shot into the back of the net to put Celtic 3-1 ahead. Jock Stein had wanted at least a two-goal lead to take to Prague, but Wallace almost extended the team's lead and, in the process, net a hat-trick, but his shot from a Stevie Chalmers cut-back hit the bar and was then cleared to safety.

There was to be no further scoring in the match, although Ronnie Simpson came to Celtic's rescue late in the game to deny Dukla a second goal their efforts would barely have deserved, and it was a delighted Celtic team who celebrated on the park at the final whistle while supporters were jubilant on the terraces, many of them no doubt now beginning to work out how they were going to get to Lisbon for the final. Indeed, one advert which appeared in the *Celtic View* for a hotel in Lisbon tried to entice would-be customers with the following appeal: *'If you are going to see the final in Lisbon on May 25th do it right – take your wife and stay a few days at the Miramonte Hotel... You have no fear of a Lisbon tummy with us.'*

However, while supporters could begin looking ahead, albeit there was still the small matter of the second leg to come in Prague, there was little time for Celtic's Scottish national team contingent to celebrate the victory over Dukla as they had to report for international duty ahead of the clash against England at Wembley. While Ronnie Simpson, Bobby Lennox, Tommy Gemmell, Willie Wallace and Stevie Chalmers all joined up with their Scotland team-mates, one of the stars of the victory over the Czech champions, Jimmy Johnstone, withdrew from the squad due to injury. On the one hand, having five Celts in the squad brought kudos to the club – and four of them would play in the match – but the absence of other key players such as Billy McNeill, Bertie Auld and Bobby Murdoch also highlighted the deficiencies in the selection process for the Scotland squad at that time, when the best centre-half and best central midfield partnership in European football were not picked to represent their country.

The paucity of Scotland caps for the Lisbon Lions has been something which baffled Celtic fans down through the years, and continues to do so. The number gained for each player is as follows: Simpson (5), Craig (1), Gemmell (18), Murdoch (12), McNeill (29), Clark (4), Johnstone (23), Wallace (7), Chalmers (5), Auld (3), Lennox (10). It makes for a total of 117, which also includes the two caps Willie Wallace won while still at Hearts.

The four Celts who were selected for the game against England at Wembley on Saturday, April 15, helped produce an iconic result that continues to be spoken of in fond, and often reverential tones, by supporters of the national team who remember the game. Ronnie Simpson, Bobby Lennox, Tommy Gemmell and Willie Wallace all played in the game as Scotland won 3-2, allowing their fans to declare Scotland to be the unofficial champions of the world. Denis Law gave Scotland a first-half lead and Bobby Lennox doubled that lead with twelve minutes of the match remaining. Jack Charlton and Geoff Hurst scored for England either side of a Jim McCalliog goal, and the Scottish fans in the crowd of just over 99,000 celebrated with gusto.

Again, there was little time for the Celts in the squad to celebrate, however, since they were quickly returning to club action. Four days later, all four of them were in the team that drew 0-0 with Aberdeen at Celtic Park – it was the eleven men who would become the Lions of Lisbon just over a month later who took to the pitch for the game – and it may well have been that the midweek exertions at Wembley affected the performance of the team, who failed to score a goal for only the second league game that season; the other time was a goal-less draw against Kilmarnock at Rugby Park. The game was, of course, a dress rehearsal for the Scottish Cup final meeting between the sides at Hampden ten days later, but both the league result and the forthcoming cup final were put to the back of the players' minds, as they prepared to fly out to Czechoslovakia to take on Dukla Prague in the second-leg of their European Cup semi-final clash.

The 3-1 victory gave the Hoops a strong but not insurmountable lead, but the Celtic squad would have been imbued with a sense of unbreakable confidence from their manager, which he expressed through the club newspaper which came out on the day of the game.

'We are within striking distance of a great day for Celtic – entry to the final of the European Cup, a distinction which has eluded every British club. How fine it will be if Celtic, who have created a great deal of football history, add another page to the story. The semi-final against Dukla at Celtic Park proved, in my opinion, two things in particular. First, Dukla clearly deserve to have reached the later stages of this important competition. The other is that Celtic, near the end of a very strenuous season, are as capable as they were months ago of winning matches and at the same time entertaining the spectators.

'I was especially pleased with the lads' display because Dukla had had 10 days' special preparation for the game and no match in that period, whereas Celtic had a Scottish Cup semi-final and a replay and a hard league game at Motherwell during that time. Yet it is true to say that our boys were running the Czechs into the ground at the end. There were, of course, other features to bring joy to Celtic hearts. Injury and illness have been troubling us, so how good it was to see Bobby Murdoch making a fine return to the team and Jimmy Johnstone showing such sparkle. I think we can take it that both will be in even better fettle for the return game in Prague.

'We got off to a good start with Jimmy's goal after a strange decision had knocked off one he made for Steve Chalmers. Then after indecision in defence had let Dukla in to equalise, two great goals by Willie Wallace in the second half gave us a convincing victory. There were several 'near misses', and all in all, the fans had a great night. We shall, of course, leave nothing to chance for the return game, even though I personally feel that not only shall we win the match on aggregate, we might even win the second game too. I don't mind telling Dukla how we shall approach our task – we shall play to a tight safe pattern for something like 20 minutes and then open up.'

Conscious of the fact that the team faced a Scottish Cup final just four days after their European Cup semi-final, the Celtic directors announced the team would fly home immediately after the game in Prague. With the League Cup already in the Celtic Park trophy cabinet, and the team top of the Scottish League Division One, there was an opportunity for a clean sweep of domestic silverware for the first time in the club's history, and the custodians were keen to assist in that by adjusting travel plans accordingly. They also asked for the fans help in this regard too, perhaps anticipating the reaction to a successful result in the Czech capital, asking supporters not to turn up to the airport to welcome the team home; '…By refraining from going to the airport you will assist the authorities considerably and help to get the players home as quickly as possible. The quicker the players are in their own homes, the better will their chances be in the Scottish Cup final.'

The game in Prague had an afternoon kick-off due to the lack of floodlights at the Juliska Stadium, and it saw Celtic appearing to adopt a much more cautious and defensive formation, out of character with their normal style of play, with Stevie Chalmers ploughing a lonely furrow up front for most of the ninety minutes. It was perhaps a twin acknowledgement from Stein that this was the most important game his team had yet faced – and, indeed, possibly the most important game in the club's history – and also that Dukla Prague were a very good side who were going to provide the toughest of tests, although several of the Celtic players who played that night stated later that it was simply Dukla's attacking qualities which had forced them into a defensive rearguard. Stein himself said immediately after the game, 'I'll never resort to tactics like these again – never!'

However, whether by accident or design, the defensive discipline of the Celtic side limited Dukla to three clear chances, two of which they squandered and one which relied upon the brilliance of Ronnie Simpson, who denied Stanislav Strunc with a great save. That chance came in the first couple of minutes, and had it gone in, it could have been a much more difficult night for the Hoops. As it was, Dukla's frustration at their inability to make any headway saw a flurry of bookings for the Czech side. Celtic's goalkeeper was outstanding on the night, while Chalmers' tireless running won praise from his team-mates, but it was the colossus in the heart of the Celtic defence who led by example and organised all around him to ensure an impregnable defence. Reflecting later on the Prague game, Billy McNeill said:

'In the early part of the game they just besieged us. That's what caused everyone on our side to spend their time chasing and sorting things out. In the first twenty minutes, they had a couple of shots at Ronnie. I remember one going screaming past me and thinking, 'God, I hope Ronnie is in the road of that one... and he was. Latterly, we just frustrated them as much as anything. It was a very uncharacteristic performance by us as a team, but it was the nature of the game, and it was dictated by the circumstances... We knew it was always going to be something of a rearguard action, but it was never intended to turn out like that.'

For Stevie Chalmers, the final whistle not only brought a welcome end to his relentless running shift, but also uncharacteristic praise from his manager, as he explained in his autobiography, *The Winning Touch*.

'Before the match, given that we were looking after a two-goal lead from the first leg, Jock Stein told me that I would be up front on my own, keeping the Dukla defenders busy all the time. He felt that by deploying only one forward we would be more strongly equipped in midfield to preserve the team's lead. Such a role suited me – indeed any role in the team in that game would have suited me. I was so delighted that we were a fraction away from making the final that I would have run until I was dead wherever I was fielded … That was the one game in which Jock was really pleased with me. He was effusive in his praise of me after it and he really hugged me right for the one and only time. He said that my performance had been great and that I had done everything he had wanted me to do … I had run around up the park so many times it had been, for me, almost a test of stamina and athleticism as much as a football match – like running a long-distance race – but Jock was always a man who saw the bigger picture. He was delighted with what I had done for him and the team and it was after that performance, I think, that he decided he had to make sure I was playing in the final. The fact that I had also scored more goals than anybody else in the run to the final must have helped.'

At the ninth time of asking, a British team had progressed from the last four and reached the European Cup final. Where Hibernian, Manchester United (three times), Rangers, Tottenham Hotspur, Dundee and Liverpool had all faltered, Celtic Football Club triumphed, and having already made history by reaching the final, they were just ninety minutes from immortality. Who stood between them and European football's ultimate prize remained unknown. Inter Milan and CSKA Sofia had drawn 1-1 in the first leg in Bulgaria, and the second-leg, the night after Celtic's Prague triumph, also finished 1-1 in Milan. A play-off was, therefore, scheduled for May 3 in Bologna to decide Celtic's opponents in the final.

There would have been a sense of unreality amongst the Celtic squad, most of whom could remember finishing eighth in the league just two years previously, but they barely had time to draw breath, never mind take five minutes to appreciate any of their successes. The enormity of reaching the European Cup final at the first time of asking was something that the players were aware of, but while supporters, gripped by their own sense of being in the middle of the greatest dream ever experienced, began to plan trips to Lisbon by planes, trains or Hillman Imps – or started counting down the days until families, friends and neighbours could gather together in the house of whoever owned a television, and huddle round the black and white set with nervous anticipation – Jock Stein's squad flew home from Prague, tired but proud, and in between bouts of sleep, already looking forward to a trip to Hampden that Saturday for the Scottish Cup final.

It was a competition that Celtic as a club, and its supporters, had long held a great affection for; it was the first major trophy the club had won in its history, way back in 1892 with a 5-1 victory over Queen's Park; Celtic would soon go on to enjoy more Scottish Cup success than any other club, a record that still stands in 2016, while the 1965 triumph, beating Dunfermline Athletic 3-2 in the final, had been the club's first silverware success in eight years, the first trophy of Jock Stein's reign, and the start of what was already proving to be something special in football terms.

So, regardless of the extraordinary prize that was up for grabs on May 25 in Lisbon, the Celtic players and their manager were determined to lift the famous old trophy at Hampden, which would represent the first time the club had won both domestic cup competitions in the same season. Aberdeen were the opponents and they had proved to be a match in the two league matches that season; the first, at Pittodrie on Christmas Eve, had finished 1-1, with Bobby Lennox's opener cancelled out by Harry Melrose, while the corresponding fixture at Celtic Park ten days before the final had finished goal-less.

A crowd of 126,102 packed into Hampden for the final, with Stein naming a starting XI that would soon become etched in the minds of every Celtic supporter for generations to come – Simpson, Craig, Gemmell, Murdoch, McNeill, Clark, Johnstone, Wallace, Chalmers, Auld, Lennox – and the Hoops controlled the match almost from the first minute, with Stein switching Chalmers out to the right wing and deploying Johnstone alongside Wallace. Aberdeen struggled to cope with Celtic's attacking prowess, not helped by the absence of their manager, Eddie Turnbull, who missed the game through illness.

It took Celtic until three minutes before half-time to score the opening goal that their dominance deserved, and it was Bobby Lennox who was the provider. He dribbled to the goal-line inside the penalty area and then cut the ball back to the edge of the six-yard box where Willie Wallace was on hand to side-foot the ball home. The second goal of the game came just four minutes after half-time and confirmed Celtic's control of the match. This time it was Jimmy Johnstone who supplied the pass for Wallace to score, cutting the ball back from a similar position to Lennox in the first-half where Wallace, from about eight yards out, fired home beyond Bobby Clark in the Aberdeen goal.

The full-time whistle saw the Celtic fans who made up the majority of the Hampden crowd celebrate what was the team's fifth trophy since Jock Stein took over – seven if the Glasgow Cup was included – and the Scottish Cup triumph not only meant that Celtic were closing in on an historic first domestic treble, but they were still on course to become the first club to win every competition they entered in a single season.

Jock Stein was fulsome in his praise of the players' efforts, both domestically and in Europe, also acknowledging in the *Celtic View* that the tactics he deployed in the Czech capital were not ones he would normally or comfortably adopt, though it did display a pragmatic side to a manager whose team had entertained fans throughout Scotland and the continent with a breathtaking brand of attacking football; Stein knew the importance of reaching the European Cup final, and while he hadn't been at the club when they had surrendered a three-goal lead in the semi-final of the Cup-Winners' Cup in 1964, the lessons of that capitulation certainly appeared to have been absorbed by the Celtic manager.

'Since this column last appeared, Celtic have made gigantic strides. We have qualified for the European Cup final and four days later we won the Scottish Cup – on a day when our league position became almost unassailable. The Scottish Cup final victory and the merit of it were especially pleasing to me in view of the fact that only four days earlier we had travelled home from Prague. There is tremendous spirit in the team, even though they have had a most exciting season.

'In the European Cup semi-final second-leg we tried, as usual, to make a quick summing-up of what our opponents would try to do. Our players very quickly decided that Dukla were going to be aggressive and bold, and our answer was to concentrate on defence. We had not intended to be so defensively-minded, but in the circumstances we had no hesitation in deciding as we did. We had, of course, played in a very different way in the first game against Dukla, but I think we showed the Czechs that we can alter our methods to suit the occasions and do so very profitably.'

The month of April had proved to be a momentous one for Celtic, booking their place in the European Cup final and winning the Scottish Cup, as well as maintaining top spot in the league. Events in May would dictate whether season 1966/67 would be a good one, a great one, or perhaps even the greatest of them all.

LISBOA
25 DE MAIO DE
1967
CELTIC 2-1 INTER
50° CELTIC FC
ANIVERSARIO

THE LIONS OF LISBON

Jock Stein's side were brought right back down to earth at the beginning of May when they suffered only their second league defeat of the season, and their first at Celtic Park, losing 3-2 to Dundee United. It was the same scoreline as the previous meeting between the sides, at Tannadice on the last day of 1966, and gave Dundee United the distinction of the being the only side with a one hundred per cent record over the Hoops that season. Celtic had twice taken the lead in the match, firstly through a Tommy Gemmell penalty in the first-half and then again through Willie Wallace just after the hour mark, but United battled back and scored a winner through Jackie Graham.

That same night, Celtic also discovered their opponents in the European Cup final, as Inter Milan edged out CSKA Sofia in a play-off at the Stadium Renato Dall'Ara in Bologna, with Renato Cappellini scoring the only goal of the game after twelve minutes. The game had originally been scheduled for Graz in Austria, but Inter's offer to give two-thirds of the gate money to their Bulgarian opponents saw the match switched to Italy. CSKA's financial gain proved to be football folly as they lost out on a place in the final. It meant that the Hoops would face the Italian champions, led by their legendary Argentinian manager, Helenio Herrera, who had already steered them to back-to-back European Cup triumphs in 1964 and '65. Inter had seen off Torpedo Moscow, Vasas of Hungary, reigning champions Real Madrid and, finally, CSKA Sofia, to set up the showdown with Celtic at the Estadio Nacional in Lisbon on Thursday, May 25, and they would go into the game as favourites to lift their third European Cup trophy.

While Inter were still battling with Juventus for the Serie A title – they would ultimately lose out after a shock 1-0 defeat to Mantova on the final day of the season, which came six days after the Lisbon final – Celtic, despite that unexpected home loss to Dundee United, had the chance to secure their second Scottish title in a row just three days later when they travelled across the city to take on Rangers at Ibrox. The advantage for Stein's side was that they knew a point would be enough to confirm their status as champions. The day of the game saw Glasgow drenched in torrential rain to the extent that some doubt was cast over whether the game would be played or not. In the event it did go ahead on a quagmire of a pitch and under the watchful eye of Helenio Herrera, who had travelled to Glasgow to check out his European Cup final opponents.

Stein had made two changes for the Dundee United game, with Charlie Gallagher and John Hughes coming in for Bertie Auld and Stevie Chalmers, but they were both restored for the Glasgow derby. A crowd of 78,000 packed into the stadium, rain continuing to fall heavily throughout the fiercely-contested ninety minutes. Sandy Jardine opened the scoring for the home side, blasting home from the edge of the box, but that lead lasted all of sixty seconds before Jimmy Johnstone equalised for the Hoops, bundling the ball home on the line after it had come back off the post. Johnstone, as always, was proving to be a handful for the opposition, and his characteristic unpredictable jinking was still evident, even on the heavy pitch. If Jinky's first goal was a scrappy affair, then his second of the afternoon, on 74 minutes, was spectacular. Gathering a Stevie Chalmers throw-in, the Celtic winger cut in from the inside-right channel before unleashing a stunning left-foot shot from the edge of the area which left Norrie Martin in the Rangers goal with absolutely no chance.

It was a goal worthy of winning any game never mind league title, and the drenched Celtic fans inside Ibrox began celebrating the first domestic treble in the history of Scottish football. Nerves were perhaps stretched when Roger Hynd equalised with nine minutes of the match remaining, but there was to be no further scoring in the game and the final whistle confirmed Celtic as champions for a second consecutive season. There would be one more league game to complete the fixtures – a 2-0 home win over Kilmarnock on May 15 – and it set the seal on a remarkable league campaign for Jock Stein's side.

They had played thirty-four league games, winning twenty-six and drawing six. They lost just two fixtures throughout the campaign, both of them against Dundee United, and both by a 3-2 scoreline. In securing the title, finishing three points clear of Rangers in second place, Celtic scored an impressive 111 goals, conceding just thirty-three.

The meteoric rise of Jock Stein's side remains an incredible football achievement, even in purely domestic terms, and even after fifty years have passed. Stein took over at Celtic on March 9, 1965, and while just twenty-four hours later his new team beat Airdrie 6-0 at Broomfield, that league campaign was another forgettable one for the club. They finished eighth in the league, having won fifteen games, drawing five and losing thirteen. The team scored seventy-six goals but conceded fifty-seven. Not even the most wildly optimistic Celtic supporter could have imagined that the team would be champions within twelve months, never mind that they would soon win every domestic trophy and stand on the verge of greatness with a European Cup final to compete in.

That was done with, more or less, the same group of players that Stein had inherited, which only served to further emphasise the importance of the new manager in the success and his ability to get the best out of every individual player within the team structure. Of the eleven men who took to the field on March 10, 1965 in Stein's first game in charge, seven of them would be in the line-up for Lisbon. The team was: Fallon, Young, Gemmell, Clark, McNeill, Brogan, Chalmers, Murdoch, Hughes, Lennox, Auld. And it was Bertie Auld, who had returned to Celtic in January that year from Birmingham City for his second spell with the club, who must have immediately caught the eye of the new manager at Broomfield, scoring five of Celtic's six goals, including two penalties; John Hughes scored the other goal.

Watching Celtic clinch their second consecutive league title in the rain at Ibrox on May 6, Helenio Herrera could not have failed to be impressed by Celtic's resilience, skill and determination in battling their city rivals and the elements. What his scouting notes said about the game and Stein's team in general were not known, nor whether what he had seen would dictate how his team would play on May 25. Herrera's team employed the 'Catenaccio' style of football that had become synonymous with the Italian game and which, to be fair, had garnered an impressive degree of success for the Inter Milan side, with three league titles and two European Cups during Herrera's reign.

Catenaccio placed a strong emphasis on defence – the word means 'door-bolt' in Italian – with the focus on nullifying opponents' attacks and preventing any goalscoring opportunities. This was particularly effective when defending a lead, when the team would deploy an ultra-defensive formation to stifle the opposition and the game. Herrera's Inter Milan side had four man-marking defenders playing in front of a sweeper, who was there to mop up anything and anyone who managed to break through the defensive line. Herrera, however, would later dispute the dour, defensive reputation that Catenaccio got, saying, 'the problem is that most of the people who copied me copied me wrongly. They forgot to include the attacking principles that my Catenaccio included. I had Picchi as a sweeper, yes, but I also had Facchetti, the first full back to score as many goals as a forward.'

Some students and historians of football would claim that it was the 'total football' of Holland in the early 1970s, pioneered by Rinus Michels, first at Ajax and then with the Dutch national team, which blew the theory and practise of Catenaccio apart – and Ajax did beat Inter 2-0 in the 1972 European Cup final after the Italians had edged out Celtic following a penalty shoot-out in the semi-final – but it was Stein's cavalier Celtic side of 1967 which had first exposed the weaknesses, showing others how Inter, and Catenaccio, could be beaten, even when conceding the first goal.

Jock Stein's first action, after seeing his side clinch their second consecutive title, was not to organise or take part in any championship celebrations. Instead, he was booked on a flight to Italy to see Inter take on Juventus in a top-of-the-table clash the following day in Turin. There had been an offer from Helenio Herrera that the Celtic manager could return with him in the private jet that had brought him to Scotland, but that offer dissipated, as was Herrera's promise of a car to pick Stein up from his hotel to take him to the Stadio delle Allpi and have a ticket waiting for him. It might have been the Argentinian trying to play mind-games with his Scottish counterpart, but he was taking on an opponent who would prove to be more than a match.

Celtic, having retained their league title to go with the Scottish Cup, League Cup and Glasgow Cup trophies already garnered, now had two competitive games left that season – the league game against Kilmarnock on May 15 and the European Cup final ten days later. However, there was also the small matter of an international friendly match between Scotland and the Soviet Union at Hampden, arranged for Wednesday, May 10. The paucity of Scotland caps amongst the Lisbon Lions has already been documented in this book, but for this meaningless game, six Celtic players found themselves in the starting XI – Simpson, Gemmell, Johnstone, Clark, Lennox and McNeill – while Willie Wallace came on as a substitute for Denis Law. Remarkably, there was not a single Rangers player in the squad, with the Ibrox side having been allowed to withdraw their players in order to take part in a friendly match in Toronto, a fixture that had been arranged after the Scotland match was announced.

The Scottish champions, meanwhile, who were in the midst of preparing for the European Cup final, had seven players in action for a friendly match. The crowd of 53,497 at Hampden saw the Soviet Union win 2-0, with Tommy Gemmell netting an own goal, lobbing Ronnie Simpson with a pass-back from the halfway line. Celtic supporters in recent years have sung 'That's why we're paranoid,' over various perceived grievances in relation to the Scottish football authorities, but they certainly could have done so with some legitimacy in relation to this decision. Thankfully, the Celtic players returned to the club injury-free which would have been a relief to Jock Stein and the Celtic fans.

Writing in the *Celtic View* on the same day that the Scotland game was to take place, the Celtic manager addressed the issue: 'Well, we've completed the clean sweep of the Scottish senior football competitions and I don't need to emphasise how happy I am. My first duty now is to give my great thanks to the players who have fought so nobly for the club and to the Celtic directors who have given me magnificent support in trying to build a team to enhance the club's reputation.

'Never before in modern times have a Scottish club won all the competitions open to them. Now the league championship trophy remains in our boardroom and stands alongside the Scottish Cup, the League Cup and the Glasgow Cup. We have, of course, one more job to do. We cannot relax for long, for the European Cup final at Lisbon lies ahead and we are going to try to win this one just as hard as we did the others. It was, of course, especially pleasing to win the title finally at Ibrox against the only team who have been challenging us for many weeks. It was also gratifying to see so good a match in such difficult circumstances. So heavy was the rain in the hours before the kick-off that I wondered if the game would go on. I think that if the torrential rain had continued for another half-hour there would have been a postponement. As it was, we were fortunate in that while the rain did not cease throughout the match, it became much less heavy.

'What a mess the league authorities would have been in had the game been postponed. When could we have played it? Not this week, because of the Scotland-Russia international match, and not the next again because our remaining game with Kilmarnock had been re-arranged for Monday, May 15. And we certainly could not have been asked to play before we left for Lisbon at the beginning of the week in which the final is to be played. One of the real snags, of course, was the choice of no fewer than nine Celtic players for the Scottish pool of 16 for the international tonight. Compare that with the situation regarding Rangers players and the game with Russia. The international was arranged long before Rangers fixed up to play a friendly match in Toronto. Yet their players are released from international commitments while ours get the heavy end of the stick. If the position weren't so serious, it would be laughable.

'I make no apology for continuing to be critical of the set-up in Scotland. Winning the Scottish Cup or the League Cup is fine, but winning the league championship is the most important of all for any club. It enables them to play in the most important club competition in Europe, if not in the world. Yet the one competition which gets knocked about in the matter of dates is the league championship! Let's have a much more realistic, sensible approach as soon as possible.'

Just one week before the European Cup final, Jock Stein was named Britain's Manager of the Year for the second consecutive season in a ceremony at the Café Royal in Piccadilly, London. It was a fitting honour for a man who had already moulded a team to dominate Scottish football, and who, along with his players, stood on the verge of greatness. By that time the team was ensconced in its now traditional seaside retreat of Seamill, where they'd headed the day after completing their league fixtures with the 2-0 home win over Kilmarnock in front of a crowd of 21,000. They would remain there until the Saturday before the game, May 20, and after a few days at home the Celtic party would fly out to their Portuguese base in Estoril, a beach resort just over fifteen miles from Lisbon. They would be staying at the Hotel Palacio, which had actually been booked by the club following the 3-1 victory over Dukla Prague in the first leg of the semi-final. Whether through confidence or foresight, it proved to be a good move by the Celtic board.

Seamill provided some welcome relaxation, with golf at the nearby West Kilbride course popular with the players, along with snooker and card games in the complex, all of this in between focused training sessions at a nearby facility in Largs, where the Celtic manager began to drill into his players what they could expect from their defensively-minded Italian opponents. Jim Craig explained: 'Jock built us up very well. There was no kidding that an ordinary performance would be fine. He let us know that Inter, with an eight-man defence, would be hard to beat. All the training was directed towards ways of drawing such a defence out and piercing it.'

The Celtic manager also organised a screening of the by-now legendary 1960 European Cup between Real Madrid and Eintracht Frankfurt, played at Hampden. Real Madrid had won the match 7-3, and many of the Celtic players hoping to emulate the exploits of Puskas, Di Stefano, Gento et al had either been on the terraces at Hampden for the match or had managed to catch the black and white footage on television. Stein desperately wanted that European Cup, but while pragmatism had ruled in the away leg of the semi-final when his team had a 3-1 lead to defend against Dukla Prague, he was going to send his team out to play to their strengths and expose Inter's weaknesses, not the other way round. It was shaping up to be a classic battle between two different football philosophies.

Writing in the *Celtic View* under the headline 'Tradition', the chairman Robert Kelly reflected on what Celtic's most successful ever season meant to him, and to the club. Kelly had joined the Celtic board in 1932 following the death of his father, James, a former player, chairman and latterly a director of the club, and he became Celtic chairman in 1947, a position he held until his death in 1971. He was a figure who divided opinion amongst the Celtic support, and continues to do so. On the one hand, the blame for the club's stagnation in the twenty years following the end of the Second World War can be firmly placed at Kelly's door. Interference in team selection, at a time when there were plenty of talented footballers at the club, saw occasional triumphs – the Coronation Cup in 1953 and subsequent league and Scottish Cup double the following season, and the 7-1 League Cup final victory over Rangers in 1957 – overshadowed by consistent mediocrity and underachievement.

However, his handling of the so-called 'Flag Controversy' in 1952, when he strongly resisted attempts to force Celtic to stop flying the Irish Tricolour over Celtic Park, did win praise from supporters, as would his later stance against playing teams from Eastern Europe following the Soviet invasion of Czechoslovakia in 1968. But it was his decision to appoint Jock Stein as manager in 1965, and also give him the full control over team selection and tactics, that was undoubtedly his greatest ever decision as Celtic chairman. While it's subsequently been suggested that it was with reluctance that Robert Kelly made the decision, apparently favouring Sean Fallon, who was already on the coaching staff at the club, for the managerial role, he was as good as his word in allowing Jock Stein to manage, and it paid handsome dividends from the day Stein walked back through the front door at Celtic Park.

Stein and Fallon both enjoyed a good relationship with the Celtic chairman. They had known him previously when they'd both played for the club, and there was always a strong respect for his position and commitment to Celtic, regardless of the fact his stewardship hadn't always brought the success he obviously craved. His death in 1971 deprived Stein of his strongest supporter on the Celtic board, and his relationship with the custodians of the club was never as close or as cordial after that.

Robert Kelly's pride in Stein's Celtic team was evident in the words expressed in the *Celtic View*, which displayed a strong pride for the club, but also for the country.

'It is no exaggeration to say that all of those who love Celtic are in happy, thankful mood – happy with the great successes in the club's greatest season, thankful that the players and the management have been blessed with fine health and spirit. I, as club chairman, am, of course, particularly delighted – for three principal reasons. Having been reared in a Celtic family – my father, James Jelly, played in the very first Celtic team and when his playing days were over, became a director and then chairman of the club – I am steeped in Celtic tradition. In my father's day, and in mine, Celtic have always preferred to play attacking football whenever it was possible. Who would say we have not maintained that tradition in the past season?

'Secondly, though we have bought senior players when the need arose, Celtic have always preferred to rear our own players. The backbone of all our teams has been the young man brought up to believe in the club and to feel honoured in playing for the club. Again, we have fully maintained the tradition. Last, but not least important, is the third principal reason. Celtic will play in the European Cup final with an entirely Scottish eleven. It is often claimed that a club which reaches a final in European competition represents their country as well as club. I claim that Celtic can most fittingly represent Scotland because we are an all-Scottish eleven. Few, if any, of the famous teams of Europe, Real Madrid, Inter Milan and the rest, can make such a claim – in some degree they have become international clubs. You will, therefore, understand why I and my directors and all at Celtic Park are very happy at this proud moment of Celtic's history.'

The same issue of the club magazine also carried words from the Celtic manager, under the banner headline, 'Fitness'. The tone of the piece was confident but realistic, with Stein highlighting Inter's strengths, both in terms of their technical ability and their experience of playing at this level. His own side didn't lack technical ability themselves, and the manager knew that, but he also highlighted one area he'd obviously identified as a key strength in the Celtic side – that of fitness. Helenio Herrera could have done worse in the run-up to Lisbon than to have subscribed to the *Celtic View*, because in those words were the blueprint that Jock Stein had surmised could beat Inter Milan. What transpired over the ninety minutes in the Estadio Nacional provided a perfect illustration of Stein's shrewd football brain and, of course, the supreme talent and fitness of his players.

'Everyone connected with Celtic knows how much effort the players have made in the past few months; they have done a magnificent job. They have one more effort to make – the greatest of them all – before they enjoy a well-deserved rest. And make it they will. I shall probably surprise many people by saying in the week before the European Cup final that capable players as the Celtic lads are, they go into the final inferior in the skills of the game to their opponents. We in Britain are still behind the best of the European clubs in the arts and crafts of the game. That does not mean to say I am pessimistic about our prospects against Inter Milan in Lisbon on May 25 – far from it.

'It does mean that we shall have to play with all of our traditional spirit, to be able to play at the greatest pace we can find and – most important of all – to be in 100 per cent physical condition, prepared to play till we drop for the club and the wonderful supporters we have. It is a manager's dream to have a team of great skill and superb physical fitness. It would be foolish to say now that we have such a combination. But we are on the way – no-one would deny us that. And our efforts to match the best in the world will be intensified whatever happens in Lisbon. Inter have a clear advantage, of course, in that they have considerable experience of the great occasions in Europe. We are only beginning to get to know them. Next Thursday night will make us much richer in experience and, who knows, perhaps champions of Europe also.'

Preparations at Seamill complete, the players had a few days to spend with their families before meeting up again on Tuesday, May 23 for the flight from Glasgow to Lisbon. A squad of twenty players was on the chartered plane – a De Havilland Comet from Dan Air – with the eleven men who would soon become immortalised as the Lisbon Lions joined by reserve goalkeeper John Fallon, and outfield players Willie O'Neill, Charlie Gallagher, John Hughes, David Cattenach, Ian Young, Jim Brogan and John Cushley, while Joe McBride was also included in the travelling party, even though he was still recovering from injury and wouldn't be playing in the final. Before boarding the flight, the Celtic manager told reporters at the airport: 'I plan to name my team on our arrival in Lisbon, later today. The players already know the team, but I will not name it until I see how they fare on the flight. Some of them are not the best travellers, and it could be I will delay naming my side if some of them are not too happy about the flight."

Stein's confidence in his team was something that he wanted to make sure his players sensed, and his decision to name his team 48 hours before kick-off was an illustration of that. Having checked into their hotel, the Celtic players headed to the Estadio Nacional for their first training session, scheduled for 5.30pm, which was the same time as the final would kick off, allowing the players to not only familiarise themselves with the stadium and the playing surface, but also the temperature in the Portuguese capital; the early kick-off had been dictated by the absence of floodlights in the Estadio Nacional. That training session took place under the watchful eyes of the Inter Milan squad who, having finished their own practice on the pitch, stayed in the stadium to watch their opponents.

Jock Stein's line-up for the European Cup final has, over the past fifty years, become like a litany of saints for Celtic supporters, instantly repeated in reverential tones upon request. When Stein named the team, it was only the sixth time that those eleven men had taken to the field together as the Celtic starting XI. Simpson, Craig, Gemmell, Murdoch, McNeill, Clark, Johnstone, Wallace, Chalmers, Auld, Lennox. Significantly, three of the games that they had played together had been the second leg of the semi-final against Dukla Prague, the Scottish Cup final victory over Aberdeen and the league clincher at Ibrox; the other games had been a 4-0 victory at Muirton Park over St Johnstone on January 14, 1967 – the first time those eleven men had been selected – and a goal-less draw against Aberdeen at Celtic Park in the middle of April.

Revealing his team, Stein told reporters: 'We are going to play not one, but three types of game at the National Stadium. This is a special match. It is the most important game in Celtic's history and, for the first time, we are going to have to work to win inside ninety minutes. So we are going to attack as we have never attacked before. We will also defend when we have to defend, and we are going to keep control of the midfield when we have to keep control of the midfield. We aim to win by teamwork alone ... Cups are not won by individuals, no matter how great they are. They are won by men in a team, men who put their club before personal prestige. I am lucky. I have the players who do just that for Celtic.'

Interestingly, the injuries picked up by Inter's two foreign players Jair da Costa (Brazilian) and Luis Suarez (Spanish), certainly a blow to Inter's attacking plans and whose absence may well have influenced how Herrera and his team approached the match, meant that Celtic's all-Scottish starting XI would face an all-Italian line-up, with extra-time scheduled in the event that the match finished all-square at the end of the 90 minutes. If that didn't produce a winner, then a replay was scheduled for Saturday, May 27 in the Estadio Nacional.

The stadium has not changed much in appearance since 1967, and it looked pretty unusual even back then. Designed by Portuguese landscape architect Francisco Caldeira Cabral, along with fellow Portuguese architect Jacobetty Rosa and German architect, Konrad Wisner, the Estadio Nacional was inaugurated on June 10, 1944 – Portugal Day – by the country's prime minister, António Oliveira Salazar. It wasn't a traditional oval-shaped stadium, but a three-sided construction, with the east side of the stadium open.

Situated in the municipality of Oeiras, six miles from Lisbon city centre, in woodland that manages to conceal the stadium until visitors are almost upon it, the stadium used to host matches for the Portuguese national team, but while it's no longer a venue for these games, it continues to be the setting for the Portuguese Cup final, the Taca de Portugal, with the 2016 final between Porto and Braga played at 5.15pm local time on Sunday, May 22 in front of a crowd of around 39,000 – the capacity for the stadium now, though back in 1967, an estimated 55,000 gathered for the most famous game in the stadium's history.

And back then, it had no floodlights, while a small temporary stand had been erected for the European Cup final facing the main, imposing edifice of the ground, which housed the assembled press, and in front of that were the respective benches of Celtic and Inter Milan. The Estadio Nacional was an all-seater stadium, the stone terraces designed for fans to sit rather than stand – though not many Celtic fans would do that during the tense 90 minutes of the final – while the eye-catching feature of the main stand which ran the length of one touchline, was the marble rostrum held up by a series of marble pillars. It was here that the dignitaries of the day would sit and it was here that it was proposed the winning captain would lead his team to lift the trophy.

While the Celtic players were relaxing in their Estoril base, and acquainting themselves with the arena they would enter on May 25, the Celtic supporters were already on the move to the Portuguese capital, with many of the estimated 10,000 expected to travel already there and making friends with the locals to the extent that Celtic became the team of the Lisboetas. This included the famous Celticade which left from Glasgow's George Square on a 1,750-mile trip to Lisbon, a 100-car convoy led by legendary *Evening Times* journalist John Quinn, who was driving a Hillman Imp that had been specially painted green and white for the trip, and waved off on the trip by Celtic captain, Billy McNeill; Quinn had only been driving for six months prior to the pilgrimage to Portugal. The Celtic captain later recalled seeing that pilgrimage party bound for the Portuguese capital.

'There were so many things that made the final such a wonderful occasion for us and that was one of them. Looking back, it seemed to be an eternity before the game, and I remember the green and white Hillman Imp leading the convoy away. It would be a big undertaking even now, but car technology being what it was then, it was an incredible journey. I'm convinced to this day that, although they were setting off on this marathon, not one of those people had any idea of what they were letting themselves in for.'

For many Celtic fans, the trip to the European Cup final was their first time abroad and the *Celtic View* offered a helpful guide for anyone planning the trip.

PASSPORT

Visitors must carry a valid passport. Applications (with two passport photographs) to 14 Princes Square, Glasgow, C.1, must be made in person.

CLOTHING

Climate at this time of year pleasantly warm; light clothing is best. The Portuguese are more formal than most in the matter of clothing; men do not go about without wearing a jacket; shorts are not encouraged.

CURRENCY

Coins – for 1, 2 ½ 5, 10 and 20 escudos; notes for 20, 50, 100, 500, 1,000. One escudo (100 centavos) = 3d. Count on that basis or on 80 to £1. Remember that Scottish bank notes will not be accepted.

RESTAURANTS

Aviz, Negresco, Solmar (beer and shellfish), A Gondola (Italian cooking), Montes Claros. For cheaper meals, the numerous small restaurants in the streets leading off the Rossio, a large square in the centre of the city, are particularly good.

CUSTOMS

You are limited to 200 duty free cigarettes (or 1 ½ lb, tobacco) on entering Portugal. Everything else for your personal use can be taken in free.

TIPPING

Hotel service charges cover everything, but give 3 escudos per bag or case to whoever brings up your luggage. Fifty escudos per week to chambermaid. One or two escudos for minor services – doorman calling a taxi, for instance. Nightclub waiter expects 5 to 10 per cent in addition to service charge.

SHOPPING

Most shops open 9am to 1pm, and from 3pm to 7pm (lunch and siesta between 1 and 3)

LANGUAGE

Should present little difficulty; English is spoke fairly fluently and understood almost everywhere.

It probably helped that one of Lisbon's big two football clubs – Sporting Lisbon – played in the same green and white hoops as Celtic, producing an instant affinity between Celtic and Sporting supporters, but the fans who arrived in their thousands from Scotland and elsewhere also made a great impression on the locals; a reputation gained by Celtic supporters and enhanced over the years of travelling throughout Europe in support of the team perhaps has its roots in the 1967 European Cup final and the trip to Lisbon.

Supporters, like the Scottish press, also had easy access to the Celtic hotel, and could mingle and chat with players whenever the occasion arose. It made for a relaxed atmosphere within the Celtic camp, which also helped settle any pre-match nerves that might have been festering within the squad.

The day before the final, Jock Stein offered his final thoughts on the impeding clash with Inter Milan. Writing in the *Celtic View*, the manager said: 'It is important for the Celtic players to think they can win every match they play. But it is equally important for them to keep in mind that there is always a possibility of losing. Now it is a 'must' that they remember that though we all hope we win the European Cup – and believe we can win it – there's more than a slight chance that we won't.

'If it should happen that we lose to Inter Milan, we want to be remembered on the Continent and indeed all over the world (because of the televiewing public) for the football we have played. Never has good behaviour on the playing field been so important. Winning or losing tomorrow night in Lisbon, I want our great club's name to be even more respected than it is at present. Our players have had this drilled into them. But at the same time they have not the slightest feeling of inferiority; all that they have to remember – and all of them agree – is that we might not win yet we might achieve great distinction.

'The Celtic officials are confident that those who go as supporters to Lisbon will treat the occasion as the players will. This will be the smallest Celtic support ever at an important Cup final. But we know that many thousands back home will be with us in spirit. To everyone who has already sent good wishes, the players and I send our thanks. It is impossible to acknowledge the vast number of messages we have received. But we hope we can give all our well-wishers a fitting reward. The Celtic party in Lisbon ask the View to wish the supporters at home very happy viewing on television or listening to the radio tomorrow night. The great majority of the club's supporters had little or no chance of attending the final. To them even more than to the luckier minority who have been able to travel to Portugal, we promise our biggest ever effort to conclude an already great season in the best possible manner.'

There was also an appeal from the club, similar to the previous round, not to go to Glasgow Airport to welcome the team home from Lisbon. Depending on whether the game was played to a finish on the Thursday or Saturday, the Celtic squad would return home and go directly from the airport to Celtic Park, with the ground being opened to allow everyone who wished to give the team a good reception.

The Celtic manager no doubt penned his notes before a bizarre incident the night before the final, one that summed up the relaxed atmosphere within his squad, while also illustrating the endearing naivety of a side making their first appearance in a European Cup final. Stein had a friend, Brodie Lennox, who ran a country club in Estoril, and the Celtic squad had been invited up to his house on May 24 to watch an international match that was on television that night. The house was a short walk from the Hotel Palacio, and the players had strolled up there in the afternoon sunshine. When they made the return journey, however, it was dusk and this was where the problems began, as Jim Craig explained. 'All we had to do was go back down this country road, cut along the sea front for a few hundred yards, and then we were back at our hotel. It was getting a bit darker by this time, and Neilly Mochan suddenly said, 'There's our hotel over there. It's just on the other side of this field. Let's take a short cut'. We could see the lights of the hotel and, to be fair to Neilly, it didn't seem like a dangerous notion to anyone. There we were on the night before the European Cup final, and the whole first-team were clambering over a wall into this field, and across a couple of fences. There could have been anything there – barbed wire on the wall, a bull in the field – and someone could have broken a leg in a ditch or tripped over a rock. There was no thought or calculation on our part about this being the night before the European Cup final. It was just the quickest way back to our hotel.'

Thankfully, the players returned to the hotel unscathed, and settled down for a night's sleep before facing the biggest game in their career.

And so, as dawn broke over the Portuguese capital, the stage was set for Celtic to make history. They would become the first Scottish, British and non-Latin side to lift the European Cup since its inception back in 1955 if they could see off the might of Inter Milan, who had already lifted the trophy twice. The competition's roll of honour was already an impressive one, and Celtic would be in extremely good company if they did win. Real Madrid (6), Benfica (2), Inter Milan (2), AC Milan (1).

Thursday, May 25, 1967 was also a Holy Day of Obligation in the Roman Catholic calendar – the Feast of Corpus Christi – and the day began for many of the Celtic players and supporters with Mass before attention turned fully to the game taking place that afternoon. The task for Jock Stein and Sean Fallon was to keep the players relaxed, yet focused on what lay ahead. Before too long, however, it was time to head to the Estadio Nacional, and as they boarded the bus which would take them to the game, they spotted Alfredo Di Stefano talking to Jock Stein, the legendary Real Madrid forward having turned up to wish the Hoops good luck; that might have had something to do with the fact he wanted Celtic to be the opposition for his upcoming testimonial match at the beginning of June. Bizarrely, the coach driver, having picked up the Celtic squad, initially started driving in the wrong direction, and so the team arrived at the stadium about an hour before kick-off. As Bobby Lennox explained in his autobiography, the delay actually worked in Celtic's favour. 'Habitually, we would get to the ground a good bit earlier than that, but our latecoming did us good. By the time we had had a walk on the pitch – which was in excellent condition – and got changed, it was time for the match to begin. There was no sitting around and no time for a build-up of nerves.'

The players had already been acquainted with the Estadio Nacional from their training session at the stadium earlier in the week but now, when they returned, the stadium was full of supporters, many of them having successfully made the journey from Scotland, including family and friends who were there for this momentous occasion.

Back in the dressing-room, which was divided in two by a shower in the middle which meant that the defenders were changing in one section and the attackers in another, the last few words of encouragement were offered by their manager before the Celtic players made their way across a courtyard to line up alongside the Inter Milan players. The tunnel at the Estadio Nacional was actually underground and at one end of the stadium, to the left of one of the goals, and the players would emerge out of the ground and into the searing Lisbon heat before walking across the pitch to the centre-circle.

It is built into the legend of Lisbon that, while both teams were lined up that tunnel, seeing the sun shine down the stairs and drawing them towards the arena where battle would commence for the greatest prize in club football, they were eyeing each other up. Well, the Celtic players were, observing the pristine, well-groomed appearance of their Italian counterparts, stern, focused, like catalogue models. It took the Glaswegian gallusness of Bertie Auld to puncture the aura of superiority that was beginning to take root in the tunnel when he burst into the opening lines of *The Celtic Song*. He was quickly followed by the rest of his team-mates, their voices strong, proud and confident bouncing off the walls and bemusing the Inter players. They would never have encountered anything like it before. Whether it unnerved them or made them think they were facing a team of jokers is not known, but Auld's impromptu singalong dispelled what vestiges of nerves remained in the Celtic squad. They were ready for the game and, more importantly, they were ready to win.

The destination of the European Cup would, of course, be decided on the field of play, but Jock Stein struck the first psychological blow of the afternoon even before the whistle sounded for the start of the ninety minutes. When the Celtic manager and his backroom staff, along with substitute goalkeeper, John Fallon, made their way to the benches on the touchline facing the main stand, they discovered that Helenio Herrera and the Inter staff had taken the home bench which had been allocated to Celtic. Stein was not going to accept that. With the help of defender John Cushley acting as interpreter, Stein told his counterpart to move. It wasn't a debate, a discussion or even a polite request, and Inter's manager quickly realised that, ushering the rest of the Inter group to follow him as they trudged along the touchline to where their bench was located. This encounter, brief and over in a matter of minutes, was witnessed by the Celtic players as they strode across the pitch. Their manager had shown them he was playing second-best to no-one. Now it was time for the players to do the same.

If there was no sense of inferiority amongst the Celtic players, there was still an appreciation that they were facing one of Europe's top sides, and as the two lines of players headed across the pitch, Jimmy Johnstone could be seen gesturing to Giacinto Facchetti that he wanted to swap jerseys with the Italian defender at the end of the game. Facchetti was a world-class full-back, whose defensive skills were matched by his attacking prowess, though on the day in Lisbon, it would be the two full-backs in green and white Hoops who provided all of the offensive impetus.

It was Inter who got the game underway and the 10,000 Celtic supporters in the Estadio Nacional, and the millions watching or listening around the globe offered up one final prayer for the cause.

The early exchanges between the sides did not necessarily give an indication of how the game was going to unfold, given that it was Inter who had the first chance in the match, Sandro Mazzola's header from the edge of the six-yard box well saved by Ronnie Simpson. However, Jimmy Johnstone was proving a handful for the Inter defence, despite having a constant shadow wherever he was on the pitch in the shape of Tarcisio Burgnich, the full-back given the thankless task of trying to stop Celtic's No.7. First, Johnstone had a left-foot shot before his header from a Lennox cross was saved by Giuliano Sarti in the Inter goal, which produced the first corner of the game. Those chances were encouraging for Jock Stein's side but on seven minutes disaster struck when West German referee, Kurt Tschenscher, gave the Italians a penalty.

Mazzola had picked up the ball in the centre of the park and surged forward before feeding a ball into the penalty area for Renato Cappellini, who had made a run across the box from the left-hand side. Celtic right-back Jim Craig had tracked the run, but as the ball reached the Inter forward, with Craig at his shoulder, he tumbled over and the referee pointed to the spot. While a few Celtic players voiced their dismay over the decision, Craig walked away from the crowd in the area. He explained: 'I didn't go overboard in my protestations when the referee awarded the penalty … What would have been the point? He was hardly likely to change his decision once he'd pointed to the spot. It was never a penalty, absolutely no way. The referee got it totally wrong. Some people said that I tackled with the wrong foot, while others said I should have tried to play Cappellini offside, but it was never a penalty. He was a big bloke but he went down far too easily when I challenged him. He was looking for a penalty and the referee duly obliged.'

Sandro Mazzola, Inter's experienced and prolific striker, duly stepped up and rolled the ball coolly into the right-hand corner of the net as Ronnie Simpson dived to his left. Given Inter Milan's skill in deploying Catennacio to defend slender leads, it certainly wasn't how Jock Stein would have wanted the game to pan out, but the loss of the early goal did not deter or deflate Celtic. Instead, it only served to galvanise the Scottish champions, who launched wave after wave of attacks on the Inter goal, though finding their opponents' defence and, in particular, goalkeeper Sarti, to be impregnable foes.

Half-time saw Inter disappear back below ground at the tunnel with their one-goal lead still intact, while the Celtic players would have wondered just how they could break down the Inter defence and get back into the match. Jock Stein was pleased with his side's first-half performance, and encouraged his side to continue in a similar vein in the second forty-five minutes, telling the players he sensed Inter Milan were wilting and that it was only a matter of time before the equaliser came.

It duly arrived just after the hour mark – sixty-two minutes to be exact – and it was the two Celtic full-backs who combined, with Jim Craig sliding a pass across into the path of Tommy Gemmell who blasted home a shot from the edge of the Inter box into the top corner of the net, leaving the excellent Sarti with absolutely no chance of stopping it. Celtic were level and while the players celebrated the goal with a visible determination to press home their advantage, the Inter players looked drained. They had managed to stem the Celtic tide up until this point, but having lost one goal, it looked as though they realised the game, and the European Cup, was slipping away from their grasp. Still, Celtic continued to attack without getting a second goal, but just as it looked as though extra-time was looming, Stevie Chalmers scored what proved to be the winning goal, and the most important in the history of Celtic, nudging home a Bobby Murdoch shot with five minutes of the match remaining. The players celebrated, Jock Stein and the Celtic bench celebrated on the touchline, the Celtic fans in the Estadio Nacional hugged and kissed friends and strangers, and all across the world, Celtic supporters jumped for joy. The team formed by Irish immigrants to raise money to help alleviate poverty in the East End of Glasgow were now on the verge of becoming the best team in Europe.

A tense, nervous five minutes followed, but the full-time whistle brought scenes of jubilation in the stadium as Celtic fans leapt over the moat which surrounded the pitch and flocked on to what was now hallowed turf to celebrate with the players.

While the only statistic that ultimately matters in any game of football is the final scoreline, the match statistics for the 1967 European Cup final do tell of Celtic's domination, where the scoreline might suggest to anyone who hasn't seen the game that it was a closely-fought affair. Celtic had a total of forty-five shots, to Inter Milan's three, with sixteen of those shots on target to Inter's three. Celtic also had twenty-nine shots off target which included three which hit the woodwork. Jock Stein's side enjoyed sixty-four per cent possession, while they had ten corners to Inter's grand total of zero. They also delivered forty crosses into the Inter penalty area, while their opponents managed just four. Celtic had 310 successful passes, compared to 224 for Inter, while they only passed back seven times to the goalkeeper (in the days when keepers could pick up the ball from a passback), while Inter made twenty passbacks.

The match report filed from Lisbon by Hugh Taylor for the *Daily Record* sums up the magic of that day in May, under the banner headline 'CHAMPIONS OF EUROPE', a joyful, celebratory account of one of the great victories in a European final.

> *'Celtic were crowned football kings of Europe in the exotic National Stadium here tonight. The scenes under the setting run at the end were fantastic − but so was the match. Celtic came back from what seemed an early crippling disaster to annihilate the once proud Inter Milan with a hurricane of attacking football.*

Every one of the 60,000 crowd here tonight knew that Celtic were really great ... and the fans paid them tribute. How Celtic came back from disaster will become an epic in European football history. They were a goal down in exactly seven minutes from a penalty – and then they spend many minutes of frustration as the most brilliant moves and the fiercest shooting anyone in Europe has ever known, failed. Failed not because this was a great Inter defence – but failed mainly because of bad luck.

In the end, however, it was a triumph of Celtic's football – the new football pattern manager Jock Stein has set – the pattern that must be adopted from now on in Europe. Celtic gave Europe a new conception of football. This was shown by that explosive character, Tommy Gemmell, hero of the afternoon. He capped a highly successful season with a super goal, the goal of the season, the goal that sent all Celtic frustrations flying. What a goal!

And it showed that Celtic had all the accent on attack as Jim Craig joined Gemmell in the assault. It was a night of wild triumph and now Celtic are unquestionably the greatest team in Europe. And if they play with this heart and courage they will be kings of global football. For I cannot see any South American team matching them.

Inter are dead – dead in European football. They were hissed, hooted, and booed for their negative tactics, and Celtic became the idols of Portuguese fans, among the most knowledgeable in Europe, with their brilliant play.

Before the kick-off the heat was tremendous. But this foreign stadium became a little bit of Parkhead, for everyone was cheering on Celtic. There was not a cheep from Inter fans. It seemed that Celtic had taken over Lisbon.

But in seven minutes the banners of green dropped around the terraces when tragedy hit Celtic. In one of Inter's few raids, Cappellini was running through and into a menacing position when he was pulled down by Jim Craig. The referee was well behind in giving the penalty play – but he had no hesitation. Celtic protested but they couldn't move him, and Mazzola scored neatly from the spot. This should have been a crippling blow for Celtic. For it compensated Inter for the loss of Suarez.

But this was when Celtic came into the picture, the brave new Celtic, the Celtic of wonderful skill, amazing stamina, and courage. They hit Inter with everything – high crosses, wonderful moves, cunning feints, and neat flicks.

Lennox did the running and Auld supplied neat moves. But it all seemed in vain. Inter were pale shadows of the once great blue and black team. Their defence was anything but tight, anything but confident. But they packed every man into their goal. Only Mazzola and Cappellini were left up front. It was frustrating. Celtic could not get the goals they so richly deserved. Nothing went right. Auld hit the bar and then Sarti saved a terrific Gemmell shot.

At half-time we wondered just what more Celtic could do to bring equality in a match when they should have been so far ahead.

But it wasn't long until Celtic showed that they had everything a great team needs. Their spirits should have been depressed when they were refused what seemed a justified penalty against Burgnich. Then, from the indirect free-kick the ball appeared over the line but the ref waved on play.

Bang, bang, bang – went Celtic. But still the luckiest defence in the world held out.

THEN TOMMY GEMMELL STRUCK.

What a great goal it was and it shows you how much in command were Celtic that it was made by right-back Jim Craig. Gemmell to Craig and back, and what a shot from Tommy. His first-time right-foot shot thundered into the back of the net like a flash. The great Sarti was beaten and the exotic stadium turned into a green and white inferno.

Helenio Herrera, who had been bawling instructions all afternoon from the bench, put his head between his knees and wept. And the Inter players knew in their hearts this was the end, the end of a once great team.

It was only a matter of time until Celtic got the winner. Inter could not burst into attack when attack was called for. They did not have the know-how, the courage, the stamina to hit back again against superb Celtic. Anxiety set in, however, as the minutes ticked away and the winner Celtic deserved did not come. But the attacks grew fiercer and fiercer. Inter had never met a team like Celtic before. Were these footballers or robots, they wondered? They soon got their answer.

With only five minutes to go, Celtic scored the goal that made history – the goal that made them the first British club to win the European

Cup. Bobby Murdoch was the man behind it. In yet another fast and fascinating attack, Inter's defence were ripped apart and Bobby slammed in a low hard angular drive.

As Sarti moved to cover it, Stevie Chalmers stuck out a foot to deflect the ball into the goal. And what joy there was. For, with the ball in the net, the European Cup was in the bag. Be proud of Celtic. This was history, and what terrific history it was.

I think only Super Celts could have come back from such a disastrous start – a start that would have knocked practically every other team in Europe out of the ring. But not this Celtic. They played all the harder, all the better. And they were entitled to call themselves great champions, for great champions they were.

It would have been the travesty of all-time if Inter had won the Cup. For they took the lashing of a lifetime. This was no cool, contemptuous defence. This was Inter at panic stations. This was Inter meeting more than their match. Burgnich, Sarti and Facchetti stuck grimly to their tasks – but in vain.

They had no answer to Celtic, a Celtic going at top speed, a Celtic who have given the world a new conception of football. No wonder Di Stefano paid a special visit to Lisbon to see the final to try to plead with Celtic to play at his benefit match in Madrid.

It was wonderful to be in this beautiful tree-lined stadium. To see the joy of the green and white bedecked fans at the end. They took over the stadium and they deserved their minutes of delirious joy.

Every Celt was a hero. On an afternoon like this, on an afternoon of triumph, of triumph never achieved by a British team before, every Celt deserved praise – from Ronnie Simpson, who had hardly a save to make all afternoon, to the fast-moving Bobby Lennox.

This was also a triumph of tactics. Celtic proved they were master of all the moves, of sophisticated raids as well as spectacular high crosses. It was a triumph for football with a real kick. It was the defeat, at last, for the method men of Inter to whom defence is law.

It was a game packed with drama, incident, excitement – and it all came from Celtic. Apart from their goal, Inter were never in the picture. Their *main hope was to try and hold on to their lead at all costs. But against Stein's men, it was a forlorn hope.'*

However, it wasn't just the Scottish press which heralded the victory as a well-deserved triumph for attacking football over the defensive philosophy of Inter Milan's that had previously proved successful if not entertaining. Gino Palumbo's report in the Italian newspaper, *Corriera della Sera*, on Friday, May 26, declared 'Inter worn out – Celtic's European Kings'

'Inter have failed. The European trophy has gone to a new team of the soccer aristocracy. The hymn of victory which rings out in the Portuguese stadium is British. The joy-crazed fans who have invaded the field are Scots. The colours which wave triumphant in the warm sunset are the Green and White of Celtic. The captain who raised the Cup towards the heavens is not Armando Picchi – his name is Billy McNeill.

In their bid to regain the title, Inter eliminated the great teams of the Continent; the Russians of Torpedo, the Hungarians of Vasas, and the Spaniards of champions, Real Madrid. Here, in the final they were brought to their knees.

Do not be misled by the narrow margin. There are no complaints, no excuses, no questions. This was total defeat, annihilation. After gaining the lead with a doubtful, disputed penalty, the 'Nerazzurri' (Black and Sky-Blue) could not hold out against the incessant attacking fury of the Scots.

At times, Inter looked like a boxer at the mercy of his opponent. The fact that they hung on for an hour, and kept vain hopes alive until a few moments from the end, was due to the sensational prowess of goalkeeper Sarti, man of a dozen incredible saves, and to the gallant defenders, Picchi, Guarneri, Burgnich and Facchetti, heroically and more and more desperately, resisting the relentless pressure of the Scots.'

It might have taken Hugh Taylor nearly 1,300 words to convey to incredible triumph of Lisbon, and reading it again sends a tingle down the spine at the excitement and sheer joy of the writer at what he had just witnessed.

Celtic manager Jock Stein put it more succinctly. 'We did it by playing football; pure, beautiful, inventive football.'

KINGS OF EUROPE

LISBOA
25 DE MAIO DE
1967
CELTIC 2-1 INTER
50° CELTIC FC
ANIVERSARIO

KINGS OF EUROPE

'John, you're immortal now.' Those words, uttered by then Liverpool manager, Bill Shankly, in the Celtic dressing room immediately after the 1967 European Cup final to Jock Stein, quickly became one of the most famous quotes in Celtic's history, a perceptive and precise soundbite from a man who was delighted for his friend, but who would also have wanted to achieve the same success. Jock Stein had achieved greatness in football and the world knew it.

On May 25, 1967, Celtic became the best team in Europe. It wasn't just that they had lifted the European Cup with the 2-1 victory over Inter Milan. That was an indisputable statistic, and would record Celtic's triumph in the history books for all-time. But Stein's side were more than just the winners of the European Cup because of the manner of the victory. It was a triumph for football, pure, beautiful inventive football, as the Celtic manager declared, and the rest of the football world, managers, coaches, players and supporters rejoiced. Celtic's victory was a triumph for the beautiful game and the positive attacking football Stein extolled, and it is no coincidence that European football would see subsequent success in the tournament from Manchester United (1968), Feyenoord (1970, unfortunately against Celtic), and the triple triumph of Ajax between 1971-74. Jock Stein's side led the way, and others followed gratefully behind Celtic.

The team that emerged triumphant from the Estadio Nacional soon became known as the Lisbon Lions, and it is a tribute that has remained with them to this day, their legendary status assured when referee, Kurt Tschenscher, put his whistle to his lips and blew for full-time. The immediate post-match melee, when the pitch disappeared as thousands of Celtic fans rushed from the stands, meant that the players were eventually ushered back to the dressing-room, many of them minus much of their match kit, which they'd been relieved of by jubilant supporters wanting a memento of the momentous occasion. It was left to Cesar himself, Billy McNeill, to make the long journey up to the podium, accompanied by assistant manager, Sean Fallon, to collect the trophy.

It remains an iconic image, Celtic's captain, a colossus of a man, gripping the massive piece of silverware and holding it aloft. The trophy, for a long time now an iconic prize, was actually making its debut in the competition that season, with the previous trophy being retained by Real Madrid the previous year following their sixth success in the competition. It was another first for Celtic, over and above the fact that they were the first British side to win the European Cup. Billy McNeill raised the trophy, at 27-years-old in the prime of his career and at the pinnacle too, a champion of Europe and a leader of men. The rest of the team, meanwhile, waited in the dressing-room for his triumphant return, and to get their hands on the trophy for the first time.

A post-match banquet had been arranged in a Lisbon restaurant, the Verando De Chancellori, and it was here that the Celtic players were presented with the medals, Billy McNeill handing them out without fanfare; they had been delivered in a shoebox to the restaurant by UEFA officials. Bobby Lennox recounted the immediate aftermath in his autobiography, *Thirty Miles From Paradise*.

'A lot of people were milling in and around the dressing-room when we eventually found our way back through the crowds. After a while we began to ask each other, 'Where's the Cup?' and 'Where's Billy?' It was only once he arrived back with the trophy that we found out he had been forced to collect the European Cup without us. So many people had thronged the pitch that, automatically, we had sought refuge in the dressing-room and that had precluded any chance of us going up to receive our medals and lift the trophy. Billy had struggled through the supporters to receive it and eventually brought it back to the dressing-room.

'The strange design of the poky little dressing-room meant that the ensuing celebrations were slightly odd because the team was split in two to a certain extent. In one photograph taken soon after the game the only people pictured are Bertie, Jimmy, Stevie and me because the two halves of the team were compartmentalised. The enormity of conquering Europe certainly had not sunk in during those moments – winning games, even the biggest games, such as that one, often produces a more subdued feeling than you might expect. The feeling of elation in victory is nothing like the feeling of despair when you get beaten.

'Exiting the dressing-room, we again had to wade through a mass of people to reach our coach, which took us into Lisbon and up to a lovely restaurant where the two teams were to eat together. Once there, Billy produced a shoebox and distributed the winners' medals, one to each of us. We had to wait for about an hour-and-a-half for the Italians because they had spent so long in their dressing-room being harangued by Helenio Herrera. We still managed to enjoy ourselves before heading off to another restaurant where the wives and girlfriends were having a meal.'

The Celtic party saw off their wives and girlfriends at the airport, though they soon made a hasty exit back to the Hotel Palacio as word of their presence in the airport spread. The players were drained, emotionally and physically, so celebrations were muted, although attempts to get some sleep before the journey home were curtailed when news reached the hotel that the plane due to fly their partners home to Glasgow had been delayed until the morning, and so the group were on their way to Estoril.

Friday, May 26 saw the triumphant European champions head home to Glasgow where a welcome fit for heroes awaited them. When their plane touched down at Abbotsinch Airport, the squad were met by Rangers chairman, John Lawrence, who offered his congratulations to his Celtic counterpart, Robert Kelly, and the rest of the Celtic party. Then it was on to a coach and the relatively short trip back to Paradise.

In his 1969 autobiography, *Fire In My Boots*, the legendary Jimmy Johnstone recalls that day. 'We drove in from Glasgow Airport through streets lined with thousands upon thousands of people. We were cheered all the way. When we arrived at Celtic Park we met a scene to bring a lump to your throat. There they were – the thousands who hadn't been able to make the long trip to Lisbon, the thousands who had followed us through thick and thin and had been denied the greatest moment of all. They were determined to be part of this great 'Welcome Home' party.

'More than 60,000 men, women and boys were packed into the arena as we boarded a lorry for the lap of honour. We drove round that park to cheers that must have been heard all over the city and far beyond. They wouldn't let us go. There wasn't a man among us who wanted to go anyway. There had never been a night like this in all the great history of Parkhead and everybody was determined to make the most of it.'

Writing in the *Celtic View* just six days after he had watched his side win the European Cup, Jock Stein said: 'One of the things we did at Seamill while we were making our final plans to try and win the European Cup was to watch from start to finish the film of that great match at Hampden in 1960 between Real Madrid and Eintracht Frankfurt in the European Cup final of that year. All of us had seen it several times, but none of us tires watching the very fine play that is portrayed in it.

'Seeing it once again enabled me to urge the Celtic players to try to emulate the very high standard of attacking football, the entertaining football which made the match memorable. We of Celtic, I said, should try our utmost to emulate the teams and the players of that 1960 final. Now on reflection I think we were at least partly successful. I said in the recent souvenir issue of the View that, generally speaking, we in Britain were behind the top club sides in Europe in terms of skill and that we had to offset that disadvantage by being at our fittest, playing at our top speed, and showing our club spirit.

'I think it is fair to say now that we beat Inter Milan in the way we thought we might, but that we also matched them and even defeated them in the skills of the game. The reason for that is that we did not permit them to use the skill on which they have depended so much – the highly-technical defensive skill which enables them to dictate the pace of a game and to strike suddenly in attack by means of the long ball. I might add that Inter Milan's manager, Helenio Herrera, might have been better off if he hadn't come to see us playing Rangers when he did. That day he saw Celtic, in dreadful conditions, display their great stamina. I am sure he went home a very worried man, because weeks before the European Cup final he was preparing excuses. In the event we were the carefree side and the more famous, more worldwide experienced Inter Milan the troubled one.

'Now, our lads who have brought so much credit to the club have one more game before they go on a well-deserved holiday. We play Real Madrid in Spain a week today, and one of the reasons is that the Celtic players after watching that 1960 final were again full of praise for that wonderful player, Alfredo Di Stefano. When 'Stef', as they call him, made the journey to meet us in Estoril and ask personally that we play in his benefit match, all the players were eager to do so. That, and the fact that a game with Real will add further to our experience of world football, helped us to make the decision to go to Madrid.

'I have thanked the players one by one for their great effort for Celtic. Now I want to thank all the supporters, those who sent us messages before and after the final – Celtic Park has been flooded with telegrams as well as letters – and those who were with us in Lisbon or with us in spirit far from Portugal. I am grateful for the presence at the final of former Celtic players, I met Charlie Tully, Billy McPhail, Alec Burns, Frank Williams and Jim Kennedy, and I understand there were several more. To everyone who helped to make Celtic's name great in the world, my heartfelt thanks.'

While the Celtic players would have preferred to head off on holiday after their triumphant return to Glasgow, they still had one more game to play that season. Jock Stein had accepted that invitation from Real Madrid legend, Alfredo Di Stefano to provide the opposition for his benefit match in the Bernabeu Stadium on June 7. It was a tough game for Celtic, not least because they were playing the reigning Spanish champions and the six-time winner of the European Cup, their most recent triumph coming in 1966, a year before Celtic's Lisbon success. Real Madrid had been eliminated by Inter Milan at the quarter-final stage of the 1966/67 competition, and the Spanish press, in the build-up to the game against Celtic, had started to promote it as a contest between the current European champions and the 'rightful' European champions, with Real set to win and prove that Celtic's success was an aberration.

It was perhaps in recognition of the risk that his newly-crowned European Cup winners and recently-named Lisbon Lions faced that Stein made two changes to the line-up which had beaten Inter Milan, with John Fallon and Willie O'Neill replacing Ronnie Simpson and Stevie Chalmers respectively. The Celtic manager had apparently been overheard telling Bill Shankly after the Lisbon final 'that team will never be beaten', and it was a phrase which had puzzled the Celtic players who heard it on the team coach at the time.

Those eleven would only play five more times – four League Cup ties at the beginning of the following season in the League Cup as well as the home leg of their European Cup tie against Dynamo Kyiv, a game that saw the cup holders knocked out at the first stage of their defence of the trophy. The Lisbon Lions played together a total of 11 times, winning six games, drawing four and losing just the once against Kyiv. There was a further game in February 1968 when Stevie Chalmers came on as a substitute for John Hughes in a 1-0 victory over Motherwell at Fir Park, and then the final game of the 1970/71, on May 1, when Stein himself billed the game as the last time the Lisbon Lions would all play together. This wasn't quite true, given that Ronnie Simpson had already retired due to a shoulder injury, but the veteran goalkeeper walked out along with the rest of his team-mates and took part in the warm-up before Evan Williams took his place in goal for the game – which Celtic won 6-1 in front of a crowd of 35,000 at Celtic Park, with Bobby Lennox scoring a hat-trick, Willie Wallace netting twice and Stevie Chalmers also getting on the scoresheet.

There was a sense that Jock Stein was protecting his legacy and that of the players who triumphed in Lisbon by trying to ensure the invincibility and immortality in his reluctance to play them together, although the Celtic boss was also having to manage the extraordinarily talented young footballers coming through the ranks at the club and pushing for a first-team place – the Quality Street Gang of Davie Hay, George Connelly, Lou Macari, Kenny Dalglish, Danny McGrain amongst others – as well as players he signed for the club.

The newly-crowned kings of Europe walked out on to the pitch at the Bernabeu Stadium in front of 135,000 Real Madrid supporters, all of whom believed that the European Cup was 'their' trophy. The Spanish side had won the tournament for the first five years of its history, with Alfredo Di Stefano playing a key role in that success, alongside the likes of Ferenc Puskas and Francisco Gento, and the club's sixth and most recent success had been twelve months previously when they had defeated Partizan Belgrade in the final. Now they wanted to show these upstarts from Scotland who were the real kings of Europe.

The match was a benefit for the great Di Stefano, a player universally admired amongst the Celtic squad, and the 40-year-old played the first fifteen minutes of the match before going off to the acclaim of the crowd, to take his place in the directors' box for the rest of the match. Very quickly, with the departure of the guest of honour, the game became a serious and physical contest, so much so that Bertie Auld and Amancio Amaro were both sent-off for trading punches. Amaro had been identified by Stein as Real's best player, and Auld had been tasked with negating his attacking threat. As he trudged off the park following his sending-off, Auld remarked to his manager, 'Problem solved, Boss!'

The game itself proved to be a triumph for Celtic, and Jimmy Johnstone in particular, who produced one of his trademark mesmerising performances, so much so that the Real Madrid fans eventually stopped berating their own players for failing to stop the flame-haired winger and instead heralded a performance of sublime skill, greeting every touch from Johnstone with chants of 'Ole!' The plaudits, of course, were welcome, but even more so was the only goal of the game, which came courtesy of Bobby Lennox, who latched on to a through ball from Johnstone to fire home in the second-half. Now the season was over, and it had finished with a bang rather than a whimper.

Celtic had played a total of 62 competitive games in season 1966/67 (League 34; League Cup 10; European Cup 9; Scottish Cup 6; Glasgow Cup 3). They won fifty-one, drew eight and lost just three. The goals for tally was extraordinary, with a staggering 196 goals scored and forty-eight conceded. In addition, there were three friendly matches – a 4-1 victory over Manchester United at the start of the season, a 1-0 defeat to Dinamo Zagreb in the second half of the campaign, and the 1-0 victory over Real Madrid in the Bernabeu Stadium at the beginning of June. It was, as Billy McNeill would later say, the stuff of fairytales, and even fifty years later it remains one of the greatest sporting stories ever told.

RONNIE SIMPSON

LISBOA
25 DE MAIO DE
1967
CELTIC 2-1 INTER
50° CELTIC FC
ANIVERSARIO

RONNIE SIMPSON

Ronnie Simpson's career reads like it's been taken straight from the pages of a *Boys' Own* adventure book or a *Roy of the Rovers* comic strip, although it may be that it was his life that produced the inspiration for many a fanciful tale. A first-team goalkeeper with Queen's Park at the age of fourteen, a double FA Cup winner with Newcastle United in the early 1950s, by which time he'd also represented Great Britain at the Olympic Games. He was a part-time player with Hibernian in the mid-1960s when he was sold to Celtic by then Hibs manager, Jock Stein. Within a year, the two men were reunited when Stein took over at Celtic. Two years later, they were European champions, Stein's Celtic side having beaten Inter Milan 2-1 in the European Cup final. That same year, 1967, Simpson made his Scotland debut in their famous 3-2 victory over the reigning world champions, England, at Wembley. For good measure, in season 1966/67 he was also voted Player of the Year by Scotland's football writers, no mean feat when playing in a team that had won every trophy they competed for, scoring 196 goals in the process.

Football had been part and parcel of Ronnie Simpson's entire life. His father, Jimmy Simpson, had been a footballer himself, most notably for Rangers, while he'd also represented Scotland, famously captaining his country to a 1-1 draw against England at Wembley in 1936. Jimmy Simpson had also been part of the Rangers team who had played Celtic at Ibrox on September 5, 1931, when Celtic goalkeeper, John Thomson, was fatally injured following a clash with Rangers forward, Sam English. But while son would follow father into football, Ronnie Simpson excelled as a goalkeeper whereas Jimmy Simpson had been a centre-half.

Ronnie signed for Queen's Park on June 2, 1945, aged fourteen, and made his debut for the amateur club at the age of fourteen years and 304 days, while his first competitive appearance against Celtic came on Christmas Day 1946 when he was in the Queen's Park side that lost 1-0 at Celtic Park. His natural ability between the sticks soon caught the eye of other clubs, and just over two years later, his father, by now a player-coach with Highland League side, Buckie Thistle, was invited back to Ibrox for a meeting with Rangers manager, Bill Struth. The offer of a job as club trainer was put before Jimmy Simpson, an offer he gladly accepted. There was one condition, however. He was to get his son to sign professional forms with Rangers. Ronnie Simpson later recounted his father's answer in his 1967 autobiography, *Sure It's A Grand Old Team To Play For.*

'My father didn't hesitate. He said: 'I'm sorry Mr Struth but I cannot help you. What Ronnie does with his football career is his business. It is his life and he will do with it as he pleases. I have never forced him to anything so far and I cannot start now.'

It was an extraordinarily principled reply by Jimmy Simpson, and one which cost him the job at Ibrox, as it was announced the following day that Jimmy Smith, another former Rangers player, had been appointed trainer. However, while that answer did not guarantee Ronnie Simpson would one day become a Celtic player, it ensured that that particular door remained open throughout his career.

It was during this period that he was selected for the British Olympic team, who were being coached by Manchester United manager, Matt Busby, one of seven Queen's Park players in the amateur squad. The football tournament was staged between July 31 and August 13, and the British team managed to reach the semi-final, though they lost that game 3-1 to Yugoslavia and subsequently lost 5-3 to Denmark in the bronze medal match.

Returning to Queen's Park, Ronnie Simpson was then called up for National Service with the Royal Armoured Corps based at Catterick in Yorkshire, where he would remain for the next seventeen months, although most weekends he was able to return to Scotland to play for his club side. His first action as a Private in the British Army was to play for the Army team against Scotland at Tynecastle, a match that the Scots won 7-1. Simpson became a Corporal P.T.I in the Army Physical Training Corps, and it was this that persuaded him a planned career as a sub-editor on a Glasgow newspaper was not for him, and instead, upon being demobbed from the army in July 1950, he joined Third Lanark as a professional footballer.

It was a short stint with the club based on the South Side of the city, not far from his former club's base at Hampden, before Newcastle United came calling in February 1951. That same season, Newcastle won the FA Cup, although Simpson was a spectator on that day. However, he did play at Celtic Park for Newcastle in September of that year when the Scottish and English Cup winners fought out a 3-3 draw. Twelve months later he was at Wembley as the club retained the trophy with a 1-0 victory over Arsenal, and he picked up another winner's medal in 1955 when Newcastle beat Manchester City 3-1 in the final. It remains the last major honour the club has won. Newcastle's league form did not match their cup exploits, however, and eighth was the highest that the club reached during Simpson's nine years at St James' Park.

In 1960, he returned to Scotland and Hibernian. He had been due a benefit from Newcastle for ten years' service, but instead the club gave him a free transfer, allowing the player to negotiate a deal with Hibs himself. He joined at the start of October, but was probably grateful to miss out on the game against Celtic in the middle of the month, when the Hoops won 6-0 at Easter Road, though he was between the sticks in the corresponding game that season, on February 18, 1961, when a Stevie Chalmers double gave Celtic a 2-0 victory. On April 1, 1964, Jock Stein was appointed manager at Easter Road following four successful years with Dunfermline Athletic, but by that time the thirty-three-year-old goalkeeper was beginning to contemplate a life outside of football, and was working as an industrial representative of an oil company. When the end of the season came, Simpson ceased training, and didn't report back for the new season, having done no fitness work over the summer.

By September, Simpson was simply turning up every week to collect his wages, and seemed to be drifting inexorably out of football. Berwick Rangers had made enquiries about his services and had been given permission to speak to the player by Jock Stein. It looked as though he was heading down the divisions of Scottish football when fate intervened in the shape of Sean Fallon. The Irishman was assistant manager at Celtic to Jimmy McGrory at the time, and following a phone-call between the men, facilitated by Stein, Ronnie Simpson, a month shy of his thirty-fourth birthday, signed for Celtic for a fee of £4,000. He believed he was going there primarily to pass on his experience to the promising young players coming through the ranks at Celtic Park, and he was initially unable to dislodge Celtic's No.1, John Fallon, from the position.

However, on November 18, 1964, he got his opportunity when he was selected to make his debut in a Fairs Cities' Cup tie away to Barcelona. The Catalans won the match 3-1, while the second leg was a goal-less affair, but it did give him a run of first-team games between November and January 1965. Interestingly, as well as Simpson, six of the Lisbon Lions played in that game against Barcelona – Tommy Gemmell, John Clark, Billy McNeill, Jimmy Johnstone, Stevie Chalmers and Bobby Murdoch.

John Fallon had been restored to the starting XI in the middle of January, and would remain first-choice goalkeeper up to the end of the season, which included the famous 1965 Scottish Cup final triumph over Dunfermline Athletic at Hampden. By that point, Jock Stein was manager at Celtic Park, having been appointed on March 9. Simpson feared it would signal his imminent departure from the club, with Stein having already dispensed with his services while at Hibernian, but nothing could be further from the truth. Whatever had happened before was forgotten, and from the moment he was selected to play against Aberdeen on September 21, 1965 – a game the Hoops won 7-1, Ronnie Simpson missed just one more match for Celtic that season as they secured their first league title in twelve years. At the age of thirty-five, he was now a league winner and for good measure had also picked up a League Cup winner's medal as the Hoops beat Rangers 2-1 in the October '65 final.

That success, however, was only a precursor for what was to follow the next season, and there was no doubt as to who was Jock Stein's first-choice goalkeeper that season. Ronnie Simpson played in all but one of Celtic's league games in 1966/67 as they retained the title – that was the final game of the campaign, ten days before the European Cup final in Lisbon. The only other competitive game that he missed was the Glasgow Cup semi-final victory against Queen's Park, although he also missed Alfredo Di Stefano's benefit match in the Bernabeu at the beginning of June. It was an astonishing display of consistency across five different competitions for a man who was now thirty-six, but Simpson was certainly enjoying a new lease of life under Jock Stein at Celtic.

While much of the plaudits were being directed towards the outfield players and the attacking style of football that Jock Stein was deploying to such great effect, Celtic's defensive unit was an integral part of the team's success, and they took great comfort from the assuring presence of the man they now called 'Faither' in acknowledgement of his seniority within the squad. Billy McNeill's assessment of his friend and colleague remains prescient.

'Ronnie was the perfect goalkeeper for us, and he had this wonderful knack of pulling off terrific saves whenever they were needed. His easy-going nature and relaxed style made him an ideal man to have on your side in a crisis. Ronnie gave the impression of being calmness personified but kept what we called a snifter box in the dressing room at Celtic Park and he was in the habit of having a small whisky just before going out. Heaven knows why he needed it because he at least gave the appearance of being cool, calm and collected and, as our last line of defence, that was a vital factor in our success.

'Ronnie wasn't what I would call a stylist, but he was quick and agile and could make the most difficult of shots appear easy to save. His concentration levels were also quite remarkable, given the way he could suddenly spring into action after lengthy periods of inactivity. Because of the way we played, pushing forward all the time, there were occasions when we were caught on the break, but Ronnie had this wonderful knack of being able to make saves with just about any part of his anatomy – knees, elbows, anything but his hands at times. Ronnie was the oldest member of the team and he was held in special affection by the rest of the lads.'

The 1966/67 was an extraordinary one for Celtic, and one that Ronnie Simpson could never have dreamt of when he joined the club in 1964, despite the exploits of his career to date. The League Cup was retained with a 1-0 victory over Rangers in October, the Glasgow Cup won the following month with a 4-0 win over Partick Thistle. The Scottish Cup duly arrived in April with a 2-0 victory over Aberdeen at Hampden, while the league was retained when the Hoops drew 2-2 with Rangers at Ibrox on May 6. And then there was the European Cup final, the greatest day in the history of Celtic Football Club. For Ronnie Simpson, just five months short of his thirty-seventh birthday, it was a remarkable achievement, just as it was for the rest of his team-mates.

While certainly the quieter of the two goalkeepers throughout the ninety minutes, as Celtic dominated possession and created a wealth of chances, it was actually Ronnie Simpson who was first called into action in the early stages of the Lisbon final, saving well from a Sandro Mazzola header from the edge of the six-yard box. He could do nothing about Mazzola's penalty, however, as the Italian forward confidently stroked the ball home to give Inter Milan the lead after just seven minutes, but it was a lead they were not able to maintain until the end of the game.

Celtic's veteran goalkeeper remained alert to any possible danger from the Italians, and coped well with anything that came his way. There was one moment of supreme skill and confidence which probably caused palpitations across the Celtic-supporting world. That moment came in the first-half when Simpson raced out to get the ball ahead of Angelo Domenghini as Inter tried to mount a rare attack. Under pressure from the Inter forward, and facing his own goal, the Celtic goalkeeper would have realised any slip-up would, in all probability, lead to a second Inter goal, yet this was the moment he decided to produce a piece of impudent skill, back-heeling the ball to John Clark and fooling his opponent in the same instant.

It showed supreme confidence and nerve to execute the move, given the magnitude of the occasion and the consequences had it not come off, yet Ronnie Simpson did it to perfection. The years of experience, playing at the highest level in Scotland and England, gave him a sense of what was needed at that particular moment, and the wherewithal to do it. That moment remains one of the many highlights of the game, although what Jock Stein thought of his goalkeeper's antics is not recorded.

The following season, Simpson remained first-choice goalkeeper at Celtic, as the team won the league championship for a third consecutive season and also retained the League Cup. Both the Scottish Cup and European Cup were relinquished, the latter disappointingly in the first round against Dynamo Kyiv. Season 1967/68 also saw a controversial trip to South America to take on Racing Club of Argentina in the World Club Championship Final. The first leg at Hampden saw Celtic win 1-0 in a tough game that was a precursor for two controversial ties in South America.

The first of those games in the Argentine capital, Buenos Aires, saw Ronnie Simpson struck by an object thrown from the crowd as he warmed up before kick-off, and he was replaced by John Fallon, who was also in goal for the play-off game in Montevideo, a game in which six players were sent off and Racing Club won 1-0.

Season 1968/69 was another treble-winning campaign for Jock Stein's side, but it was in February 1969, in a Scottish Cup second round tie against Clyde at Shawfield, that Ronnie Simpson dislocated his shoulder early in the match, being replaced in goal by Tommy Gemmell. He had been battling with John Fallon for the No.1 jersey, but had to relinquish it until October of that year, but in the third game back – the League Cup semi-final against Ayr United at Hampden – he dislocated his shoulder again while making a superb save late in the game to deny Ayr United an equaliser. His heroics ensured Celtic were through to their sixth successive League Cup final, although it was Gemmell again who pulled on the goalkeeper's jersey. For Simpson, however, the recurrence of the injury effectively ended his playing career.

He did take one final bow at the end of the following season, May 1, 1971, when the Lisbon Lions appeared together in Celtic colours for the last time in the final league game of the season against Clyde. Ronnie Simpson ran out alongside his legendary team-mates before the game although, once the match started, it was Evan Williams who was in goal for Celtic. It brought down the curtain on a truly remarkable playing career which had finished with some incredible highs at a time when the player himself believed his playing days were almost at an end. He made a total of 188 appearances for Celtic, recording ninety-one shut-outs – an impressive forty-eight per cent success rate – and he garnered an impressive haul of medals; four league titles, two League Cups, one Scottish Cup and, of course, the European Cup in 1967. He also gained five Scotland caps, and a Player of the Year Award … and, of course, there was that back heel!

A brief spell in football management followed at Hamilton Accies, before Ronnie Simpson ended his career in football. He was the elder statesman of the Lisbon Lions, and they looked up to him as such. He had already done so much in the game even before he arrived at Celtic Park in 1964, and his team-mates knew and acknowledged that. While he played his part on the pitch in the remarkable success the team was enjoying under Jock Stein, he was also able to use his years of experience to help the younger men in the squad, although despite everything that had happened him beforehand, nothing could probably have prepared Ronnie Simpson for what he was to experience at Celtic.

Sadly, in April 2004, Ronnie Simpson passed away at the age of seventy-three. The Lions had lost one of the youngest members of the team, Bobby Murdoch, three years previously. Now the elder statesman was gone too.

Ronnie Simpson was 'Faither' to his friends and team-mates, a quiet, unassuming, intelligent man whose football career could be bettered by few players. That day back in the 1940s when his father had told Rangers he would not influence his son's football career and it was up to Ronnie who he played for, was to prove a pivotal moment in Celtic's history. We have a lot to be thankful for due to the principled stance taken by Jimmy Simpson.

IN HIS OWN WORDS...

'I'm not being funny when I say I had the best position in the ground for the European Cup final because I had very little to do. It was just one of those games which turned out that way and the Inter Milan goalkeeper, Sarti, was bombarded. He had an exceptionally good game and if it hadn't been for him we would've won much easier. But it was a wonderful position to be standing that day, right in the centre of the goalmouth and watching the boys play and they played really out of their skin that day. I don't think I'd ever seen another team play quite so well – not just Celtic – and it was something I always remembered.

We were always attacking but there was always the chance they could come back in the last three or four minutes and equalise. Bertie Auld was really tremendous, he was the kind of player you needed for that situation because if he got the ball he'd take it and make for the corner flag every time and whether he knocked it against the corner flag or against the player's leg he kept it down in that very tight area. That was the most important thing – to keep it down there and keep a hold of it. That's all part of the game. It's not a time-wasting thing. The ball is in play so it's up to the other team to get a hold of it.

I was crying (*At the final whistle*). I couldn't stop myself. The tears came rolling down my cheeks. I was standing under the lingering sun of Lisbon in the Estadio Nacional, completely helpless to my emotions. The European Cup final of 1967 was over! Referee Kurt Tschenscher of Germany had blown for the last time and Celtic were champions! Champions of all Europe for the first time at their first attempt. And I, Ronnie Simpson, at the age of thirty-six years and seven months had become the first British goalkeeper to win a European Champions Cup medal. I couldn't believe it. I was overcome.

I wasn't alone for long. In seconds I was smothered in the arms of manager Jock Stein, then reserve 'keeper John Fallon, the player who had stripped for every European tie and never been called up. The three of us were locked together, crushing each other, scared to open our months in case we all burst into tears again.

Suddenly I realised there were more people running around us than there should have been. Our supporters were on the field. This was their greatest moment as it had been ours and they were going to make the most of it. But the fastest man of all at that moment was our outside-left Bobby Lennox. He came sprinting straight at me as though Herrera himself was chasing him. I held out my hands, thinking he was coming to join in the goalmouth celebrations, but Bobby kept going right into the back of the net. Then it dawned on me.

Before a match I take out my false teeth, and stick them in my cap which I keep in the back of the net. It's a habit I have adopted in important matches, just in case I have to meet someone at short notice or at the end of a game. Then I can always pop my teeth in. Bobby noticed this habit of mine and as he also had false teeth, he asked me before the Lisbon final to keep his set of choppers inside my cap. And this is what Bobby was racing for – and I suddenly knew why.

The fans, Celtic, Portuguese, Italian and the others were desperate to get some sort of souvenir from this remarkable final. Players were getting jerseys and pants torn from them bodily, fans were cutting lumps out of the turf, the corner flags were already on their way to places well away from Portugal. My cap, with two sets of false teeth, was too obvious a trophy.

Bobby won his race, grabbed his teeth and ran for the tunnel leading to the dressing-room. I quickly grabbed my cap and teeth and tried to make it – and did so after what seemed like an eternity. I was half-strangled and almost crushed as a tug-of-war went on for my jersey. But this was one jersey I was keeping. I fought with my remaining strength to make the tunnel and I made it with my jersey, cap, pants, boots, hair, gloves, false teeth and body intact.

I was met in the dressing-room by Bob Rooney, our physiotherapist. He threw his arms around me, dumped me on a seat and the two of us burst into tears. We couldn't help it. The happiest moment of my life and I cannot raise a smile!

I admit now that there is one moment from the game which has given me a couple of sleepless nights and has made me think quite a lot – the moment when I back-heeled the ball to John Clark across my goal out of my penalty area. A loose ball had come up into our area, some thirty yards from goal and I went for it as almost every other member of our team was up in attack. I had plenty of time, or so I thought, and my intention was to give the ball a good old-fashioned wallop up-field. But as I ran towards the ball I could hear Domenghini chasing me from the other side of the field and he was gaining very quickly. It was then that I got it into my head that if I kicked the ball, I might kick it against the Italian, and it might rebound towards my goal, which was unguarded.

As I was running I could see John Clark running to the other side of the penalty box, obviously to cover the goal. I made up my mind then. As I got the ball I threw my left leg over it and back-heeled across the penalty area to John Clark. 'Luggy' promptly cleared it and that was that.

Since then I've woke up twice in the night and asked myself: What would have happened if that hadn't come off? Supposing I had muffed the kick and Inter had scored? Would I be where I am today? Would I have been able to live it down? Remember, this was the first-half and Inter were already leading 1-0! It would have been a tragedy for me, for Celtic, for Scotland. What a chance to take – but I got away with it.

We understood that we won a big cup but it was only later that we realised the magnitude of the thing. You look back and think it's a huge cup to win. Not many teams had won it up until then, never mind a British or Scottish team being the first to win it. It was a magnificent thing to win, really looking back on it. It was big enough at the time but I would say it's bigger now.

I dare say it's feasible for a Scots team to win the European Cup again. We might not think that but it's feasible, but you won't get that within a thirty-mile radius – eleven players from that area. I don't think that would ever happen again.

We were absolutely mobbed at Celtic Park. They had a truck waiting for us to take us around the perimeter of the ground inside and the stadium was nearly full capacity. It really was tremendous. I was lucky I had experienced it twice before, bringing back English cups to Newcastle but it brought back a memory just similar to that.'

JIM CRAIG

LISBOA
25 DE MAIO DE
1967
CELTIC 2-1 INTER
50° CELTIC FC
ANIVERSARIO

JIM CRAIG

Jim Craig played a central role in the 1967 European Cup final. He conceded the penalty which gave Inter Milan a seventh-minute lead, while it was his pass into the path of Tommy Gemmell which led to Celtic's equaliser just after the hour mark; his tireless running up and down the right flank in the sweltering heat of late afternoon Lisbon was a feature of the contest – Gemmell was doing the same thing on the other flank – and contributed to the relentless waves of attacks which Jock Stein's side launched on their Italian opponents. He was always an outlet for his team-mates, while he also created space for the likes of Jimmy Johnstone to exploit. The performance of Craig and Gemmell was a masterclass in the art of the overlapping full-back, and that in a game in which one of football's finest exponents of the skill, Giacinto Facchetti, was on the same pitch, albeit in the blue and black of Inter. Despite the result, and the manner of the defeat, once the dust had settled on the game, Facchetti would no doubt have appreciated the performance of his counterparts in green and white Hoops, just as the Celtic players admired the Italian's resolute defending, tireless running and goalscoring talents.

Having turned twenty-four just over three weeks before the final, Jim Craig had less first-team experience behind him than might have been presumed for a man of his age, and certainly less experience than his team-mates. That wasn't due to a lack of ability, however. Far from it. The lack of first-team opportunities was due to his decision to pursue an academic career in tandem with his football aspirations. At the time of the Lisbon triumph in 1967, Craig was a newly-qualified dentist, having sat his final university exams the previous summer, which prevented him going on the North American tour with the rest of his team-mates.

That close-season tour was cited as a pivotal event in creating the cohesive team unit which would serve Celtic so well in the all-conquering 1966/67 season, but Craig was back home studying and sitting exams. The tour was a great success, not only in terms of results but also in terms of team-bonding, and it meant that Craig would have to show patience in the reserves before he got his chance in the first-team again in early 1967.

He had already shown an independent streak since Celtic had first pursued and then signed him, and allied to well-placed confidence in his ability as a footballer meant that not only did he bide his time, but when that time came, he seized it, not only for that season but for the rest of his career with the club, remaining first-choice right-back up to his final game in the 1972 Scottish Cup final.

Sean Fallon, with his unerring eye for football talent, had long identified James Philip Craig as a player who belonged at Celtic Park, and having impressed in Under-18 international matches against England, he was invited to sign for the club he supported. That he did so as an amateur was due to the fact that in October 1961 he had began a five-year dentistry degree at the University of Glasgow. Here was a player with talent in his feet and brains in his head. Trying to balance the demands of a rigorous academic degree with his football commitments must have been tough for the young man, but he managed to combine both successfully, which eventually led to him signing as a professional in January 1965, though he still had eighteen months of his studies left. While his mother wasn't too keen on him committing himself to Celtic, perhaps worried that the twin demands would prove too much to cope with, Jim Craig's father articulated what his son was feeling, as the Lisbon Lion explained in his book, *A Lion Looks Back*. '… I thought I had missed my chance at senior level. By then I was halfway through my fourth year and felt that I could cope with whatever was thrown at me and spare some time for training. Mum wasn't too keen but Dad was quite blunt: 'There are a lot of dentists, son, but not everyone gets a chance to play for Celtic.'

It would be October of that same year when Jim Craig would make the first of his 224 appearances for the Celtic first-team. The occasion was the second leg of Celtic's European Cup-Winners' Cup first round tie against Dutch side, Go Ahead Deventer. The Hoops had thrashed their opponents 6-0 in Holland, with Bobby Lennox hitting a hat-trick, and for the return leg in Glasgow, Craig came in to replace Ian Young at right-back. Nine of the Lisbon Lions would play in that match. Only Bertie Auld and Willie Wallace, the latter of whom had not yet signed for the club, were missing. It meant that it was the first time that Ronnie Simpson had played behind a back line of Craig, Clark, McNeill and Gemmell.

Jim Craig later described the game as one of his proudest moments as a Celtic player when he spoke to the *Celtic View*. 'To get my debut against Go Ahead Deventer in 1965 was absolutely amazing. The night before I had been told I was playing by Jock. I didn't have a car at that time so I took the bus from underneath the Heilanman's Umbrella to Celtic Park – the number 62. The fans didn't know me from Adam, as I had never played for the first-team before, and they were all discussing who the team was going to be. And I was sitting there thinking, 'I'm playing and no-one knows anything about it!' So when I went out there, I was really chuffed. We had won 6-0 in the first leg and I didn't travel as I wasn't allowed to travel as the Dean of the university wouldn't give me permission. And on the night we weren't very good. I got some good press as they were quite kind to the new guy but it wasn't a very good night as we only won 1-0. But for me, it was a very proud moment to wear the Hoops. It was fantastic.'

There were also further European appearances that season, against Danish side, Aahrus, and then Dynamo Kyiv in the last eight of the competition. Celtic travelled to the Soviet Union with a 3-0 first-leg victory and confident of booking their place in the semi-final of the competition. The second-leg was a feisty affair, finishing 1-1, and Craig was sent off in the second-half, along with Dynamo Kyiv's Khmelnitsky, following a touchline tussle when the Celtic player was punched and sought out the guilty culprit who wasn't Khmelnitsky, incidentally, though he was punished by the referee. As well as a sore jaw, however, the dismissal meant that Craig missed both legs of the semi-final against Liverpool.

Having made the breakthrough into the first-team, Jim Craig would go on to make a total of fifteen league appearances for the Hoops that season. Crucially, one of those games came at Fir Park on May 7, 1966 when Celtic won 1-0 thanks to a last-minute goal from Bobby Lennox. The significance of the victory was that it confirmed Celtic as Scottish champions for the first time since 1954. Jock Stein's transformation of the team was continuing apace, and Craig now had the first of what would be seven league winner's medals. Indeed, it was his cross from the right into the six-yard box which enabled Lennox to bundle the ball home for the title-winning goal.

However, while there were celebrations at having won the league after a long gap, the Celtic players were soon off on their close season travels across the Atlantic, which didn't benefit Jim Craig, who was left behind, and so, when the new season began, he was back in the reserves and waiting for the opportunity to impress again and stake a claim for a regular first-team place.

Apart from a couple of appearances in the first half of the season, it wasn't until the start of 1967 that Jim Craig became the first-choice right-back. Up to that point in the season, Tommy Gemmell had been occupying the position, with Willie O'Neill at left-back, but the introduction of Craig into the starting XI allowed Gemmell to switch flanks, and he looked a much more comfortable and confident player in that position. The catalyst for the change had been the 3-2 defeat at Tannadice to Dundee United on December 31, and a week later, when Dundee came calling to Celtic Park, Jim Craig was in the team.

It meant, too, that he was able to play his part in the run to Lisbon from the quarter-final stage onwards when Celtic faced the Yugoslavian champions, Vojvodina Novi Sad. Domestically, Celtic were closing in on a second consecutive league title – which would be Craig's second title in a row too, and while he had missed out on the previous two League Cup final successes, he would pick up the first of four Scottish Cup winner's medals that season when he helped the Hoops beat Aberdeen 2-0 in the final.

Celtic had progressed, too, in the European Cup, with Jim Craig now having made four appearances as the team saw off Vojvodina and Dukla Prague to set up a final showdown with Inter Milan. While the game in Czechoslovakia had been an uncharacteristically defensive 0-0 draw, in this case the ends justified the means for the Celtic manager. They had achieved their aim of reaching the final. However, with a Scottish Cup final looming that weekend, Jim Craig was worried he was going to miss the game due to flu symptoms he was displaying on the flight home. He managed to shrug them off by the time the game at Hampden came around although, by his own admission, it wasn't one of his finest performances. Still, it was another trophy in the cabinet for Celtic and the target now was to complete the domestic treble and then focus on the European Cup.

When Celtic stepped into the Lisbon sunshine on May 25, 1967, minutes away from the 5.30pm kick-off, they did so as Scottish champions, having gained the solitary point they needed to retain the title in a 2-2 draw against Rangers at Ibrox. Now there was only one trophy left to collect. It was the big one, however, and Inter Milan, a side who had won the European Cup twice in recent years, were determined to make it a third triumph. For the dentist in Celtic's ranks, as for the rest of his team-mates, it was the opportunity to make history.

On the day of the final, as the players relaxed at the Hotel Palacio in Estoril, Jim Craig was on the receiving end of trainer Neilly Mochan's disapproval. The club had recently signed a sponsorship with sporting giants Adidas, and Jim Craig was the only player who wore black Puma football boots. So Mochan had to paint out the white Puma flash with black paint and then re-paint the iconic three white Adidas stripes on the side of the boots. He may have done an impressive job upon first glance, but in the course of the game, the white strips slowly began to disappear and the Puma logo re-emerge, although not too noticeably, and it didn't appear to affect Craig's performance.

That was impressive, all the more so given the start he and Celtic had made to the game. Just seven minutes were on the clock when he made a challenge on Renato Cappellini inside the box. The West German referee pointed to the spot, Mazzola scored and Inter had the lead. The Celtic defender was adamant then, and has remained so, that it was not a penalty, though while several of his team-mates protested the decision, he took up his place on the eighteen-yard line. For one thing he knew the referee wasn't going to change his mind, while he was also thinking of his father, who had made the trip to Lisbon and had just witnessed his son conceding a penalty in the biggest game that Celtic had ever competed in. Jim Craig recalled: 'My Dad was sitting in the stand with my Uncle Philip and when the penalty was given, he turned to him and said: 'I've come all this way, just to see that!'

Thankfully, for Jim Craig and his father, that moment in the Celtic penalty area was not to be their abiding one from the European Cup final. That came in the sixty-second minute when the right-back rolled a pass across the park and into the path of Tommy Gemmell, who blasted the ball into the Inter Milan net for Celtic's equaliser. A mixture of joy and relief would have flooded through Jim Craig's mind, but there was no time for him or his team-mates to enjoy the moment – they had a European Cup to win. And the winner came courtesy of Stevie Chalmers' goal with five minutes of the match remaining.

Having battled his way back into the starting XI at the beginning of 1967, Jim Craig was now a European Cup winner. His haul of honours during his time at Celtic makes for impressive reading. Seven league titles, four Scottish Cups and three League Cups to go with the medal he won in Lisbon. There were only six goals from 224 appearances, but his first job was always to prevent the other side from scoring, and those statistics don't tell the full story of the amount of goals he created for his team-mates.

And he even used his intellect to great effect, helping a Celtic team win the BBC sports quiz show, Quiz Ball, on two occasions – 1969/70 and 1970/71 – in a team that also included Billy McNeill, Willie Wallace and actor and Celtic fan, John Cairney.

The following season, 1967/68, Jim Craig made thirty-two appearances, including twenty-two in another successful league campaign. The treble-winning 1968/69 season saw Jim Craig's name barely absent from the team, though one of the games he did miss was the early season 4-2 loss to Rangers at Celtic Park in the league. Celtic had another opportunity of European glory in 1970, having battled their way to the final where they faced Feyenoord in Milan's San Siro Stadium. There was to be no repeat of the success three years previously, however, as the Dutch side triumphed 2-1 after extra-time, with Jim Craig a frustrated spectator on the Celtic bench that night.

Season 1970/71 was a double-winning one for Jock Stein's side, while they fell at the quarter-final stage of the European Cup to a Johan Cruyff-inspired Ajax side. Season 1971/72 would be Jim Craig's last season at Celtic. Competition for the right-back position was fierce, with the Lisbon Lion battling Davie Hay and Danny McGrain for the No.2 shorts. He still made twenty-nine appearances that season, with his European swansong against the team he'd helped defeat five years previously in Lisbon. This time it was the semi-final of the competition, and after both legs had finished goal-less, including the thirty minutes of extra-time at Celtic Park, the tie was decided by a penalty shoot-out. While Sandro Mazzola, the man who'd scored for Inter in 1967, netted his side's first penalty, Dixie Deans blazed his effort over the bar. Jim Craig was next up for Celtic, and he netted his effort. Indeed, every other penalty was converted by both sets of players, meaning Inter Milan won 5-4 and reached the final, denying Celtic their third European Cup final appearance in five years.

At the end of the campaign came Jim Craig's final appearance for Celtic, and it was fitting that it came in the Scottish Cup final at Hampden against Hibernian, the team his father had grown up supporting. It was a traditional 'Battle of the Greens', in the days when both sides still wore their traditional home kits for the match, although it was less a battle than a rout, with Celtic trouncing their Edinburgh rivals 6-1, which included a Dixie Deans hat-trick, in front of a crowd of 106,000. Jim Craig recalled the occasion: 'The day before we had stayed at the Marine Hotel rather than Seamill and had gone for a walk along the edge of the golf course, along the sand-dunes. Jock told us all to take a seat and announced the team and said, 'This is Cairney's last game for the club, because he's leaving us next week'. I hadn't mentioned it to anybody and there was a general consternation and everybody was determined to give me a good send-off. It really was a wonderful way to end your career.'

Having bid farewell to Paradise, Jim Craig headed off to South Africa, joining Hellenic FC. It was a move that generated some headlines and a degree of controversy, given South Africa's apartheid regime at the time, but Jim Craig later explained to the *Celtic View* his thoughts on the move: 'The thought-police told me I shouldn't go and I occasionally get rants from people who want to turn Celtic into some sort of political organisation. Celtic's a football club, which does a lot of work for charity and brings people together, but let's keep it a football club. I went out there to see what it was like and I would say it was fascinating and appalling. What I did discover was that there were a lot of white South Africans who were working very hard to change the system from within, like my boss at the time who treated people irrespective of their colour. I had a friend there, who worked in the same building as me as a caretaker and had a degree from one of the black universities and we used to go to the racing, but had to go in through separate doors, stand at separate bars and go to different windows. It was absolutely crazy and thank God it's gone, but it was fascinating to see it, even for five months.'

Returning to Britain, the Lisbon Lion joined Sheffield Wednesday in December 1972, before he hung up his boots just over a year later, in March 1974. There was a brief spell as Waterford manager later that year, but he opted to concentrate on his career as a dentist while also forging a successful second career in the media, both of which he continues to do while also maintaining his reputation through writings and talks as a Celtic historian par excellence.

IN HIS OWN WORDS...

'I was kicked in the face when I was in my final year at school and broke my front teeth. I was in the dental hospital for a while and that got me interested in dentistry. I qualified in 1966 and signed for Celtic when I was halfway through my course. I played in the European Cup final not long after qualifying as a dentist and I was surprised nobody did a feature on that at the time. There were no features in those days but when I speak to journalists they all say it would be a dream nowadays. Ever since I have checked every European Cup final and to my knowledge I think I'm the only dentist to have played in it.

I wasn't in the team at all at the start of the 1966/67 season, which was the real problem. I had been sitting my finals that year so I missed out on the North American tour of '66, so when the team came back and the season started again I was in the reserves. I beat a path to Jock Stein's door week in, week out asking why I wasn't in the team because I'd been the guy in charge of the position before they went to America and now I was out the team. I didn't think they were playing all that well although they were winning, but anyway I went into see him. Somebody told me to always make a nuisance of yourself, but it does help. People remember you when you do that. Anyway it took me to January before we had a bad game and I got in. But it was fine from then on and I was in there from January right through to the final moments of the season.

It was a great day in all our careers. The setting was good too, the Estadio Nacional in Lisbon. Back in 1967 it was a stadium more or less specially designed for the purpose and it was very scenic. I think we all got a boost from coming up the steps from the darkness down below into the sunshine to see this mass of green and white. I've never walked on to a stage but I can imagine that is what it feels like. But the story about Bertie singing is very true. I think he recognised a bit of nerves among one or two and he's quite an astute fella and I think he knew something needed to be done to break the nerves at that point. We all joined in and it did something to us. We actually approached from different steps and I remember standing in the tunnel and thinking how tall the Inter Milan players looked when, in actual fact, it was the stripes making them look taller, whereas the Hoops make you look smaller. In fact, throughout my years as a Celtic player and the years that followed, supporters used to often speak to me and say that they never realised I was this tall. So I can only put it down to the Hoops.

By the time we got to walk up the steps of the stadium, we could not believe the number of Celtic supporters there. We had no idea that so many had made it because we'd only been from Estoril to the national stadium which were both just on the outskirts of Lisbon. We hadn't been to Lisbon itself so we had no idea of the numbers who turned up there, and just to see the masses of green and white was amazing. So when we won, you can imagine the reaction. We knew the support was there and thereafter it was up to us. We were back in the dressing room and I don't think Billy wanted to go up and get the cup. The crowds were everywhere and we were all inside the dressing room and Billy had to go out. In fact they got a car to take him round the other side of the stadium to allow him to get up and get the cup. It was only after the game when we went for a meal and we were sitting there for a good hour until an official from UEFA turned up and placed what looked like a shoebox down and inside were the medals, and they were then passed around the players.

I remember when I was back in Glasgow going for a walk one night with my Dad and he said to me, 'I was really worried in that second-half because I was worried about going through life being the father of the guy that gave away a penalty.' And I said to him, 'Well Dad, at that particular moment my own worries were a lot worse than that because I was that guy!' It was beginning to kind of loom in my mind during the game because, try as we might, it wasn't happening, but fortunately we got the breakthrough.

What delighted me was not only that we won, which was a big deal for me because I'd given away the penalty, but that we won it playing attacking football. But just at that moment for us when we'd won, it was simply wonderful for all of us. We reacted in the way anyone would and then the fans came on and celebrated with us. The only unfortunate thing was that we were deprived of doing a lap of honour. Many a football authority has said since that we won it with such style and I think that is really important. I think if the Italians had won it, it would have been another triumph for a defensive-minded team and this time a team had chosen to challenge that system and had shown how football could be played. What followed was Manchester United, Ajax, Bayern Munich who were all attack-minded teams, so maybe that day sparked off a change in football.

Jock Stein was something special. He and I had our moments when he arrived because he liked a master-servant relationship and in my sort of unusual position – I'd been seven years at primary school, six years at secondary school, I was in the fourth year of a five-year course with people telling me I've got to think for myself and make my own decisions. And then I got to Celtic Park and there's this guy there saying, 'Never you mind thinking, I'll do the thinking for you. You just do what you're told.' Well, it was hard to change your thinking, so we had our moments all through the time I was there. But he was an amazing man because it would never have happened without him.

I arrived in 1965 a couple of months before Jock came and I got to know some of the first-team guys. Quite a few of them were hoping to leave. They were going to go to England to different teams down there, or maybe different teams in Scotland. They thought Celtic was going nowhere. Suddenly Jock came in and revolutionised the whole thing. We would never ever have done it without him. He really does deserve all the credit he gets.

Jock made a colossal difference as Jimmy McGrory was a very self-effacing man and Bob Kelly basically made all the major decisions, whereas when Jock came in he knew who was boss and had a great presence. And you were under no illusions as to who was in charge in the dressing room. He was just very impressive in how he analysed the game and told you what he wanted you to do. This all happened just a few weeks after I got there, so it made a real difference for me.

He encouraged me to come forward. He said to me, 'You realise the way you play, coming forward, is chancing it as if things don't work out, but you've just got to have the confidence in your ability, and if you make a mistake, put it behind you, and if I'm happy with it, that's all you need to bother about – it's me you need to satisfy'. And I was very happy to do so. And I know that Tam Gemmell got a boost with Jock coming in as well, by just getting the chance to come forward.

The best player I played alongside was Bobby Murdoch. He had wonderful control of game. He was always available if you were in trouble. There were those terrible moments for a full-back when you were chasing back to your own goal and you were on your own, but Bobby Murdoch was great at just coming into position for that. You could just slide the ball for him and he would hold it for a minute or two, wait for you to get into a better position and then give it back to you. He was really good at that kind of thing. It was a pleasure to play beside him.

You could sum it up in one simple phrase: when he played, the whole team played. When he was on song and spraying passes around, the whole team rose to the challenge. More so than anyone else as he played that bit deeper, unlike Bertie Auld who was about fifteen or twenty yards further forward and was equally good at getting the forward line into operation or the backs coming through. From where Bobby played as a deep-lying player, he was able to bring everyone into the equation. He was just a real talent, no doubt about it. He had two great feet and could spread the game very well. Everybody in that team had their own talents in one way or another so it's a good accolade.

Having said that, I am also very proud to be a member of the Craig, McNeill, Clark and Gemmell back four. People say to me that football is all about scoring goals but I would extend that very slightly and say that's it about scoring goals at one end and keeping the gate shut at the other. That's the hardest thing to do. If you look at the record for that time, not only were we scoring roughly 90-100 in a season, we were only losing less than a goal a game at the other end which is a very difficult thing to do. I was very proud of that.

The 1967 European Cup final is the highlight from my playing days at the club. That had become the 'Holy Grail' for British teams over the years and a few had got close, the likes of Manchester United and the Spurs side of 1961. For us to do it in the first attempt, you really can't do any better than that.

My most memorable moment at Celtic Park, though, was the day after we came back from the final in Lisbon and I met my wife, Elisabeth, downstairs, outside the boardroom. She was the daughter of Jimmy Farrell, the director. She attended the occasional game and then the night we came back from Lisbon she came to pick up her parents who had been there. I bumped into her, literally, and she said congratulations. We got talking and she said she was going to work in Paris. I told her she should make sure she got her teeth checked before she left and funnily enough her dentist had just retired. I told her I would look at them for her. After that I drove her home and started thinking, 'How do I see her again?' I phoned her up and told her according to National Health regulations she had to come back and get her teeth polished after a check up. It was a pack of lies but it got her back into the practice. That was it after that and I asked her to marry me after ten days. She went home and told her mother that she'd met a fruitcake! It was on the fifty-third occasion that she finally said yes!'

TOMMY GEMMELL

TOMMY GEMMELL

Tommy Gemmell enjoyed scoring in a European Cup final so much that he repeated the feat in another final. The Celtic left-back produced a blistering finish to draw the Hoops level in their 1967 clash with Inter Milan in Lisbon. It helped propel them to victory, the winning goal coming courtesy of Stevie Chalmers. Three years later, Gemmell was on target again, firing home from the edge of the box after half-an-hour of the 1970 final against Feyenoord in Milan. This time, however, there was to be no fairytale ending for Jock Stein's side, though it did mean that Tommy Gemmell joined a select band of players who have scored in more than one European Cup final. He would gladly have swapped that distinction had it meant a second winner's medal, but sadly it was not to be.

Like many of Celtic's best players during the 1960s and '70s, Tommy Gemmell has Sean Fallon to thank for bringing him to Paradise, the Irishman being tipped off about the promising young player who was attracting scouts from a number of clubs both north and south of the border. Gemmell's own dream was to sign for the team he supported – Motherwell – but it was Celtic who first came in with an offer to train with the club a couple of nights a week, and Gemmell signed a provisional form in October 1961, the same night, incidentally, as another Lanarkshire boy – Jimmy Johnstone. While serving his apprenticeship as an electrician, the young player spent the 1961/62 season playing for junior side Coltness United, but after a year he became a part-time Celt, playing for the club's third-team and quickly progressing into the reserves.

It was a sign of Gemmell's potential and progress that, before too long, and while still a part-timer, he made his first-team debut just over three months after he turned nineteen. That came in a game against Aberdeen at Pittodrie on January 5, 1963. It was a successful outing for the young player as the Hoops won 5-1, with John Hughes scoring a hat-trick, while it was also the first time he'd played alongside Billy McNeill and Stevie Chalmers, the two other future Lisbon Lions in the team that day. Gemmell would play two more first-team games that season – a 5-2 away win against Queen of the South in the league and a 2-0 Scottish Cup victory over Falkirk at Brockville.

Despite still only being signed as a part-time player, and continuing his work as an electrician at Ravenscraig, Tommy Gemmell was a regular in the first-team in the 1963/64 season, playing forty-nine times for the side. Indeed, only Stevie Chalmers made more appearances that season. Among those forty-nine appearances were eight in the European Cup-Winners' Cup, which saw Celtic progress all the way to the semi-final stage. Despite winning the first leg 3-0 against MTK Budapest, Celtic collapsed in the return match in Hungary, losing 4-0. That game perhaps sums up perfectly what was wrong with the club at that time. For one thing, it was the chairman, Bob Kelly, who picked the team rather than the manager, Jimmy McGrory, and it had often led to inexplicable team selections to the detriment of the team on any given occasion. For the game in Hungary, Kelly wanted his young Celtic side to go out and attack, to showcase their talents and play in a manner befitting a Celtic side. It was naivety of the highest order, as MTK overturned what should have been an impregnable lead and progressed to the final. While experiences such as that only served to sow the seeds of dissatisfaction amongst the squad at that time, it was also a lesson that they – six of the Lisbon Lions, including Tommy Gemmell, played in Hungary – and the man who would soon take over as manager remembered, particularly when it came to the 1967 semi-final clash with Dukla Prague in Czechoslovakia.

For a player who would go on to score sixty-four goals for Celtic, an impressive total for a defender, it took Gemmell until October 28, 1964 before he scored his first goal for the club, though it came in a 5-2 defeat to Kilmarnock at Rugby Park, and he only scored three in total that season, though the tally continued to rise, particularly once he'd taken over penalty-kick duties in the all-conquering 1966/67 campaign. That 1964/65 season, however, was also a pivotal one, not only for Tommy Gemmell's own career but also for Celtic as a whole, because it saw the arrival of Jock Stein as manager in March 1965. The appointment was the key to Celtic's subsequent success in Scotland and Europe, and Bob Kelly's acceptance that he had to relinquish control or interference in first-team matters, which marked a sea change in how things were governed at Celtic. It's unlikely that Stein would have accepted the job if he'd had to work under the same limitations as his predecessor, Jimmy McGrory, and having previously been a player and then reserve coach at the club, Stein knew exactly what was required and what needed to happen on and off the field.

The change was instant, and Celtic lifted the 1965 Scottish Cup – their first trophy in eight years – with a 3-2 victory over Dunfermline. Tommy Gemmell was one of seven of the starting XI in Lisbon who played in that Hampden triumph, and it represented his first major honour at Celtic. It's unlikely, however, if he or any of his team-mates realised they were on the cusp of greatness. They were just glad to have won a trophy, for themselves and for the long-suffering Celtic support.

In his autobiography, *Lion Heart*, Gemmell stated: 'We were hungrier than Dunfermline in wanting to win it, and it was Jock Stein who had created that hunger. Winning that final was a transformation in itself because previously we had kept getting to semi-finals or finals and losing them. Now we had won a final at Jock Stein's first attempt and everything just snowballed from there. Once you start winning matches, confidence builds; an average player becomes a good one, and a good player a great one. Jock's cleverness lay in recognising individual abilities and piecing the whole thing together. He asked everyone to play to their strengths and never asked them to do anything they couldn't do … He bonded eleven players into a team and made us realise that, although we were playing different roles, we all depended on each other. It sounds so simple – but that simplicity was the key to everything.'

Jock Stein's first full season in charge at Celtic saw him deliver two trophies to Paradise and guide the team to a European semi-final. One of those trophies was the league championship, Celtic's first title success since the double-winning 1953/54 season, when Stein had been captain. A 1-0 victory over Motherwell at Fir Park on the final day of the season confirmed Celtic as champions. Tommy Gemmell was one of only two players – the other being John Clark – who played in every one of Celtic's thirty-four league fixtures, while he also netted his first European goals for the club, scoring in both legs of the quarter-final victory over Dynamo Kyiv. Celtic were desperately unlucky not to reach the Cup-Winners' Cup final that season, losing 2-1 on aggregate to Liverpool, though a late Bobby Lennox goal at Anfield in the second leg was controversially disallowed, denying Celtic victory on the away goals rule.

Celtic's reward for winning the league was entry into the following season's European Cup, and it was Tommy Gemmell who had the honour of scoring the club's first goal in the competition, firing home from about thirty yards out in a 2-0 victory over FC Zurich at Celtic Park. In the return leg in Switzerland, which the Hoops won 3-0, Gemmell scored twice, the first a near identical strike to his Paradise goal, while the second came from the penalty spot.

Given the fact that he could hit a shot which registered at a speed of almost seventy miles an hour, it was no surprise that Tommy Gemmell was eventually given responsibility for Celtic's penalties. Being able to hit a dead ball twelve yards into the net at that speed meant it was a brave or foolish goalkeeper who put himself in the way on that thunderbolt. In his 1968 autobiography, *The Big Shot*, one of three that Tommy Gemmell has published, he offered an explanation of his spot-kick technique – 'You just run up and give it a terrible dunt!'

He continued: 'There are two ways of taking a penalty-kick. You can stroke the ball carefully, trying to place it as far away from the keeper as possible. Or you can use the 'terrible dunt' method. If a goalkeeper throws himself in the right direction he will probably save the first kind of kick because the ball is not travelling fast and so is easily deflected. With the second method, the keeper should have no chance unless you shoot straight at him. If he dives and gets a hand or an arm to the ball, the power of the shot will still carry it over the line in most cases. A keeper's only chance, therefore, is to move before the kick is taken and hope to get his body in the line of fire – and after taking penalties for about a year I began to realise this was happening.

'The good goalkeepers, knowing I always hammered the ball, were taking a chance and moving along the line as I ran up to take the kick. They knew the kick would be retaken if the referee spotted them, but this is a trick which a ref can often miss. There was one game where I took a penalty and when the ball struck the keeper's leg he was practically at the post. He had obviously moved, but as the ref let him away with it, I knew it was time I found my own remedy. The next three times I placed my shots and scored easily as the keepers were obviously expecting a full-blooded drive. Today, I vary my penalties according to which keeper I'm facing, but I'm still convinced the best way to score from the spot is to give the ball a terrible dunt!'

Whatever the technique, it obviously worked for Gemmell as he only missed three out of the thirty-four penalties he took for Celtic.

The free-scoring forwards for Celtic might have been getting many of the plaudits that season, and rightly so, but Jock Stein had emphasised the importance of the team, and every player made a vital contribution to every success Celtic enjoyed that season... and it was noted. At the turn of the year, Gemmell came sixth in the European Footballer of the Year (Ballon D'Or), one of only two Celtic players to make the list – the other was the boy who'd signed provisional forms for Celtic that same night in October 1961, Jimmy Johnstone, who came third behind Bobby Charlton and the winner, Florian Albert of Hungarian side Ferencvarosi. There were also two Inter Milan players in that list – Sandro Mazzola and Giacinto Facchetti – both of whom finished below the two Celts.

In season 1966/67, Tommy Gemmell scored sixteen goals across all competitions, eight of them from the penalty spot, and while three of his four European Cup goals came in the first round ties against FC Zurich, he saved the best 'til last in the heat of Lisbon. By then, of course, Celtic had swept all before them in Scotland, having secured four trophies – the League, Scottish Cup, League Cup and Glasgow Cup before they faced their biggest test of the season.

Jock Stein had travelled to Italy back in the early 1960s when he was still in charge of Dunfermline Athletic, and he'd observed the training methods of Inter Milan's coach, Helenio Herrera. Inter had one of the world's best full-backs in Giacinto Facchetti, resolute in defence but renowned also for his attacking prowess and his ability in front of goal. Perhaps it was having seen the player at close-hand which convinced Stein to demand so much of his own full-backs in an attacking sense, while always reminding them that their first priority was always to defend, and if they raced up the park, they would have to race back.

In the Estadio Nacional on May 25, 1967, Jim Craig and Tommy Gemmell produced a masterclass in attacking full-back play, with the crowning glory being their combination play which led to Celtic's equaliser. It was also a goal that provided an unexpected bonus for the scorer as he'd been promised fifty gallons of petrol free by Billy Skelly, brother of Motherwell car dealer, Ian Skelly, if he scored. That promise was duly kept when Celtic's conquering hero returned home to Lanarkshire.

The season after the Lisbon triumph was a disappointing one for Celtic as they relinquished their hold on the European Cup at the first time of asking, being knocked out in the first round by Dynamo Kyiv. It wasn't the best preparation for their World Club Championship clash with Racing Club of Argentina. The first leg in Glasgow was duly won 1-0, thanks to a Billy McNeill goal, and the team headed out to Buenos Aires intent on becoming world champions. Despite losing Ronnie Simpson before the game after he was struck on the head by a missile, Celtic settled into the game and Tommy Gemmell gave the Hoops the lead with a twenty-second minute penalty, although that lead lasted just eleven minutes before Racing Club equalised. Their second goal, which came just after half-time, meant that a play-off would have to decide the outcome of the clash, and it was scheduled for the Uruguayan capital, Montevideo. There had been debate within the Celtic camp as to whether or not they should play the third game, particularly given the behaviour of the Racing Club players in the first two games; that they ultimately opted to travel to Uruguay was something that many in the club would rue.

Gemmell, in his 1968 autobiography, described Racing Club as 'the dirtiest, most ruthless, and despicable bunch of soccer hatchet-men ever gathered together under the one set of jerseys.' After the game in Buenos Aires, which left the Celtic players with a sense of injustice that the illegal tactics their opponents employed had been given free reign by weak officials, chairman Robert Kelly initially indicated that he would not allow the team to play a third game. It was a decision that met with widespread support within the squad. However, that decision was reversed, in part due to assurances given that the game, and the men officiating it, would make for a fairer contest in Montevideo. How wrong that proved to be.

The Paraguayan referee proved to be even worse than the Uruguayan officials in Buenos Aires, and the game descended into near anarchy. Celtic had three players sent off – John Hughes, Jimmy Johnstone and Bobby Lennox, while Bertie Auld refused to leave the field when ordered to do so by the referee. Racing Club had two players sent off, while they scored what proved to be the only goal of the game ten minutes into the second-half. Tommy Gemmell stayed on the park, though television cameras did catch him surreptitiously kicking a Racing Club player during yet another melee on the pitch. It was an image that preceded Celtic's return to Scotland, and created negative headlines for Gemmell and his team-mates, all of whom were harshly fined £250 by the club for their behaviour in that third game.

Gemmell was a skilful and powerful player, but also a fierce competitor, and another momentary lapse in discipline, this time while on international duty with Scotland, would cost him a League Cup final spot with Celtic, and definitely strained relationships within the club. Towards the end of a game against West Germany, the Celtic left-back was sent off for what was deemed a retaliatory kick at a German player. While the indiscretion was with Scotland, it was Celtic who punished the player, dropping him for the 1969 League Cup final against St Johnstone, with Davie Hay coming into the starting XI. Gemmell only found out when he walked into the dressing-room half-an-hour before kick-off, which only added to his sense of injustice over the decision. He asked Jock Stein the following day about it, and the Celtic manager claimed it was on the instructions of chairman, Robert Kelly, who wanted the club to be seen to be doing the 'right thing', although it wasn't an explanation that Gemmell readily accepted and he requested to be put on the transfer list, a position he was to remain in until he left the club for Nottingham Forest in December 1971.

By then, of course, he had helped Celtic reach another European Cup final, and scored in that game, but it was the Dutch champions, Feyenoord, who lifted the trophy with an extra-time victory in the San Siro Stadium. However, Gemmell, like his team-mates, believed that had the game gone to a replay then Celtic would have performed much better and, in all probability, have won the cup.

The start of season 1971/72 saw Gemmell play only a handful of games for the first-team, though he was in the side that lost 4-1 to Partick Thistle in the League Cup final, playing at centre-half in place of the injured Billy McNeill, while his very last appearance for Celtic was in Malta, in the first round second leg tie against Sliema Wanderers. Just over a month later he joined Nottingham Forest. After two years away, which included a spell in Miami, Gemmell returned to Scotland, signing for Dundee. And in his first season at Dens Park, he helped his new team lift the League Cup, ironically with a 1-0 victory over Celtic in the final at Hampden. He would later manage the club for three years between 1977 and '80. His last involvement in football came with a spell as manager of Albion Rovers in the early 1990s.

Tommy Gemmell is a great Celt, a defender with an eye for goal, netting sixty-three goals in 418 appearances. His haul of medals is impressive – while there are also those two European Cup final goals to boast of. There are not too many players in the history of the beautiful game who can say they've done such a thing.

IN HIS OWN WORDS...

'In the two matches against Zurich I scored three goals – I got one at Celtic Park from about thirty-odd yards and the same at Zurich plus a penalty kick, so we won that round quite comfortably. I never thought at any time we were under pressure to get knocked out by them. In fact, they were a couple of easier games. Vojvodina beat us 1-0 and I had a poor pass-back to Ronnie Simpson which was intercepted and they stuck it in the net. To my mind Vojvodina were the best side we played that year in the European Cup and we had a hard time beating them in Glasgow. I was beginning to panic a little bit but when Billy knocked that one away in the last minute it was a great result for us, but I thought they were a tremendous side.

When we played Dukla Prague over there, Jock set us out to play a defensive formation. It was the first time and last time he ever asked us to do that. We drew 0-0 but they hit the woodwork three or four times, we cleared a few off the line and they had numerous shots at goal. How we survived I do not know but we had a good cushion of 3-1 from Glasgow from the first match and poor old Stevie Chalmers was left up there on his own chasing shadows, but it was the first and last time that Big Jock ever asked us to play defensively.

I was normally quite relaxed before the game although a lot of people approach these matches differently. My approach to all the games was that I couldn't hang around the dressing room from half past one until the three o'clock kick-off or whatever time it was. I liked to go into the dressing room about twenty minutes before kick-off and just get the gear off, get the gear on and get out on the park. It saves you thinking about it. But then you've got the likes of Stevie Chalmers, for example, who would be sitting at two o'clock on a Saturday afternoon with his gear on ready to go out and play. I couldn't handle it like that. I just liked to rush out at the last minute and that's the reason I did that sort of thing.

The system normally was that if Jim Craig was going forward, I had to stay at the back and cover for Billy and John Clark, but in the second-half of the final in Lisbon, Inter Milan were only playing with one man up front, so there was no point in three defenders and a goalkeeper marking one Inter player. There was no point in me staying back there, although the golden rule was that if Jim Craig went forward I had to stay back and vice-versa. But there was nobody to mark so what was the point? I mean, just go for it and we had to get a goal somewhere along the line. There wasn't a team in the world who could've given Celtic the ball as much as Inter gave us the ball and the goal had to come eventually. Fortunately I got it but it could've been anybody at all. We could've been three or four up by half-time if Sarti hadn't produced his acrobatics in the Inter goal.

We always thought we could beat them and we gave them a real going over. It was 2-1 going on 6 or 7. The Italian style of play at that time was score a goal, sit back soak up the pressure, hit you on the break and get another goal. That's how they played at that time. But when we got the breakthrough when I got the equaliser, their heads went down – they didn't want to know – and when Stevie tucked away the second one, the referee could've blown the whistle at any time because they'd chucked it.

I could've scored three or four goals that day in Lisbon. I hit the crossbar, the goalkeeper had two or three great saves from me and then, when I tucked that one away, I had the freedom of the park. When I was charging forward there was nobody came back with me and picked me up. If you look at the goal on film there's a defender (Picchi) who came out and, two yards from me, he stopped and turned his back. If he took another pace he'd block that shot and if they broke away and scored a goal I'd have been in deep trouble but, of course, that didn't happen and that was the breakthrough we needed. We knew as soon as we got the goal that we had beat them.

At half-time we were still behind but the Boss told us to stick to exactly the same technique, although he warned those who were crossing the ball to pull it back to the edge of the penalty box as the Italians were getting everything in their area. After the interval we really sailed into them. Everyone was going forward and Jim Craig was coming into his own. Playing with terrific confidence he was striding down the right-wing as if Inter didn't exist. Three times after the interval he moved deep into Inter territory and sent over crosses which gave them plenty to think about. Then in the sixty-second minute he went off again with a pass from Bobby Murdoch. After Bobby parted with the ball he ran away towards the inside-left position, taking a man with him. This left a wide gap in the centre of the field and I started to run.

Jim, looking as casual as ever, was still heading towards the corner flag. It seemed as if he was about to put over another cross. I started to shout, 'Cairney! Cairney!' I knew if he cut the ball back I would be in a great position for a shot and as I came near to their penalty area I was still shouting. Then, at exactly the right moment, he stroked the ball across to me. It was a great pass, coming at just the right speed, and asking to be hit. An Italian, who might have blocked my shot, shirked the tackle when he saw me running in at full tilt and I hit the ball first-time with my right. It felt good … and when I lifted my head it looked good. The ball was flying into the net. I had scored. We were level and still had almost half-an-hour to play. No wonder Cairney had a huge smile on his face.

That was the most important goal I've ever scored and the one most people will remember because it knocked the heart out of Inter. They must have known, as we did, that it was only a matter of time before we would score again. Sure enough, Stevie Chalmers got the winner six minutes from time. Later that night, when I was telling Cairney for the umpteenth time what a great pass it had been, he said, 'Ach, I knew you were coming through all the time, I just waited until you were in the right place.'

That game changed my life. If I hadn't scored that goal and if we hadn't won the European Cup we would be nonentities nowadays, but it's in Celtic's history and it will never be forgotten. People say to me in the street, 'That was some goal you scored.' I say, 'I scored a lot of goals. Which one are you talking about?' I scored a better goal against Benfica at Celtic Park in the European Cup, but people don't remember that, they just remember the big-time games.

There is no doubt that the most amazing thing about our performance – about everything we did – was this confidence we all shared. I didn't think about it at the time, but looking back now I can see that it must have astonished everyone we encountered, especially Inter Milan. By top international standards, we were just a bunch of youngsters, virtually unknown as individuals outside of Scotland. We were just about to play the most famous club in the world at that time, Internazionale of Milan. They were a tremendously experienced side, full of high-priced individuals. They had won the European and World crowns in 1964 and 1965. They were recognised at the greatest defensive side ever seen in Europe. Yet we expected to beat them! Why? I'm sure it was because we had no fear of losing to them. It didn't matter if we lost because we had already achieved everything. We had realised our greatest ambition by becoming the first British team to reach the European Cup and we had won every honour in Scotland. We had nothing to lose that sunny day in Lisbon.

We had received a tremendous send-off from Lisbon Airport; we were sped through with the European Cup and treated like the celebrities we had become. At home, the club's officials had asked supporters not to go to the airport in Glasgow to meet us. Instead, they put in the newspapers the route our coach would follow in taking us back to Celtic Park from the airport. The whole route was lined with people and when we got to Celtic Park there appeared to be around 25,000 outside the ground whilst inside, the stadium was packed to capacity to watch us parade the trophy around the track on an open-topped truck.

I did take the European Cup to Craigneuk to show it off to our neighbours. My parents were at Celtic Park when we returned from Lisbon the day after the Inter Milan game. Following all the celebrations at the park, I took a 'loan' of the silverware for the rest of the evening. Incredible! Could you imagine that happening today? I simply lifted the cup and took it over to where I stayed with my parents in Craigneuk. There seemed to be about 300 people there to welcome me home. It was just fabulous. My parents' home was a second-floor apartment and I think everyone – and I mean EVERYONE – crammed into their wee place that night.

The most important thing for my Celtic career was 1967, and apart from winning the European Cup, we won everything we played for – the Scottish Cup, League Championship, League Cup, and the Glasgow Cup. My biggest disappointment was leaving Celtic, I never actually wanted to leave Celtic at any time but my relationship with Big Jock had wavered a bit so it was better to go rather than stay, but it happened to a lot of the players that played in Lisbon. They left Celtic pretty soon after we won the European Cup and a lot of people thought that the team was possibly broken up a bit too quickly.'

LISBOA
25 DE MAIO DE
1967
CELTIC 2-1 INTER
CELTIC FC
50º ANIVERSARIO

JOHN CLARK

JOHN CLARK

John Clark may well be considered the quiet man of the Lisbon Lions, an unassuming player whose characteristic modesty reflected itself in the unfussy way he went about his business on the pitch, the last line of outfield defence, sweeping up all before him and ensuring Ronnie Simpson's goal remained protected. Yet, if John Clark didn't get the headlines that forward players inevitably garner, particularly for their goalscoring exploits – Clark only scored three goals for Celtic in 316 appearances – he was absolutely central to Celtic's success and his manager and his team-mates appreciated his talents to the full. The fact that, between April 1965 and September 1967, John Clark did not miss a single game – a remarkable total of 140 – is evidence enough of his importance to the Celtic cause; that total also included every friendly match the first-team played at that time.

His partnership with Billy McNeill in the heart of the Celtic defence was one of the strongest and toughest in football at that time, and it was a relationship that would later prove just as beneficial to the club when the Lisbon Lions stepped into the managerial hot seat at Paradise. Indeed, to say that John Clark has devoted his working life to Celtic is no exaggeration. From the moment he joined the club from Larkhall Thistle in October 1958 at the age of seventeen, he has been player, reserve coach, assistant manager and in more recent years, the club's kit controller.

When he originally signed for Celtic back in the later 1950s, just a year after the club's momentous 7-1 League Cup final victory over Rangers at Hampden, he did so as a left-half, although he also found himself in the right-half position on many occasions. Like so many of the young players at Celtic during that time, it was Jock Stein's arrival at the club in March 1965 which transformed John Clark into a world-class sweeper. Indeed, one of three nicknames he acquired – The Brush – was in recognition of his new position, while the more obvious one has been 'Clarky'. Perhaps the most famous, though, is Luggy, apparently coined after he ended up with a cauliflower ear following a training ground collision with Billy McNeill. If the player himself was never too fond of it, the moniker has become one of affection amongst the rest of the squad.

John Clark's first-team debut came in a league match away to Arbroath on October 3, 1959, a match that Celtic won 5-0, with his future Lisbon team-mate, Stevie Chalmers, netting two of the goals; as well as Clark and Chalmers, Billy McNeill and Bertie Auld were both in the side, as was the legendary Neilly Mochan, who would be the club's trainer in Lisbon nearly eight years later. The memory of the 7-1 game might still have been fresh in the minds of the supporters, but the reality of that season, like most others, was one of abject failure. Clark only made two appearances that season – the other was in a 1-1 draw at home to Aberdeen the week after his debut – as Celtic finished ninth in the league. The following season, John Clark pushed himself into the first-team on a few more occasions, even scoring his first goal for the club – the extra-time winner in a Scottish Cup quarter-final replay against Hibernian at Easter Road, when Ronnie Simpson was in goals for the Edinburgh club – and he was also in the side for the Scottish Cup final against Dunfermline Athletic, then managed by Jock Stein, who had first spotted the young Celt when he took part in a trial game. After a replay, Stein's Dunfermline triumphed, giving the Fife side their first success in the tournament, which was also the case for their promising young manager.

John Clark, however, was continuing to make steady progress at the club, which included gaining valuable European experience, playing in the club's first home tie – a Fairs Cities Cup game against Valencia in October 1962, when he missed a penalty – while he was an integral part of the side that reached the semi-final of the European Cup-Winners' Cup the following season, albeit that campaign was to end in heartache as Celtic surrendered a 3-0 first leg lead, losing 4-0 in Hungary to MTK Budapest. By the time season 1964/65 arrived, Clark was a regular in the side, and he would enjoy happier memories of a Scottish Cup final against Dunfermline Athletic this time around.

Celtic faced Dunfermline in the Hampden showpiece, with the Hoops now managed by Jock Stein who had arrived at the club from Hibernian six weeks before the final. Celtic had to come back twice in the match, with Bertie Auld providing the equaliser on each occasion, before Billy McNeill's goal on eighty-one minutes won the cup for the green and white Hoops. It was a first winner's medal for every one of the Celtic players, a first trophy as Celtic manager for Stein, and the catalyst for the incredible success that was to follow, even if none of the players were anticipating such an incredible turnaround in such a short space of time.

Speaking in a book to celebrate the fortieth anniversary of the Lisbon success, John Clark reflected on the importance of the 1965 Scottish Cup final. 'We had to shake off the stigma of never being good enough to walk up those stairs at Hampden and hold aloft a trophy – any trophy. So, it is obviously understandable that the support still talks about Big Billy's wonder header and wee Bertie's two efforts. How many remember a John Clark clearance off the line when the game was deadlocked at 2-2, though? One of their players – I think it was a bloke called John McLaughlin – beat John Fallon and the ball was heading goalwards until I managed to get a kick in the way. The ball spun up into the air and there was a bit of a melee before someone thumped it clear. Not a headline-grabber, I agree, but critical to what was to come later. If that had gone in, it could – and, knowing our luck, probably would – have been an entirely different outcome.'

Celtic were now a team of winners, and in Jock Stein's first full season in charge they set about proving that, securing a first league title in twelve years and delivering the League Cup for the first time since 1957. Now comfortably settled in at sweeper, John Clark was in the midst of his remarkable run of consecutive games. It had actually started the previous season, on April 17, 1965 in a league game at home to Partick Thistle, a match that Celtic lost 2-1, and it would continue until September 27, 1967 when he missed the League Cup quarter-final second leg against Ayr United. In that title-winning 1965/66 season, both Clark and Tommy Gemmell played in every single game in all four competitions. That included the European Cup-Winners' Cup, when Celtic reached another semi-final. There was to be no disastrous semi-final collapse from the Hoops this time around, although there was still the same sense of sadness as Liverpool won 2-1 on aggregate.

However, Celtic could console themselves with the fact they were now the best team in Scotland, winning the league by two points from Rangers, the decisive victory coming on the final day of the season against Motherwell at Fir Park. The reward for that success was, of course, qualification to the European Cup tournament the following season. It would be Celtic's first participation in the competition, and Swiss side FC Zurich were first up for the Hoops.

By this time, John Clark had also gained international recognition, making the first of five appearances for Scotland on June 25, 1966 against then world champions, Brazil, at Hampden, as part of their preparations for the forthcoming World Cup tournament in England; Scotland had failed to qualify for the competition. The match ended 1-1 and Clark did an impressive job in marking the legendary Pele, so much so that, when their paths crossed later in a New York hotel lobby, it was the Brazilian who recognised the Celt and stopped to talk to him.

Celtic began season 1966/67 full of confidence. The close season tour of North America had given the team a sense of unity and purpose, as well as supreme confidence in their manager and in what he was trying to achieve. Even before the season started there was another sign of Celtic's growing strength and potency when, on August 6, they thrashed Manchester United 4-1 at Celtic Park. A week later, the competitive action got underway, and two Joe McBride goals gave the Hoops a 2-0 win over Hearts at Tynecastle in the opening League Cup sectional game. The first trophy of the season duly followed with a League Cup final win, and that was quickly followed by the Glasgow Cup. And maintaining a vital presence in his new sweeper role was John Clark, wearing the No.6 shorts.

Celtic's attacking statistics in season 1966/67 make for incredible reading – a staggering total of 196 goals across five competitions (League, Scottish Cup, League Cup, Glasgow Cup and European Cup) – but the defensive record is worth acknowledging too. In sixty-two games, the Hoops conceded just forty-eight goals, and that helped create the foundation for Jock Stein's side to conquer all who came before them. Indeed, there were only three competitive defeats that season – two against Dundee United in the league, and the away leg against Vojvodina. Throughout all of those games, John Clark was always there, a model of consistency, a beacon of calm, the epitome of a Celtic player, always proud to wear the green and white Hoops, and always doing so to the best of his ability.

Anchoring the defence was the formidable duo of Billy McNeill and John Clark, a partnership forged from their earliest days at Celtic, two Lanarkshire Bhoys both determined to play for their team. In the early days of that friendship, they travelled in from Lanarkshire by bus, but on the way back, the journey took a little longer. Clark explained: 'None of us, including Jock Stein, had a car at the time and we used to go up to Parkhead Cross to get the bus home. The first bus that came along was ours, the Wishaw bus that dropped Billy at Bellshill and me at Holytown. But, Jock held us back and wouldn't let us on it until his bus came along. His bus came along going to Hamilton and he'd jump on it and we'd have another forty-five or fifty minutes to wait on our bus coming again. And he did that every night we were training, we would stand there talking to him and notice our bus going the other way into Glasgow knowing we'd have to wait on it coming back out the other way. But when Big Jock got a car, he used to drop us off at our houses, so he returned the favour.'

John Clark ended his Celtic career with a game against Clyde on the last day of the 1970/71 season, when the Lisbon Lions took their final bow as a team, although Ronnie Simpson only ran out alongside his team-mates before the game. John Clark won three league titles, three Scottish Cups and four League Cups during his time at the club, as well as the European Cup. There were three goals in 316 appearances, although he did score one more goal for Celtic – in a 3-1 victory for the green and white Hoops over the blue and white hoops of Morton, when the Lisbon Lion put through his own net for one of Celtic's goals; Celtic wore an all-green strip that day.

'I just wanted to keep playing and stay here,' he later told the Celtic View. 'Once I got in I didn't want to lose my place and that was all down to my hard work and ability. It's important to stay injury-free and that can sometimes be the difference between success in the long-run. That's what eventually ruined me at the end, I was out for a year and the team couldn't wait for me. The team can't wait a year for anybody. I had a good career, though, and I enjoyed it.'

He returned to Celtic as a coach in 1973 before he linked up again with his former captain and central defensive partner, Billy McNeill, who had taken over at Aberdeen in January 1978. Just over a year later, the two men were back at Paradise, succeeding Jock Stein, and in their first season in charge produced an incredible title triumph, beating Rangers 4-2 in the final game of the season on a night that became known as '10 Men Won The League'. There were five years at Celtic before the two men left, and John Clark had spells with Cowdenbeath, Stranraer and Clyde as manager, before he returned to Celtic as the club's kit controller. It was a position he held for many years, making him an integral part of the many successes the club enjoyed, with his experience as a player and coach who had done it all with Celtic invaluable.

Billy McNeill gave this assessment of his friend and fellow Lisbon Lion in his autobiography, *Hail Cesar*. Celtic's legendary captain wrote: 'I was probably closer to John than to the other members of the team, because we had known each other longer. He arrived at Celtic Park shortly after me and, as we came from roughly the same part of Lanarkshire, we travelled to training together. The fact that we came through the reserve team together enabled us to develop an almost telepathic understanding, despite having somewhat different personalities. Later, he became my assistant at Aberdeen and the first time round at Celtic and I knew I could always rely on him as a steadying influence.

'John was certainly fairly quiet and sensible and, I suspect, a little shy. He was also a complete football nut, who had no other interests or pastimes than the game itself. While the rest of us read novels when we were on trips abroad, John invariably had his nose buried in a football magazine and he developed an extensive knowledge of the game and its personalities ... but it would be wrong to paint a picture of John as a football anorak. He was always good company. We roomed together on trips and there was never a shortage of Mars bars in the bedside cabinet, for the pair of us are very sweet-toothed. As a player, John was positive, determined and hard as nails, and for someone who isn't the biggest guy in the world, incredibly powerful.'

John Clark has always been immensely proud of his association with the club he supports, and at the start of the 2015/16 season, he was the guest of honour on the opening day of the season and unfurled the league flag at a packed Paradise, in front of supporters who also acknowledged everything the Lisbon Lion had done for the club, as well as celebrating another title success for the club. He explained: 'I have worked here through the 1950s, '60s, '70s, '80s, '90s and into the 2000s and '10s. I could never have imagined that I would be here that long, but I've just been lucky to have been involved in the game for as long as I have. And as a Celtic supporter myself, I've been incredibly lucky to have been at the club for so long.

'The Hoops are unique and wherever you travel around the world, people love it. They love the clean look of it and it looks great, especially on a sunny day, when you're playing in a final. It is well known and well thought of throughout the world, and working as kit man, you find that there's a real demand for it. It's a special shirt with its own history and you felt pride just pulling it on before a match. That's your team, that shirt

The captains and officials before the big kick-off.

The moment that changed the history of Celtic Football Club – Stevie Chalmers steers the ball home.

The Celts line up for the pre-match photo.

They think it's all over – it is now.

Tommy Gemmell's shot hits the back of the Inter Milan net, Celtic are level and on their way to European glory.

The Lions take to the turf at the Estadio Nacional.

The Celts go through their training routine on the eve of the final.

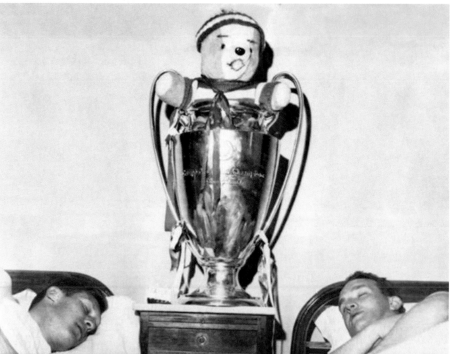

The Lions sleep tonight – with the European Cup and that hooped teddy still in their dreams.

Jock Stein and his Bhoys parade the European Cup at a packed Paradise.

It's there – Stevie Chalmers reels away after scoring the winner.

Bertie Auld flights over a free-kick.

The winning captain trying to get the cup back to his team-mates in the dressing room.

Cesar raising the cup aloft as Celtic become the first British team to win the European Cup.

represents your love for the club and as a supporter, pulling that on meant that I had achieved what I wanted to achieve and more importantly, I did with a great bunch of boys and a fantastic bunch of people to work with.

'Celtic has been my life and I have worked here in every decade over 50 years. It meant a great deal to me as a youngster, because you can only thrive if you are a Celtic supporter who gets the opportunity to play for the club, it's every supporter's ambition. I am just so fortunate that I have had the opportunity to play and work here, but I never thought that I would I enjoy such a long association with the club and could never have imagined, when I signed, the success we would have under such a great manager as Jock Stein. He pushed us to be the best we could be and drove us to the greatest honour that any club can win. It's been a major part of my life and as I said, I always attach that word 'luck' to me and Celtic.'

IN HIS OWN WORDS...

'If you're brought up being a Celtic supporter when you're a kid and you win the biggest trophy that everyone's spending millions on trying to win just now even, it's hard to describe. You feel like you're delighted to be part of it. Fifty years on, you're a better player now than what you were when you played! People love telling you that they were there. I think the Lisbon Lions will never be forgotten about and that's the thing about the supporters. Time has gone on and we're still invited to functions all over the world. It's a great feeling and you feel chuffed about it.

First and foremost, we were really well-organised as a team and we had a manager who made sure the players that played were the best players for that position. He never elaborated on 'You've got to do this or do that'. He just asked you to play the game how you saw it. He made sure he played people in the right positions. We had individual players like Jimmy and Bobby and Bertie, Tommy Gemmell who would come from the back to score, big Billy at set-pieces. We were a well-organised team, plus the fact we had a lot of ability.

It was a great achievement to be in the final. For a club like Celtic to be in the final of the European Cup was a massive thing. We didn't fear anybody and everybody had confidence in themselves. The inspiration for us was Jock Stein but he had a good staff behind him as well. I would say that we were a really confident team and we never accepted that we were going to get beat.

One of the most intense games we ever played was against Vojvodina at Celtic Park in the quarter-final. Billy McNeill scored the winning goal with the last touch of the ball – a corner kick from Charlie Gallagher. I thought that was the hardest game I'd ever played in my life because we knew that any mistake at the back and we were out. We had to be on top form that night. I still remember Charlie's corner and Big Billy's header. Vojvodina had a goalkeeper that night, Pantelic, who was absolute class and he could have stopped anything – he could probably have even stopped the wind – but he had no chance with Billy's header. There was just such an explosion of relief and joy, both among the massive crowd here and among the players and what a finish it was, a great corner and a great header.

Before the Inter game we were up in Estoril. It was very warm and we weren't allowed out during the day. We trained in the evening and weren't allowed out until then. You had to stay in the hotel during the day which was all air-conditioned. You weren't even allowed out to sit on the lawn or anything like that. Big Jock would crack up. He thought the heat took the strength out your body. I'm sitting here just now and if Jock Stein was still alive, I would know where he was in the building. He had that vibe. And all of the players knew that as well. The players loved him as a manager and a coach.

Back then, Inter had the top man in the world – Helenio Herrera. His philosophy for was playing in the 'Catenaccio' style, where the emphasis would be not losing a goal. I think Celtic deserve a lot of credit for what they did in destroying that with their attacking football. I think it was the end of it after that, as teams changed their outlook to playing football again. Before that, Inter had been the king-pins. But it just shows how football goes in cycles.

We played our own way. We didn't bother with their system. We had a lot of clever players. We had guys who could play – players with good control, good vision and the likes of Jimmy who could take players on. We had a good pool of players. We were well-covered in the full-back positions and defensively. Then you had players like John Hughes and Charlie Gallagher who could come in and offer something different as well.

In Lisbon we were all lined up and then the next thing wee Bertie starts blasting out *The Celtic Song*. It was typical of that team and the personality of the team. That was the whole thing about it. We had personalities and players who didn't lack confidence. We believed in ourselves and were determined to do well for Celtic all the time.

I'll never forget that back-heel from Ronnie Simpson. I still break out it a sweat when I think about it. It came from a long pass from the edge of the Inter Milan penalty area. Ronnie, as he often did, saw it coming and was off his line swiftly. Cappellini didn't give up the chase, however, but kept on going. Ronnie actually turned his back on the Inter forward and looked as though he was going to run towards his penalty area where he could have picked up the ball. Instead, he decided to back-heel it to me! But that was Ronnie. He was a very confident person but it was experience that made him do that. He told me he realised I was there all the time. He got away with it, but just think what would have happened if he made a mess of it. We wouldn't be talking about it fifty years on.

Our equaliser was a tremendous goal and Tommy Gemmell was capable of doing that all the time. He was one of the best full backs in the world and Stevie then got on to a shot to score the winner. I still remember that moment, it was good work and then Stevie got his toe to it to put it into the net. You're always going to have it in the back of your mind that they might equalise, like you would in any game and against any team, so we had to watch that we didn't get caught out. They tried to get back at us and had a wee spell but gradually we wore them down and we stepped up the pace again. I think our fitness, at the end of the day, overran them a bit and they were shocked by that.

The place was covered in green and white everywhere you looked. It was massive and you saw that after the game when the fans got on to the park, you just couldn't describe it. The only thing that was a bit disappointing was that we couldn't do a lap of honour for them like teams do now. We made up for it the next night, though, when we got back to Celtic Park and saw all the fans – that will live in my memory forever. It certainly sank in when you saw photographs of our captain holding up the cup. That makes you realise you are the winners of the competition.

After the final whistle Bobby Lennox came and hugged me and I don't like guys hugging me! The bottom line is that I am particular about who hugs me and when a guy like Bobby Lennox starts putting his arms around you, that should tell you a lot about how I felt at the final whistle! And I ended up with my boots getting taken off me. Going down the road after the game on the bus, there were thousands on the street and there was a guy holding up the boots – and I knew they were mine!

I have been part of Celtic for a long time and I have been attached to the club since 1958. Everything that has to be won, I have won it. Outside my family, Celtic is the biggest thing in my life. The club have been a huge part of my life and always will be. The first time I ever went to Celtic Park was in 1956 when Celtic played Manchester United in the afternoon.

My father was killed on the railways and I got a job in there. It only lasted about a few months but on my first day, I asked if I could go away earlier to go and watch Celtic play Manchester United. My boss couldn't believe I was asking that at fifteen years of age. Fortunately enough, he was a Celtic man himself, so he let me away. That was my first match at Celtic Park. I stood in the old Rangers End as that is where I came in. I had been at Hampden previously to watch Celtic play Manchester United in the Coronation Cup. We didn't have the finances to go to Celtic Park back in those days as my mother was a widow, but I went to the Coronation Cup with my uncles when we beat Man United in the semi-finals.

After that, I went back to Hampden again when Celtic played Clyde in the Scottish Cup final. I saw the first final but I never got back to replay because we never had the money. That's how it started. The next time I went to see Celtic at Hampden was the 7-1 game in October. One year later, I was signing for Celtic. I was on the groundstaff and Jock Stein was my gaffer as he was in charge of the youths at the time. Apparently, I was the first player he ever signed. He signed me at the door going into the Green Room at Celtic Park. It was down by the laundry and the kit room. It was a Thursday night and he brought a form in and I was delighted to sign it. My mother was a widow so it helped us financially, and my career went from there. I started playing more regularly and then got involved with European football. After Jock Stein came back from Hibs the whole thing seemed a lot more professional and everything clicked after that.

I had to bide my time for a first-team chance but that wasn't a problem. I was still learning and my body was still adapting to training. I was playing all the time and that helped me develop my own game. I was delighted to move up to the first-team and a lot of the older boys helped with that. I was in amongst established players but we were also a group of talented young players. After I broke in, the likes of Billy McNeill, Bobby Lennox and wee Jinky came in. Bertie Auld came back from Birmingham, Tommy Gemmell and Jim Craig came in and Ronnie Simpson came from Hibs. When we all stuck together we were a good team. We had the right man looking out for us and he put a right good team together.

From 1958 I have seen the lot. I have been part of a lot of good occasions and met a lot of really good people – players, managers, directors and supporters – and I am just one of them. The whole thing has been one long road of mostly success, not only as a player but as part of the club. God has been good to me and I have been a lucky guy as well. People like Jock Stein, Sean Fallon, Neilly Mochan and Bob Rooney were great to me, especially when I was younger. Jimmy Gribben, who was the old-time kit-man, would sit in a chair and direct things for the groundstaff.

I have met everyone I wanted to meet and played against the best players – you can't play against any better than the likes of Pele, Eusebio, George Best and Jimmy Greaves. I also saw the best managers from other teams as well. I have enjoyed it all. Whenever I stop here, I will walk out with my head held high.'

LISBOA
25 DE MAIO DE
1967
CELTIC 2-1 INTER
CELTIC FC
50° ANIVERSARIO

BILLY McNEILL

LISBOA
25 DE MAIO DE
1967
CELTIC 2-1 INTER
50° CELTIC FC
ANIVERSARIO

BILLY McNEILL

He was the leader of men, the colossus who strode into battle at the head of his green and white army and who, more often than not, emerged triumphant when the dust finally settled on the hostilities. His nickname, Cesar, may have its origins in comparisons to a Hollywood actor of the 1960s, Cesar Romero, but Billy McNeill was Celtic's Caesar who, with his team-mates, came, saw and conquered. He famously described the story of Celtic, from its humble and unique beginning, through to the many unexpected, unlikely or extraordinary triumphs enjoyed over the years, as a fairytale; that description could easily describe Billy McNeill's life. He was a man who, it seemed, was born to play for Celtic. Not only that, but he did so during the most successful era in the club's history, playing his part as Celtic dominated Scottish football and conquered Europe. Any imagery from that time has one consistent – Billy McNeill with a piece of silverware in his hand. He won nine league championships – the historic nine-in-a-row success between 1965 and '74; he lifted the Scottish Cup on seven occasions, doing so for the last time in 1975 on what was his last competitive match for his beloved Celtic. There were also six League Cup successes, along with numerous Glasgow Cup trophies.

In terms of iconic imagery, however, nothing will ever eclipse May 25, 1967, when the Bhoy from Bellshill lifted the European Cup trophy on the podium in Lisbon's Estadio Nacional, having captained Celtic to a 2-1 victory over Inter Milan in the final. It was the first ever triumph in the competition for a British team and Billy McNeill became the first ever British captain to get his hands on the trophy. It was, in fact, a brand new trophy in 1967 since the original piece of silverware had taken up permanent residence in the Santiago Bernabeu Stadium following Real Madrid's success the previous season.

Such were the chaotic scenes on the pitch after the final whistle in Lisbon that the Celtic squad beat a hasty retreat, most of them in a state of undress after jubilant spectators sought souvenirs of the momentous moment before Billy McNeill, accompanied by assistant manager, Sean Fallon, made his way up to where the trophy awaited him. The twenty-seven-year-old, in the prime of his football career, standing tall and proud in his green and white Hooped shirt, grasped the handles of the trophy and thrust it into the air; supporters around the stadium and around the world cheered, treasuring a moment that none of them could ever have imagined would happen.

Billy McNeill signed for Celtic in August 1957 – he'd been known as 'Willie' up to then but changed to Billy when he became a Bhoy – and even then Jock Stein's influence was prevalent, as McNeill explained: 'Jock was the person who impressed upon Robert Kelly that he had to sign me after a schoolboy international at Celtic Park. Jock came out to my Mum and Dad's house to persuade me to sign, but there was no need because this was my club and the one thing about my Mum and Dad was that they never interfered with anything I did, as long as it was sensible. Jock was instrumental in giving me the career I loved and was there for me from that day on.'

A year later he made his first-team debut, playing against Clyde in a League Cup sectional tie at Celtic Park. The Hoops won 2-0, with Bertie Auld scoring one of the goals. While no-one amongst the crowd of 39,000 who watched that game could have predicted they were watching the debut of a player who would go on to make more appearances than any other player in the club's history – 790 in total – it is interesting to look at the men who played alongside Billy McNeill in that game; many of them were great players who are rightly considered to be Celtic legends, yet they had the misfortune to play in an era of under-achievement due, in no small part, to mismanagement at the heart of the club. The team was: Frank Haffey; Dunky MacKay, Neilly Mochan, Willie Fernie, Billy McNeill, Bertie Peacock, Charlie Tully, Bobby Collins, Jim Conway, Sammy Wilson, Bertie Auld.

Billy McNeill was actually in the team for Bobby Evans who had picked up an injury against Clyde just three days previously in the opening fixture of the league campaign. It might have been Evans' bad luck which gave McNeill his entry into the first-team, but he did enough to impress and would go on to make a total of twenty-three appearances that season, including seventeen in the league. Celtic, as was the norm at that time, finished well off the leaders in fifth place. The following season, which saw McNeill make over thirty appearances across all three domestic competitions, was even worse as far as the league was concerned. Celtic finished ninth in an eighteen-team league, the points gap between them and bottom-placed Arbroath smaller than the gap between them and champions, Hearts.

By the time Billy McNeill turned twenty on March 2, 1960, he was an established first-team player at Celtic, and season 1960/61 saw him an almost ever-present in the team, missing only three league games in a campaign that saw the Hoops finish in the giddy heights of fourth; he also scored his first competitive goal for the club, Celtic's first goal in a 3-1 win over Ayr United at Somerset Park on March 4, two days after his twenty-first birthday. There was slightly better news in the Scottish Cup, however, as the team reached their first final in five years, although that ended in defeat to Dunfermline Athletic following a replay. The Fife side were managed by Jock Stein, who had previously coached the reserves at Celtic, including McNeill, and while it was another disappointment for the Hoops and their long-suffering supporters, it was also a sign that Stein was a manager to watch. Just five days after that Scottish Cup final defeat, Bertie Auld was sold to Birmingham City.

The season also saw Billy McNeill win the first of his twenty-nine Scotland caps when he played against England at Wembley on April 15, 1961. Like the rest of his Lisbon Lions' team-mates, it was a paltry total for one of Europe's top defenders in the 1960s and '70s. It was an unforgettable debut for the young Celt, though not a memorable one as England thrashed Scotland 9-3. It was worse for McNeill's Celtic team-mate, goalkeeper Frank Haffey, who was between the sticks for the Scots that day.

At that time, Billy McNeill was still making his way in the game, so he might not yet have identified the malaise which had gripped Celtic, though he, like his team-mates, would have been frustrated by the lack of silverware. In season 1962/63, the club took its first steps into European football, facing Valencia in the first round of the Fairs Cities Cup. The Spaniards won the tie 6-4 on aggregate, going on to win the tournament with a two-leg victory over Dinamo Zagreb in the final. The following season, 1963/64, Billy McNeill took over the Celtic captaincy from Dunky MacKay, a position he was to hold until his retirement in 1975, and the timing of that decision may have been significant, given that the player had turned down an opportunity to join Tottenham Hotspur. But while that season told a similar story of underachievement in the three domestic competitions, Celtic enjoyed better fortunes on the European stage, reaching the semi-final of the Cup-Winners' Cup; they had qualified for the competition by virtue of being Scottish Cup runners-up the previous season.

Celtic saw off FC Basel, Dinamo Zagreb and Slovan Bratislava to set up a semi-final clash with MTK Budapest of Hungary. The first leg at Celtic Park saw the Hoops record an impressive 3-0 victory, the side including six of the starting XI in Lisbon three years later – Gemmell, McNeill, Clark, Johnstone, Murdoch and Chalmers, who scored two of the goals, with Jimmy Johnstone netting the other. The return leg in Budapest, while not a formality, should have been successfully negotiated. Instead, there was a catastrophic collapse on the part of the Celtic team, who lost 4-0 and were dumped out of the tournament; MTK would lose the final 1-0 to Sporting Lisbon.

It's not surprising that Billy McNeill would have attracted interest from other suitors, and Everton were another English club whose advances he rejected. There were also rumours linking him with a move to Manchester United as Matt Busby sought a long-term replacement for defender, Bill Foulkes. Given what unfolded over the next few years, it's incredible to think that Billy McNeill was contemplating life away from Celtic. After seven years in the first-team, with no medals to show for it, and a continuing stream of very talented players leaving the club, often, or so it seemed, on the whim of the chairman, Robert Kelly, the Celtic captain had started to believe that his career might be better served away from Celtic Park. Then the club made a decision that changed everything.

Speaking in his autobiography, *Hail Cesar*, McNeill said: 'Heaven knows what state Celtic Football Club would have ended up in had Jock Stein not returned to Celtic Park in March 1965. It would be too dramatic to suggest that the ship was sinking, but it was certainly listing badly to port. The signs of decline were everywhere. The team had not won a major trophy for eight years and there was a growing sense of disillusionment among the players and our supporters ... With Jock at the helm, Celtic underwent an immediate transformation. Crucially, he knew many of the younger players like myself from his time as a coach and that made the task of putting across his message slightly easier.

'I had never seen Mr McGrory in a tracksuit; Jock was rarely out of one. Training altered dramatically and it suddenly became a pleasure instead of a chore. Jock dispensed with the tedium of players pounding round the track and replaced these mind-numbing sessions by introducing footballs into our daily fitness sessions! Daft as it may sound, under the previous coaching regime we had prepared in the manner of track athletes, rather than football players, and working with the principal tool of our trade had not figured prominently on the agenda. I felt like a man reborn and all thoughts of a move away from Celtic Park disappeared from my mind.'

Celtic had come close to losing one of their greatest assets and it is impossible to imagine where the club would have ended up had they not appointed Jock Stein as manager back on March 9, 1965. From that moment, nothing was ever the same again, and dreams that were beyond even the wildest imagination were soon to become reality. And leading all of it on the park was Billy McNeill, content once again at Paradise and on his way to a record-breaking appearance tally for the club, also becoming the only one of the Lisbon Lions who did not play for another club.

Jock Stein's impact at Celtic was instant – the team won 6-0 at Broomfield against Airdrie the day after he took over as manager – although the league form remained inconsistent and the team finished eighth in the table. In the Scottish Cup, however, the team managed to overcome Motherwell in the semi-final at the second time of asking, winning the replay 3-0 to set up a meeting in the final with Stein's former side, Dunfermline Athletic. It would be no easy task for Celtic to win, given that they'd lost 2-1 at home to the Fife side earlier in the season, and Dunfermline would ultimately finish third in the table, just a point behind Hearts and champions Kilmarnock.

On April 24, 1965, however, at Hampden, despite twice trailing in the match, Celtic showed great fighting qualities, with Bertie Auld drawing his side level on both occasions. Then, with nine minutes of the match remaining, Celtic scored what proved to be the winning goal, and it was fitting that Stein's captain should be the man who was the match-winner. Charlie Gallagher's pinpoint corner was fired into the box and on to the head of Billy McNeill, whose powerful header ended up in the back of the net. Celtic were the Scottish Cup winners – the club's first major trophy in eight years. More importantly, it was a first trophy success for their new manager and the group of talented young players he was aiming to mould into a team of winners. They didn't realise it at the time, but the victory at Hampden was the catalyst for every extraordinary thing that was to follow over the next ten years.

Billy McNeill later reflected on the triumph: 'That Scottish Cup success in 1965 was so important to the team. Jock actually said to me that day that we were going to try something different, that I'd to go forward for free-kicks and corners and that they were going to try and use my ability in the air. It was strange, because it was something which, at that point, hadn't happened very often. To score the winning goal in a Scottish Cup final was something very special.'

The new Scottish Cup holders still had one league fixture to conclude four days after the final, ironically against Dunfermline at East End Park, and that ended in a 5-1 defeat. It may have been due, in part, to the post-Hampden celebrations, but it did not take the shine off the success, while on a personal level, Billy McNeill became the first recipient of the Scottish Football Writers' Player of the Year Award.

The real evidence of the Stein factor at Celtic is most strikingly illustrated when comparing the league tables of 1964/65 and 1965/66. In the first of those seasons, as previously mentioned, the Hoops finished eighth. They won sixteen games, drew five and lost thirteen, scoring seventy-six goals and conceding fifty-seven. The following season, Celtic won twenty-seven games, drew three and lost four. They scored 106 goals and conceded thirty. The most important statistic, however, was the league placing, as a 1-0 victory at Fir Park on the final day of the season confirmed Celtic as champions of Scotland. They also won the League Cup and reached the semi-final of the European Cup-Winners' Cup before losing narrowly, and unluckily, to Liverpool, who would subsequently lose the final after extra-time to Borussia Dortmund at Hampden.

The turnaround in Celtic's fortunes was extraordinary, and while Jock Stein was the inspiration, he looked to his captain to lead the team by example once they stepped over the white line and on to the pitch. Billy McNeill never let him down. If the 1965/66 season had been an enjoyable one for the Celtic support – a first League Cup trophy since 1957 and, more remarkably for a club of Celtic's size and reputation, a first league title since 1954 – then the following season was to exceed all expectations, even those of the players, as Billy McNeill explained: 'The one year that I would say was the highlight of my time at Celtic is an obvious one, the season of 1967. It was the greatest experience that I think any of the Lions enjoyed at the club. Winning all of the domestic honours and then winning the European Cup and being the first British club to do so, is something that will live beyond any other achievements. We had hope that year – we believed we could do something – but I'll always remember Jimmy Gordon, later of Radio Clyde, who was recording a film of that particular season. He was outside our house one day filming and he said to me, 'Billy, I have a great feeling that once again the mysticism of Celtic will shine through and I have a feeling that this is going to be a great season'. It turned out to be a fabulous season, it really did.'

Billy McNeill missed just one game across all the domestic and European competitions that season – a 1-1 draw at home to St Mirren on November 5 when Bobby Murdoch was sent off – and the Celtic captain certainly needed his strength for all the trophies he had to lift that season; the League Cup was won with a 1-0 victory over Rangers, with Bobby Lennox scoring the only goal of the game. Lennox then hit a hat-trick as Celtic beat Partick Thistle 4-0 to win the Glasgow Cup, Stevie Chalmers netting the other goal. Two Willie Wallace goals beat Aberdeen 2-0 to win the Scottish Cup, while two Jimmy Johnstone goals at Ibrox gave Celtic the point they needed to retain the championship. And then there was the most momentous day in football history – May 25, 1967 – when eleven men born within a thirty-mile radius of Celtic Park became the champions of Europe, Tommy Gemmell and Stevie Chalmers scoring to beat Inter Milan 2-1. Some fifty years may have passed since those heady days, but the achievements of Jock Stein's Celtic side remain just as impressive and exciting now as they undoubtedly did back in 1967.

Billy McNeill's contribution to the Celtic cause during those years also makes for remarkable reading, and perhaps the only disappointment is that he doesn't have any other European Cup triumphs to show for his, and the team's excellence in the competition at that time. McNeill only missed a total of five European matches (which also includes the games against Racing Club of Argentina in the World Club Championship), while he played in 282 out of a possible 306 of the nine-in-a-row league matches. He won twenty-three major honours with the club, while he played 790 times – never as a substitute – scoring thirty-five goals in the process.

If his goal against Dunfermline Athletic won the Scottish Cup for Celtic and propelled the club forward on its incredible journey, then his goal against Vojvodina in the quarter-final of the 1966/67 European Cup kept the dream alive that Celtic could conquer Europe. Again, it was a header from a Charlie Gallagher corner, and that last-minute goal to win the tie sent Paradise into raptures. Billy McNeill said: 'I came flying down the middle of the park after scoring and the first thing I said to John Clark was, 'Hey, don't let us lose a goal now'. He looked at me and said, 'The game's finished, big man'. I told him, 'I don't care if it's finished or not, we're not going to lose a goal!' So the game restarted and the referee immediately blew for time up. I looked round at John and he said to me, 'See, I told you!'

When Cesar was carried aloft by his team-mates at Hampden on May 3, 1975 after lifting the Scottish Cup for the seventh time as Celtic beat Airdrie 3-1, even they did not know that it was his last game for the club, having decided to retire at the age of thirty-five. However, it would not be the end of Billy McNeill's Celtic career. After spells with Clyde and Aberdeen as manager, he returned to Paradise in 1978 as the man with the unenviable task of taking over from Jock Stein as manager. With fellow Lisbon Lion, John Clark, alongside him as his assistant, McNeill steered Celtic to the title with a stunning 4-2 victory over Rangers in the game that became known as '10 Men Won The League'. The following season his team won the Scottish Cup with a 1-0 extra-time victory over Rangers, and then came consecutive league titles in 1981 and '82. He won the League Cup in 1983, again with a win over Rangers, before leaving the club, although he returned four years later to guide Celtic to a memorable League and Scottish Cup double in the club's centenary season. Once again, the 'fairytale' element of the Celtic story was there for all to see. A further Scottish Cup followed the following year as a Joe Miller goal gave the Hoops a 1-0 win over Rangers before his second spell as manager ended in May 1991.

Speaking later to the *Celtic View*, he said: 'Looking back on my career as a player and manager I can say that I have no regrets about my time at Celtic. Yes, you have your ups and downs, your low points and bad days. That's only natural. But my era with the club was just such a wonderful time and I can say that I have no regrets whatsoever. I was fortunate enough to serve the club as a player, captain and manager and I enjoyed every experience I had at Celtic Park, I enjoyed everything. They were great times for me and when I look back on my playing days, early on, I did have an opportunity to go down to England. But luckily enough, Big Jock returned and the rest, as they say, is history.'

When Celtic announced in July 2009 that they were appointing a Club Ambassador, there was only one man who could properly fill that role – Billy McNeill. A familiar presence on matchdays at Celtic Park, and a much-loved and revered figure amongst the Celtic support, it was fitting that Cesar became the club's first ambassador – he had long been fulfilling that role anyway. He has since been joined by two other Celtic legends, Davie Hay and Tom Boyd.

Even a cursory glance through the Celtic history books will make any reader aware of Billy McNeill's contribution to the club, but for visitors to Celtic Park, they too are aware of this great Celt. While three statues stand outside the front of the stadium in recognition of our founding father, Brother Walfrid, our greatest manager in Jock Stein, and the man voted the Greatest Ever Celt by supporters, Jimmy Johnstone, what greets everyone at the start of The Celtic Way is a stunning statue of Billy McNeill holding aloft the European Cup. The statue was unveiled by Cesar and his grandchildren in December 2015 and is a fitting and lasting tribute to a man whose career was devoted to the green and white Hoops he always supported. It's unlikely that any other player will ever break Billy McNeill's appearance record for Celtic, and while everyone, including Billy himself, would love to see another Celtic captain lift the European Cup, he remains 'primus inter pares' – first among equals, Celtic's leader of men, the captain they called Cesar, who led his comrades into battle as they came, saw and conquered.

IN HIS OWN WORDS...

'The biggest highlight was winning the European Cup in 1967 – nothing really compares with that because that was us at the top of the tree. It was a fabulous achievement and particularly when you consider that most of the lads came from within a very, very tight circle of Glasgow.

We had some players in that team who were absolutely incredible. I mean, wee Jinky – I've never really seen a player in this country with the ability that the wee man had. He wasn't that big but he had powerful shoulders, powerful legs and his ability on the ball was absolutely incredible, Bobby Murdoch was fabulous. He dominated games with his passes. He was different class. Bertie was very, very clever, very shrewd. Bobby Lennox would run forever and was sharp as anything. Stevie Chalmers was sharp and neat about things. Tommy Gemmell scored goals from incredible positions. Jim Craig got up and down that park for days at a time. John Clark was as shrewd and clever as anybody and he knew exactly what things were going to happen and what to do. Ronnie Simpson was absolutely brilliant. He felt that when Big Jock came back that he would be on the way out but it never worked that way. Ronnie was an essential cog in the whole machine. Willie Wallace came from Hearts and was absolutely brilliant. We also had reserve players like Charlie Gallagher, John Hughes, Joe McBride, Willie O'Neill and John Fallon. They were good players as well. And that team had one thing which was very important – there was a pride about them. They could play with determination, they could play skilfully, but they didn't suffer fools easily. They wanted to be successful and I think that's the reason so much success came.

At the start of the season that would have seemed a fairytale but there's a thing about Celtic that fairytales often come true and it certainly came true that year and obviously nothing quite compares with the feeling of being European champions. People have asked me what I was thinking when I went to pick up the European Cup and I've tried to think. I've watched it on film, I've watched it on video and I haven't a clue! I think my emotions were just so high that I don't remember anything. The first clear recollection I've got is, I actually have the cup, been presented with it and I was showing it off to the crowd. That's the first clear recollection I've got of anything that happened after the game. The whole thing just seemed to be just a maze of different things.

We were away to America for nearly six weeks and that trip consolidated an atmosphere, an attitude, a friendship, a professional aspect that still exists to this day. That set the whole thing. We then started to believe that we could handle anybody on our day, and lo and behold, a year later we end up with the European Cup.

A British side had never reached the European Cup final, never mind won the trophy as the competition was the domain of the Latin nations. And, all of a sudden, we just marched through everything. The thing about it was the attitude of the team, in that we weren't frightened of anyone. We always had this attitude that if we went and played well, then we could cope with anybody and that worked for us right through the whole season. Obviously everything went to plan, the League Cup was the first one on the mantelpiece, then the Scottish Cup and then the Championship, but if anybody had said to us at the start of the season that we would win the European Cup we would probably have had a wee look at them and wondered about their sanity.

In the preparations for that particular game, everything went perfectly to plan. There was the excitement of all the fans travelling and the Celtic motor cavalcade leaving George Square days in advance of the game. I'm quite convinced to this day that half of those people didn't have any idea where the hell they were going! The Estoril hotel we were in was absolutely magnificent, it was a really classy establishment and Big Jock impressed upon us that we weren't going to be allowed out in the sun for any more than maybe half-an-hour. When we came back from training we would have a wee swim in the pool and then we had to go indoors. Luckily enough there were a few rooms downstairs where we could play cards or read to save us being stuck up in the bedrooms. But Big Jock was very, very strong about not going out in the sun because we weren't there to relax, we were there to play well and he didn't want the sun to take any energy from us.

Everything went perfectly, the training was terrific, the pitch was absolutely magnificent and the fans, of course had started to reach Lisbon before the game and they were already creating a wonderful scene.

We felt we could beat anybody provided we played well and Big Jock's preparation for the European Cup final was terrific. We were down at Seamill for a few days and then we came up the road and headed for Lisbon. And when we got to Lisbon, just next to the hotel we were in, there was a park and it had green and white mushrooms; when I say mushrooms I mean lights, but they were green and white and it was almost something that was signalling to us and saying you can win this game, and the Portuguese people seemed to favour us rather than Inter Milan. But it didn't matter to us who we would've played because we had prepared well for it. We had a hungry, determined team with lots and lots of ability and a very fit team.

I don't like tunnels and it was a long tunnel from dressing rooms to the pitch. You came up steps to take you on to the ground. I'm not the greatest when there's something just above my head and they stopped us, and being captain everybody else is behind. All of a sudden wee Bertie started singing *The Celtic Song* and we all joined in. I turned round and looked and all I could see was these green and white Hoops which I think is a marvellous strip but it's the white legs that go with it that take a wee bit away from it! You could see the white legs with the freckles, and freckles on the face. Some of the boys, believe it or not, had false teeth as well and they were whipped out and I had a look at that Inter Milan team – the handsome faces, the dark legs and the dark arms, good-looking, with immaculate strips that looked like they had been made by a tailor.

I could see the expression on their faces. I think they thought they were playing a pub team but it worked very much in our favour because that was typical of our attitude. I remember when we got to the top of the steps and you just burst out into the sunshine and the atmosphere in the ground was absolutely magnificent. The colours of the two teams were terrific as well because they were easily distinguished – Inter with the blue and black and us with the green and white.

The Estadio Nacional wasn't your typical football ground. It's almost like a Roman amphitheatre, but it was great. It suited us that day anyway. And it was a great venue for the European Cup final.

We were aggrieved because we didn't think it was a penalty-kick and we thought we'd been done. Having seen it a thousand-odd times since then, it was a penalty. In actual fact, I thought Mazzola actually miss-hit the ball because he seemed to put his foot right round it and it found its way into the net. Ronnie was good at penalty-kicks but he never had a chance with that one. I thought it was an injustice at the time but it certainly helped us because it left us with no other option than to take the game to them and obviously that suited us brilliantly. Big Jock had to calm us down at half-time because we all had a wee go at the referee in the tunnel and he had to calm us all down and that filled in the half-time break. Then the second-half came and we really pounded them and took total command of the game.

As it happened it was one of the easiest games that John Clark and I had, and I'm sure Ronnie Simpson as well, because we had very little to do as we had the ball most of the time and basically our job was to get the ball and immediately transfer it to Bertie or Bobby Murdoch, or to wee Jinky, and let them go on. Tommy Gemmell and Jim Craig were up and down the park all the time, and if you think about it, one full-back passed the ball and the other full-back stuck it in the net. That's unusual but it was typical of what had happened. When we got the first goal I knew the second one would follow. I expected that in the last four or five minutes of the game, we would've had our backs to the wall but Inter were gone. Whether it was just the disillusionment, or whether it was just the acceptance that we were the better team I don't know but they were finished.

We were essentially a team and as a team we had won the European Cup so it would've been absolutely brilliant to have the rest of the boys with me. I've watched Champions League finals and the captain gets presented with the trophy and he then goes to his team and they go round the pitch showing off the trophy to their supporters, and it shows how excited they are and how they love getting the opportunity and that is the one thing that I wish that I could've changed to this day – that we could all have been there together and gone round the park. Our supporters had travelled in their thousands and they were absolutely brilliant, but I just wish they could've given us the opportunity to display the trophy as a team and not just a big eejit standing himself!

I remember being up there with Sean Fallon and there was loads of police and they all wanted their photograph with the cup – not with us in – with the cup, and that's what created a real delay in getting away. We had to go right around the stadium because we couldn't go across the park, so we were in a car going right around the stadium to the dressing rooms, and by the time I got back down to the dressing room, the boys had all disappeared, so I was left myself getting a shower and then hurrying up.'

LISBOA
25 DE MAIO DE
1967
CELTIC **2-1** INTER
50° CELTIC FC
ANIVERSARIO

BOBBY MURDOCH

1967
LISBOA
25 DE MAIO DE
CELTIC 2-1 INTER
50° CELTIC FC
ANIVERSARIO

BOBBY MURDOCH

Even for those supporters not lucky enough to have seen the Lisbon Lions play, instead having to rely on sporadic and often grainy footage, along with the embellishments of eye-witnesses, there can be little doubt as to the quality of Bobby Murdoch as a footballer. The testimonies of team-mates, opponents, managers and admirers alike all point to one thing – here was a player of absolute, unquestionable world-class ability. It has long been a mantra amongst the Lions of their friend and team-mate that when Bobby Murdoch played, Celtic played. For that to be said of a man whose team-mates included the likes of Jimmy Johnstone, Bobby Lennox and Bertie Auld amongst others, says much for the high regard that his team-mates always held Bobby Murdoch, one of the youngest members of Celtic's most famous team.

Jock Stein once said, 'As far as I am concerned, Bobby Murdoch was just about the best player I had as manager. I only let him move because he had run out of challenges with Celtic,' while Inter Milan's Argentinian manager, Helenio Herrera, described the Celtic midfielder as 'my complete player.' And Jack Charlton, who took Murdoch to Middlesbrough from Celtic in 1974, stated that it was 'the best signing I ever made.' Fellow Lisbon Lion, Bertie Auld said of his friend and team-mate, 'He could do everything. He could tackle, he could shoot and he could pass. Everything Bobby Murdoch did was stamped with class and authority.' And Jim Craig offered this insight into the player. 'There's something you might not know about Bobby and that is, he was a very emotional character. He would cry if we won. He would cry if we lost. He would cry even if we drew. We just cried when he wasn't in the team.'

A Rutherglen boy, Murdoch was a pupil at Our Lady's High School in Motherwell, just like the man who would become his captain at Celtic, Billy McNeill, and he had a trial for the Fir Park side, although once Celtic showed an interest in him, there was no doubt where he would end up and he signed for Celtic on October 23, 1959, though he was then farmed out to Cambuslang Rangers. His debut came three years later at the start of the 1962/63 season when Celtic played host to Hearts in a League Cup sectional tie on August 11. It was Sean Fallon who broke the news to him two days before the game that he would be making his first appearance for the Celtic first-team, just six days short of his eighteenth birthday. The game also saw a late change in the starting XI as John Divers had turned up without his boots, which he'd left at home. He dashed home to get them and returned to Celtic Park, only to discover that his place had been taken by Charlie Gallagher. Murdoch later admitted it was a salutary lesson that no player would be bigger than the club, and it was something he never forgot.

As debuts go, it was just about perfect. It took Bobby Murdoch all of seven minutes to make an impact, bundling the ball home from inside the six-yard box following a cross from John Hughes. The overwhelming majority of the 41,000 fans who packed into Celtic Park for the match, full of renewed optimism for the start of a new season that would, unfortunately, soon dissipate, celebrated the goal, obviously not aware that they were witnessing the first steps in an extraordinary Celtic career that would see the player go on to make 485 appearances and score 102 goals. In his 1970 autobiography, *All The Way With Celtic*, Murdoch recalled that debut day. 'After the match the Celtic team went for dinner at a Glasgow restaurant where the club chairman, Bob Kelly, leaned across and said to me: 'That was quite a good performance. It was nice to see you score in your first game.' It had been a good day for me.'

Two of Murdoch's fellow Lisbon Lions were in the Celtic team that day, Billy McNeill and Bobby Lennox, while Willie Wallace lined up for Hearts. Having made his debut in the first competitive game of the new campaign, Bobby Murdoch would go on to play thirty-one times for the club that season as they finished fourth in the league and reached the Scottish Cup final. Murdoch scored in the 1-1 draw against Rangers at Hampden, equalising for Celtic on the stroke of half-time, but the replay held eleven days later resulted in a very disappointing 3-0 defeat for the Hoops.

The 1962/63 season also saw Celtic's first foray into European football as they took on Valencia in the Fairs-Cities Cup. Bobby Murdoch didn't play in either leg of the tie, although he was in the Celtic party that travelled to Spain, the first time he had been outside of Britain. However, he would make his European debut the following season – and score his first European goal for the club – when Celtic beat Swiss side, FC Basel, 5-0 in the second leg of their Cup-Winners' Cup first round tie, having won the first leg 5-1. Murdoch hadn't been included in the squad that headed out to Switzerland for the first leg, something which angered and frustrated him at the time, but he would play in every other European game that season as Celtic reached the semi-final of the competition, scoring another goal – a penalty in a 1-0 win over Slovan Bratislava at Celtic Park. The semi-final, of course, saw the Hoops squander a 3-0 first leg lead against MTK Budapest to lose 4-0 in Hungary, but the campaign was still a valuable experience on that stage for the likes of Murdoch, McNeill, Clark, Gemmell, Johnstone and Chalmers.

Murdoch later recalled: 'I'll never forget the return journey from Budapest. It was like a funeral. Nobody spoke. We all sat there on the plane with our own silent thoughts, not looking at each other. It was the longest plane journey I've been on and I've crossed the Atlantic a few times.'

By the time Jock Stein returned to Celtic Park in March 1965, Bobby Murdoch was a first-team regular, and had been joined in the January of that year by the man who would form one of the most dominant midfield partnerships in football at the time, Bertie Auld. It's Stein who is credited with moving Murdoch from inside-right to the right-half position in order to fully utilise his abilities to control and dictate the rhythm of a game. The transformation in Celtic's fortunes was immediate, with the team winning the 1965 Scottish Cup with a 3-2 victory over Stein's former side, Dunfermline Athletic. Celtic's first major piece of silverware in eight years and their first triumph in the competition since the Double-winning season of 1953/54 was done with a team that included seven of the players who would win the European Cup just two years later. Only Ronnie Simpson, Jim Craig, Jimmy Johnstone and Willie Wallace were missing from that side, and of that quartet, only Wallace was still to join the club.

Stein's arrival certainly steadied the ship at Celtic Park and prevented the departure of several players who had been contemplating a life away from the Hoops, and the instant success he delivered only added to the impression amongst many observers that something fundamental had shifted, not just in the running of Celtic Football Club, but in the very fabric of Scottish football. There were words of praise, too, for the then Celtic chairman, Robert Kelly, from Bobby Murdoch in his autobiography. 'This victory was a complete vindication of our chairman who had said, time and time again, that the youth policy laid down by himself would be a success if the supporters were prepared to give the club time. They weren't, as Sir Robert found out when he was shamefully abused from the terracing and the stand when we lost vital games because of our inexperience. The win, however, was no surprise to our new manager, Jock Stein. He had taken over just forty-six days before the match and had been quite confident that we would beat his former club, Dunfermline Athletic. When the Boss had returned to Celtic Park, via Dunfermline and Hibs, he had told us straight away that we were as good as any team in Scottish football.'

The following season, the transformation was truly remarkable. A team which had finished eighth in the league were suddenly challenging for the league title, something that Celtic hadn't won since 1954, and Bobby Murdoch was an integral part of the club's success, playing in thirty-one of the thirty-four league fixtures, and making a further twenty-six appearances across the other three competitions – the League Cup, which Celtic won with a 2-1 victory in the final over Rangers, the Scottish Cup, which was lost after a replay, and a European Cup-Winners' Cup campaign that saw Jock Stein's side reach the semi-final where they lost narrowly to Liverpool. Murdoch also hit double figures in the goals chart that campaign, scoring eleven times.

The success of the team in winning the league title gave them entry into the 1966/67 European Cup campaign, and Bobby Murdoch was an ever-present in the march to Lisbon, playing in all nine ties, including the final against Inter Milan. Like many of his team-mates, there would have been times throughout that season, particularly as the team progressed through the rounds of the European Cup, when he reflected on the progress Celtic had made in such a short space of time; a club seemingly trapped in the doldrums of mediocrity were suddenly scaling extraordinary heights. The League Cup was retained with a narrow 1-0 victory over Rangers at Hampden on a day when the Hoops were not at their best – again, a sign of the quality within Stein's side with their ability to win even when they didn't play well – while the Scottish Cup was won with a 2-0 victory in the final over Aberdeen. Celtic finished top of the league for the second season in a row, three points clear of Rangers, while the Glasgow Cup was also won.

Bobby Murdoch had only missed three league games in the campaign, played in every League Cup tie, while he was also in the starting XI for four of Celtic's six Scottish Cup matches, including the final. And, of course, he didn't miss a European tie. His goals tally for that season was eight, all of them scored domestically, while Celtic scored a total of 196 goals across all competitions, including the Glasgow Cup. How many of them were created by Bobby Murdoch isn't known, but it's safe to assume that it would be a considerable number. The most famous of those came in the Estadio Nacional on May 25, 1967 when, with just five minutes of the European Cup remaining, he fired a left-foot shot towards the Inter Milan goal which was steered into the net by Stevie Chalmers for what proved to be the winning goal. Speaking of that triumph years later, Murdoch said: 'If you look again at the television recordings of that game and, with the benefit of video machinery, freeze any close-up of me and you will see that my right ankle is almost twice the size of the left. I don't think I kicked the ball with my right foot any more than five times over the course of the entire ninety minutes' play, and I was playing at right-half. Even the shot I had at goal, which was deflected by Stevie Chalmers to give us the winner and the trophy, was struck with my left foot.'

Murdoch had picked up the knock early in the game when an Inter Milan player had stamped on his foot, but in the absence of any outfield substitutes, the only advice that the Celtic bench could give to the player was to 'run it off'. That Bobby Murdoch could produce such a commanding performance, in the most important game of his career, and against one of the continent's top club sides, while carrying an injury says much about his quality as a footballer and the strength of character he possessed. The reward was to become a European champion along with the rest of his Celtic team-mates, and it was a thoroughly deserved reward for all of them.

Murdoch's medal haul, when he eventually called time on his Celtic career in September 1973, was impressive; eight league titles – he just missed out on the nine-in-a-row collection – five League Cups, four Scottish Cups and the European Cup medal. As his captain, team-mate, friend and fellow ex-Our Lady's High pupil, Billy McNeill, later explained: 'We had come through the hard times at Celtic so, when we started to win, it was paradise. Leagues, cups, medals – that's what it was all about. It's what Bobby and I used to talk about after training in the late fifties and early sixties. It was only a dream but there was no harm in letting your imagination go for a wander every now and then. The jigsaw came together in Lisbon and no-one played a bigger part in our historic day than Bobby Murdoch.'

Throughout Murdoch's time at Celtic, which spanned from 1958 until '73, the good times far outweighed the bad, but the fact that he had broken through into the first-team nearly three years prior to Jock Stein's arrival at the club gave Murdoch an appreciation of what was being achieved after so many fallow years, and he was an integral part of the success, playing 485 times and scoring 102 goals. There are only eleven men who have played more times for the Celtic first-team than Bobby Murdoch, including three of his team-mates – Jimmy Johnstone (515), Bobby Lennox (586) and Billy McNeill (790).

It seems churlish to even mention any low points during this time, but it also serves as an indication that, despite Celtic's phenomenal success, they came close to making the story even more remarkable; Murdoch lost four Scottish Cup finals, three League Cup finals and the European Cup final in 1970, a game that was as big a disappointment to the Celtic players as Lisbon had been a great joy. Murdoch also played in all three of the World Club Championship games against Racing Club of Argentina, and was fined by the club, along with the rest of his team-mates, when the dust settled on what had turned out to be a South American debacle. The fine still seems a harsh punishment for a group of players who had endured a level of unprovoked and unprotected physical abuse rarely seen on a football pitch. Speaking in 1969, Murdoch said: 'Each of the Celtic players who took part was fined £250 as a disciplinary measure. It seemed hard to me at first, but when I realised the high standard of living Celtic had given me and that we had failed to live up to the standards of discipline insisted upon by the club, I accepted the punishment… The fine, incidentally, went to a charity, which only proves that some good always comes out of what looks so bad.'

Murdoch had been named by the referee as one of the players sent off in the infamous 'Battle of Montevideo', though it was actually John Hughes who'd been dismissed, and Murdoch was later exonerated by the SFA who dealt with the disciplinary fall-out from the games. However, he would get a red card in the 1967/68 European Cup first round, second leg tie against Dynamo Kyiv. Celtic, the tournament holders, had surprisingly lost the first leg in Glasgow 2-1, and were aiming for a positive return in the former Soviet Union. But their cause wasn't helped when Murdoch, who'd already been booked, was dismissed after showing dissent when a decision for a foul went to the home side instead of the Hoops.

'This was a bad moment for me," Murdoch later admitted. 'It wasn't a bad offence – a flash of anger when something goes against you. I knew then that Celtic were going out of the European Cup. I knew that we needed every man to win in Kyiv. We couldn't do it with ten players. I had let the club down badly and I couldn't keep back the tears as I pleaded to stay on. The Boss, however, was waving me off and I went. A green jersey was thrown over my head to cover my feelings as I left a match which I thought we could have won. It took me many a long day to forget that match, even though the Boss reckoned we lost our chance at home.'

Bobby Lennox did give Celtic the lead just after the hour mark and the ten men of Celtic continued to press for a second goal which would put them through. However, in the last minute, Anatoliy Byshovets equalised for the home side and Celtic were out, the first time in the seventeen years of the competition that the holders had been knocked out in the first round of their defence.

The closest that Celtic would come to winning the trophy again, apart from the 1970 final, was in 1972 when they faced Inter Milan in the semi-final of the competition. This time it was the Italians who progressed, winning a penalty shoot-out at Celtic Park after both legs had finished goal-less. Bobby Murdoch scored Celtic's final penalty – in those days both sides had to complete all five penalties – though by the time he trudged up to take his spot-kick he and everyone else inside Celtic Park already knew that it was Inter Milan who'd be heading for the final, given that the only penalty miss in the shoot-out had been Dixie Deans.

The following season, 1972/73, would prove to be Bobby Murdoch's last full season at Celtic, and he played forty games in that campaign as the Hoops made it eight league titles in a row. In May 1973, Jock Stein signed Stevie Murray from Aberdeen, and the acquisition was seen as a replacement for Murdoch, with Murray perhaps having more pace and energy as a box-to-box midfielder. However, in terms of football ability, Murdoch was still peerless, and at the age of twenty-nine would surely still have had much to offer Celtic over the next few seasons. However, he would make only one appearance in the new season – in a 3-1 win over Arbroath at Gayfield in the League Cup group stages. Just a few weeks later he left for Middlesbrough, who were then in the English Second Division. Two days prior to the move, Celtic played Rangers in a league game, as Murdoch later explained. 'I remember going to the game at Ibrox, a fixture I had always detested for the way the tension strangled the creativity out of the players involved, and taking a last look at the team. Jimmy Johnstone, who had been one of my best pals when that side let its hair down away from the game, scored the winning goal and I went to a family party that night as the only one who knew I would be leaving Glasgow. When I walked out of Celtic Park two days later as an ex-Celtic player I couldn't have looked back to see the place, in any case, for the tears in my eyes.'

Bertie Auld, his midfield partner who had left the club in April 1971, said: 'I couldn't see Celtic letting him go to Middlesbrough because he was still a young man and a magnificent player. Bobby would have been the ideal player to play at the back because he read the game so well. He didn't give the ball away easily and he was a force to be reckoned with. I honestly believed he would have become Scotland's Beckenbauer.'

The player himself later explained that he'd become bored with Scottish football and had lost his motivation, though perhaps a change of position and playing style would have reinvigorated him. That's all conjecture, of course, and Murdoch headed for Ayresome Park, becoming a Middlesbrough hero under Jack Charlton and a role model for young midfielder, Graeme Souness, who was at the club at the time. Murdoch's Middlesbrough connections would include a short spell as manager, although his heart always remained at Celtic Park. He had been a popular player during his time at the club, and remained so in later years, always a welcome presence at supporters' functions.

Sadly, on May 15, 2001, Bobby Murdoch died, the first of the Lisbon Lions to pass away. Among the many tributes to him was one from his former assistant manager, Sean Fallon, who said: 'Bobby was a good friend and a great Celt. He was a lovely man, truly humble. As a player, he had everything and he was also a genuine Celtic supporter. He genuinely felt for the supporters when things weren't going well and they appreciated that. Off the park, he always thought about others before himself and was as nice a person as you could hope to meet.'

His fellow Lisbon Lion and friend, Jim Craig, remembered a player who, like many others at the club during the 1960s, flourished under the tutelage of Jock Stein. He said: 'Great players are often recognised by the number of international caps that they accumulate, yet it's well known that Bobby had only twelve Scottish caps. However, I think anyone who ever saw him play would recognise just how good a player he was. He had two great feet, he was powerful, he had great vision and when he played the whole team played, and that's really the biggest tribute that anyone could give him. Bobby was a Celtic fan who had been brought up in the traditions of the club, and came to Celtic almost straight from school. He played here throughout the unsuccessful days of the early 1960s and at a time when, like a lot of young boys, he was played out of position in the inside-right position. When Jock Stein arrived at the club he moved him into midfield into the old right-half position, and that was where Bobby really found his forte.'

His captain, too, was effusive in praising the youngest member of the Lisbon Lions, saying: 'Bobby was a genuinely great guy. He always had a smile on his face, always had time to sit down and have a chat, and was a very unassuming character. He loved the Lions getting together and, if you look at all our meetings, I would bet that he didn't miss a single one. Bobby was undoubtedly a great Celt and someone who immensely proud of his association with the club. And what a player he was! He was the central cog in our team and had the rare ability to pass and shoot superbly with both feet. Anyone who saw him play will remember him as a quite immense talent. I'll prefer to remember him for the special, humble person he was.'

IN HIS OWN WORDS...

'I joined the club in 1959 from school and signed professionally in 1962. From the start it was hard work, but we were all brought up from the same area. We came through the third team, the second team then the first team together, and we were all playing against each other at school level, so the average age when we won the European Cup was a good average age. That night in Lisbon was a dream-come-true. We had won four trophies and we were going for a fifth and a clean sweep, plus being the champions of Europe. It was unbelievable. I cried. I was in tears coming off the park. I remember doing a radio interview for a Portuguese radio and the guy spoke good English but I don't think they understood what I was saying because I was crying most of the time. I think I said something like we came here to show you how to play attacking football or something like that against the Italian defensive-minded people, but that was it. Afterwards, I was so exhausted I actually had my boots on when I went into the shower.

I sometimes think that our European Cup final was one of the easiest games in Europe. Our approach to this final with Inter Milan in Lisbon was such that we were geared to success. We just didn't think we would lose the game. We were much fitter than they were and, though we lost the opening goal to Sandro Mazzola via a penalty kick, we never worried. I reckon Celtic played some of the greatest attacking football ever seen anywhere during the time we were chasing the two victory goals. Every member of the first-team pool that year got an eight-millimetre colour film of the highlights of our European Cup final, which runs for forty-five minutes. I regularly run it through at home, when friends drop in for a spot of supper or a natter, and I never cease to marvel at some of the football the boys turned on. The film is one of my most treasured possessions.

The greatest thing was when we came home and we came to Celtic Park with the trophy we got a great welcome there. By that time it had sunk in what we had achieved was unbelievable. The Celtic fans are unique. They have always known what the club represents and so did the players who played for the club. In our day there were a lot of Celtic supporters all over the place and they always had a Player of the Year award. Big Jock used to say 'You're going there, you're going there and you're going there...'

and if there was one player who maybe had a few awards to collect on the same night other players would go and collect it on his behalf if he had to go to another club. The thing was that we had an affinity with the support and the main thing was we had time for them because we respected them as Celtic fans. They're still great – you couldn't get better fans at any club and that's the reason. We know what the club represents, the fans know what the club represents and it's great to be in their company. We don't want to let them down.

I suppose I enjoyed playing in European Cup ties more than any other match because there is so much glamour and so much international interest in these games, and I must say right away that I enjoyed playing in the ties away from home! I got too keyed up prior to the ties at Celtic Park. Though we always got away to the Ayrshire coast for a few days before a big match to get away from the ticket-hunters and the general buzz, to prepare and relax, I found that tension tends to build up quickly prior to a home game. As a midfield player in the Celtic system of play I know that I simply cannot afford an off-night in a European tie at Celtic Park. My role was so vital in a home tie, where we must go out and chase goals, that I must play well.

I found that, in European ties, I had to move the ball quicker. Opponents were in on you smarter. You just didn't get the same time to think out a move as you did in a normal league game, and I was very conscious of this when I can out on to the field before a 75,000 crowd at Celtic Park, where the fans give you such a fantastic roar of encouragement. They want you to play well and they want to see the goals go in. The air of expectation is fantastic, and I think the games played under floodlights injected a sense of unreality to the whole atmosphere. You cannot see the crowd but you know they are there and they are with you to the last man.

The European Cup tie I shall never forget – apart from the Lisbon final of 1967 – was the second leg of the quarter-final against Vojvodina of Yugoslavia at Celtic Park in March of our European Cup-winning season. I have to say that Vojvodina were the hardest team we have ever met in the European Cup.

When we gathered for the first meeting the next season after Lisbon, Jock said, 'For some of you football will never be the same again.' He wanted to provoke us into proving him wrong, but it turned out to be right.'

BERTIE AULD

BERTIE AULD

Bertie Auld returned to Celtic on January 14, 1965, having spent the previous three-and-a-half years with Birmingham City after leaving the Hoops in May 1961. Just over two weeks later, on the last day of January, it was announced that Jock Stein would be taking over as Celtic manager, with Sean Fallon staying on at the club as his assistant, though Stein wouldn't take charge until the middle of March. There would have been excitement and anticipation amongst supporters at the news of a change in the management structure, although tempered by the realities of the previous twenty years and the decision to wait and see how things developed at the club once Stein took over. After all, they had watched a Celtic legend in the shape of Jimmy McGrory prove to be a largely ineffective manager under the pressure and influence of the board in the shape of chairman, Robert Kelly, who would still be in his boardroom post after the new manager was in his job.

There would also have been a positive reaction to Bertie Auld's return – he had been a popular player before his departure to England – but that would have been mixed with surprise. The circumstances surrounding Auld's transfer to Birmingham centred round a perceived problem with discipline and Robert Kelly's disapproval of such behaviour, and that hadn't necessarily improved during his time in England. However, the player had a champion in the club in the shape of Sean Fallon, who'd briefly played alongside Auld in the late 1950s when the latter had first joined the club as a teenager.

In the biography, *Sean Fallon: Celtic's Iron Man*, the Irishman recalled the events which led to Bertie Auld's return to Celtic Park. The legendary Celt, who became Jock Stein's assistant manager, explained: 'I had to plead with the chairman before he finally agreed. At first, he was adamant about it. 'Once a player goes, Sean, they're gone,' he told me. But I kept at him because I knew Bertie would make all the difference. He was an older head; tough and cunning. And he could play – Bertie could take three players out of the game with a single pass. I knew he'd put his foot on the ball and slow things down for us because our football at that time was too fast and furious. Bertie knew how good he was – he fancied himself rotten – and we needed that kind of self-belief at the time. Other players you had to work hard to instil confidence in, to help them realise how good they could be, whereas Bertie just came in with that swagger of his, believing he was the best. And he was right to have belief in himself because he was a great player with an outstanding football brain. I was delighted to get him into the club, and he didn't let me down…

'Jock and I had stayed in touch, and we still spoke often when he was at Dunfermline and Hibs. When I mentioned to him about trying to bring back Bertie, he wasn't a fan of the idea. I remember him saying to me: 'You're signing trouble there'. The whole thing had come about because of a conversation I had with Tommy Reilly, who was chairman of the Celtic Businessmen's Club at that time. He told me that Bertie wasn't too happy in England, and that was when I started making the case for bringing him back. The chairman felt the same as Jock – that Bertie could be trouble – but eventually he gave in. Bertie won everyone over in the end, of course, and Jock was very good that way – he kept an open mind about players. It was the same with Ronnie. Even though the two of them had fallen out at Hibs, Jock was fair about it and eventually gave him his chance. As for Bertie, he was never out of the team – he became one of Jock's favourites, and rightly so. It was clear from the moment he arrived back that he had matured into a magnificent player. He was such an important signing for that team.'

The player himself was delighted to be 'home', and he returned to Celtic Park older, wiser – still as confident as ever – but with four years' experience of English football that had helped him develop as a player. The pieces were slowly falling into place, although it's unlikely they would have all fitted together if it hadn't been for the appointment of Jock Stein, which represented a much bigger change of heart from Robert Kelly, who had to relinquish the control and influence over team matters that he had been so used to wielding since becoming chairman in March 1947. Bertie Auld, who had known Stein when he'd coached the Celtic reserve side back in the late 1950s, was convinced that it was the perfect appointment for the role.

He said: 'We needed someone who was strong in character, who was strong-willed and had tremendous knowledge of the game and Jock had all three. I was very fortunate in that I had played under him as a youngster before I went to Birmingham and he went to Dunfermline, so we knew his quality. We knew what type of man he was, how he loved the club and that the supporters needed success. Knowing that Jock was back, I knew that the club was heading in the right direction. Although the love for the club was there, he brought what the supporters had from the terraces, and that was the will to win. He also gave us the licence to win 50-50 balls, which before would have seen us dropped for the following game.'

Jock Stein's subsequent decision to pair Bertie Auld and Bobby Murdoch in the heart of the Celtic midfield as the fulcrum of the side was inspired, and during those six years when the two men played together in the green and white Hoops, it would be difficult to argue against the notion that they were the best midfield partnership operating in football at that time. Auld was the older of the two by six years, and had experience beyond Celtic and Scottish football, and that would prove beneficial to his younger team-mate. Auld, for his part, was, like the rest of his team-mates, a fully paid-up member of the Bobby Murdoch Appreciation Society. Asked about the best player he'd played alongside, he told the *Celtic View*: 'I would have to say Bobby Murdoch. He had a presence, both on and off the park. Everything about him was impressive, his stature, his football ability, which was second to none and he was a leader as well. A great player.'

Bertie Auld was himself a player of considerable ability. Signed from Maryhill Harp in April 1955 as a seventeen-year-old, he was loaned out to Dumbarton, which meant that, technically, when he returned to Celtic in June 1957, he re-signed for the club. His competitive debut for Celtic came on August 24, 1957 in a League Cup sectional tie against Airdrie at Broomfield, a tie that Celtic – holders of the trophy – would win on their way to a second consecutive final. Having made it into the team, Auld continued to be selected for the remainder of the campaign up to the final, when he lost his place in the starting XI to Neilly Mochan. Not only did he miss out on his first chance of a cup final, but it also happened to be the day when Celtic hammered Rangers 7-1 in a game that was only eclipsed in terms of its significance by the European Cup final ten years later.

As Auld later recalled: 'There were times in the past when I questioned the chairman, Robert Kelly's way of thinking, because he picked the team at the time. I played in a reserve game in Dumfries on the day of the final and that proved to me that I wasn't ready for it. He played Neilly Mochan instead in the cup final. Neilly was at the top of his game then and was a great friend and team-mate and he deserved to play that day. Disappointed? Naturally I was disappointed, but when I heard the result that day it took all the disappointment away.'

After six years at the club, Auld left for Birmingham City in May 1961, and while his former team-mates did gain some European experience in the early 1960s, the club continued to languish in domestic mediocrity, Auld gained a League Cup medal with his new club in 1963 when they beat Midlands rivals Aston Villa 3-1 on aggregate in the final, while he also played in the 1960/61 Inter-Cities Fairs Cup final which was played later in the year after Auld had joined the club, but which Birmingham lost 4-2 on aggregate.

Just two days after his return to Celtic in January 1965, he made his second debut for the club, playing in a 2-1 home defeat to Hearts in front of a crowd of 21,000. Two weeks later, and the day before the announcement of Jock Stein's imminent arrival at Celtic Park, the Hoops beat Aberdeen 8-0 at home. Auld scored a penalty in that game, although the star of the show was John Hughes, who scored five of the goals wearing a pair of sannies on a hard and frosty pitch. For Auld it would be one of seventy-eight goals he would score for the club in 275 appearances, and of that tally of goals, arguably the two most important strikes came on April 24, 1965, although he did also score five goals in Jock Stein's first match in charge of the club – a 6-0 win over Airdrie at Broomfield.

It was the Scottish Cup final and Celtic, now managed by Jock Stein, faced his former club, Dunfermline Athletic. Twice in that match the Fife side led, only to be pegged back both times by goals from Bertie Auld. The first equaliser came just after the half-hour mark when Auld was the first to react and head home from almost on the goal-line after a Charlie Gallagher shot was pushed on to the bar by the Dunfermline goalkeeper, Jim Herriot. The second came on fifty-two minutes when Auld latched on to a cutback from Bobby Lennox inside the box. He controlled it with his left foot and then, from about twelve yards out, smashed it home with his right, following the ball into the net and taking another, jubilant kick at it. Billy McNeill's goal with nine minutes of the match remaining gave Celtic a 3-2 victory and delivered the club's first trophy since that League Cup final of 1957 and Stein's first piece of silverware as Celtic manager.

Bertie Auld has always been aware of the significance of that game. He told the *Celtic View*: 'The cup final was the big one for us. We hadn't won many trophies in the lead-up to that final and had endured a barren period. In 1965 I had come back in January from Birmingham and there were a lot of young boys in the team like Lennox, Murdoch, Gemmell, Jinky and John Hughes, who was getting tremendous reviews when I was down south for coming in with a passion and an ability to score goals. John Clark was also there and so was Big Billy, so we had a nucleus of a team and that win got us off the mark. I'll never forget Jock's team talk before the game. He said that we had worked hard to get there and now was the time to go out and enjoy it. It was the first thing that a lot of the boys in that dressing room had won. Not a lot of the team had had the experience of winning anything. So you could picture it, it felt like something that was almost unbelievable. Each and every player was like a wean in a sweet shop.'

If every player was, in Auld's words, 'like a wean in a sweet shop', then over the next few years they devoured everything that was put in front of them. The following season the league title was captured for the first time in twelve years, while the League Cup was also won, though Auld missed that final. He played seventeen league games in the championship-winning campaign, while he played in both legs of the European Cup-Winners' Cup semi-final against Liverpool, which Celtic lost 2-1 on aggregate. The following season saw him play more games as every trophy the club competed in was duly won. That culminated on May 25, 1967 when Celtic defeated Inter Milan 2-1 in Lisbon's Estadio Nacional.

The Celtic folklore of that day starts in the tunnel when both sides were lining up before emerging into the Portuguese sunshine. The design of the Estadio Nacional was such that the players appeared out of the ground, the tunnel at one end of the ground behind a goal, and nerves would have been jangling, certainly amongst the Celtic players who were stepping out into the unknown; Inter Milan, having won the trophy in 1964 and '65, were accustomed to this kind of pressure, and also had the assurance of being pre-match favourites. While, as professionals, they wouldn't have taken Celtic lightly, Helenio Herrera's team went into the match believing that a third European Cup was theirs for the taking. Jock Stein's side had different ideas, of course, and Bertie Auld epitomised the confidence which was an integral part of a team that had already swept all before them domestically.

Billy McNeill recalled those last few pre-match moments in the Estadio Nacional: 'The atmosphere in the tunnel before the game was absolutely brilliant. I turned around because I was at the head of the team and I could see Inter standing there against the opposite wall all tall, tanned and bronzed like Roman gods and then I looked at our shower – all white with red blotches on the skin, Ronnie without his teeth … you can imagine what I thought. But as soon as we were allowed up out of the tunnel and started walking across the grass, that was the key for our big day, it really was. But before that, when Bertie started singing *The Celtic Song* in the tunnel, you want to have seen the faces of the Italian boys. They were thinking 'What in the hell are we playing against today?' But that moment walking on to the pitch, there was a determination among the boys that this was going to be our day. And obviously it turned out to be that way. Well, it didn't turn out that way – we made it that way.'

Bertie Auld's performance that day – over and above his singing ability – was in keeping with the way he'd played that season and, indeed, since Jock Stein had arrived at the club, and was a vindication, if any was needed, of Sean Fallon's wisdom in advocating a return to Paradise for the player who was both a combative and stylish presence in the heart of the Celtic midfield. If the latter attribute was evident in that dominant 1966/67 season, when he played forty-nine games, scoring twelve goals, the former came to the fore later in 1967 when the European champions took part in the ill-fated World Club Championship against Racing Club of Argentina.

The first leg at Hampden had seen Celtic win 1-0 thanks to a Billy McNeill goal, with the Argentinian side offering hints of the type of illegal tactics they would deploy to a greater degree in the two subsequent games in South America. The first of those matches took place in Buenos Aires, and Celtic suffered a pre-match blow when Ronnie Simpson was hit by a missile thrown from the crowd behind his goal, forcing him to be replaced by John Fallon. Celtic took a first-half lead through a Tommy Gemmell penalty, but two goals from Racing Club either side of half-time gave them a 2-1 victory. There were debates within the Celtic camp after that match as to whether they should head home to Scotland or travel on to Uruguay for a play-off game in the capital, Montevideo.

The decision was taken to stay and play. Hindsight, always the greatest of gifts, would suggest that a return home would have been more advisable. The game in Montevideo was calamitous, a farce of a football contest officiated by a Paraguayan referee whose grasp of the rules of the game and control of proceedings was flimsy at best. A total of six players were red-carded, two for Racing Club and four for Celtic. Bobby Lennox, Jimmy Johnstone, John Hughes and Bertie Auld were all dismissed by the referee, although Auld, given his marching orders late in the game following another melee on the pitch, refused to go and played out the remaining minutes; Lennox, meanwhile, was in the dressing-room nursing a genuine grievance, having been sent off despite committing no offence; the referee had apparently decided earlier to send off Racing's No.6, Alfio Bastile and Celtic's No.8, Bobby Lennox, for the next serious offence committed by either side, irrespective of whether the players themselves had anything to do with it. Lennox was eventually ushered off the field by a police officer, despite Jock Stein's protestations.

Auld, who had missed the second leg in Argentina, was never one to shirk a fight, and he and his team-mates battled bravely against the brutal tactics of their Argentinian opponents and the incompetence of the referee, though they lost the match and the World Club Championship when Juan Carlos Cárdenas scored the only goal of the game ten minutes into the second-half. It was a disappointing end to what had been a difficult trip to South America, and while it seemed as though the football was incidental, the experience was one that the Celtic players never forgot, as Auld later explained.

'You can get tough and then you can get brutality and Racing Club. I don't think any player in our team has ever experienced anything like that, and I wouldn't like any other club or individual to experience that. We could handle ourselves at any level of football but the referee wasn't strong enough. The officials were very poor and weak. We won't even bring Racing Club into the equation because as far as I'm concerned that wasn't a football match at all. If we had been allowed to play, we would have beaten them. Jock and Sir Robert Kelly understood what we were up against, and we knew we shouldn't get down to their level, but you are only human and you cannot continue to turn the other cheek when you are getting spat upon and hit from the back.'

Despite what they had faced in South America, the Celtic players were still punished by the club for their own lack of discipline, a decision that appears harsh when the overall experience is considered. The players had been due a £250 bonus each for having won the League Cup prior to heading out to Argentina, and that money was withheld and, instead, donated to charity.

The following season, Celtic won the domestic treble, although they fell at the quarter-final stage of the European Cup to AC Milan, with Bertie Auld not always a regular starter in the team, although he was there when it mattered – scoring a goal in the 6-2 League Cup final victory over Hibernian and being an integral part of an imperious Celtic side that beat Rangers 4-0 in the Scottish Cup final. The following season, he scored the only goal of the game as the Hoops beat St Johnstone to retain the League Cup, but it was in Europe that Jock Stein's side once again impressed, reaching the final where they faced Feyenoord in Milan's San Siro stadium. Along the way, they vanquished the English champions, Leeds United, winning 1-0 at Elland Road and 2-1 at Hampden in front of a European record attendance of 136,505. The disappointment at not following up that magnificent semi-final triumph with a second European Cup success was a heavy one for the Celtic players to contend with, and it may have been that extra-time defeat in Milan which precipitated the break-up of Stein's great Celtic side, although with talented young players such as Kenny Dalglish, George Connelly, Davie Hay and Danny McGrain waiting in the wings, there was also a need to free up some first-team spaces to allow them to break through.

Bertie Auld had been linked with a move to Clyde, something he wouldn't countenance, although his last game for Celtic was against Clyde, on May 1, 1971. It was also the last time the Lisbon Lions would appear together on the pitch as a team, although Ronnie Simpson only took part in the warm-up before being replaced by Evan William for the game. The ten outfield players, the men who had conquered Europe and changed Celtic forever, put on a typically-impressive performance for the 35,000 fans who had flocked to Celtic Park for the occasion. Bobby Lennox scored a hat-trick, Willie Wallace netted two and Stevie Chalmers also scored as the Hoops, already champions for a sixth consecutive season, ran out 6-1 winners. Five days later, Bertie Auld signed for Hibernian. A year later he was back at Hampden, coming on as a substitute in the Scottish Cup final against Celtic, which the Hoops won 6-1.

Management beckoned for Bertie Auld once he did hang up his boots, most notably with Hibernian and Partick Thistle, and while his name was occasionally linked with the Celtic job – there had been talk of him taking over in the late 1970s from Jock Stein although, in the event, it was Billy McNeill who got the job. Ever popular during his playing career with Celtic, Bertie Auld has remained so in the intervening years, synonymous with Lisbon and that tunnel rendition of *The Celtic Song* but remembered and appreciated for so much more that he did on the pitch for the green and white Hoops.

IN HIS OWN WORDS...

'It makes me proud to be a Lisbon Lion and what a special bunch of players that was. Just being in the tunnel with that side was special. You had Jimmy Johnstone, who prepared in his own way, you had Bobby Lennox, who was a machine, while Bobby Murdoch would grow in width and height as he stood next to the opposition in the tunnel. Big Billy was a brilliant captain and the pride you saw in that team was hard to replicate. Sure, we had our off days, but when that happened, the Celtic support was the twelfth man.

In the dressing room in Lisbon before the game, Jock said, 'You've achieved something that no other British team has done – you got to the final. Now remember the Celtic support has come to see you,' and his last words to us were, 'entertain – you have the ability'. I had signed for Celtic when I was sixteen and that Hoops jersey became so tight when he was saying these things. The chest swelled.

In our time Inter were the kings of Europe. They were a very well-organised and well-drilled team and they played a system that all Italian teams did but they had two or three players that could hurt you, given the chance. We went out to entertain, score goals and play attacking football. We played with individuals that were the best in Europe in every position. They were tremendous individuals and they could have played at any level at any time. That's something that Celtic always had – entertainers – and the boss was the main man behind that.

It wasn't until Celtic took us all back to the Estadio National in 2007 for the game against Benfica that I really started to remember the build-up to the European Cup final. Standing in the tunnel, the memories began to flood back. I could remember sitting in this big, dark dressing room, with the noise and excitement all around me. The ones who looked the least excited were the ones who were going to play, they all had this calmness about them. Then we walked out into the tunnel, thirty yards up to the steps leading out to the pitch and they kept us there until everything was ready. I can remember wee Jimmy looking them up and down and talking about the size they were. Now when we were at home, on the bus going to games, we used to sing Celtic songs and that's what came to me that day. It was second nature and I we just started to sing *The Celtic Song*. We started in a quiet, low, deep voice and then, by the final verse, Pavarotti would have been proud of us!

The marvellous thing about the Celtic players' bus back in the late 1950s and the '60s there was always someone who knew the Celtic songs and the Irish songs. So when it came to '67 it just came natural. You were out to play football and out to entertain the people who came to watch you. And to get into the same frame of mind as they were, *The Celtic Song* seemed appropriate. And the thing about it was that everybody was in song, just standing and waiting to get on to the park. It's like everything else. The adrenalin was going because of the occasion. To sing the song was because the occasion was that big. It was part and parcel of you getting prepared to go on to the green stuff, the turf. It was green just like everywhere else in the stadium.

The great thing about the tunnel was the acoustics. When we started to sing, everybody sung the song and you looked over, and I won't kid you, the Inter players went the same colour as their teeth. I was going to say the same colour as our teeth but some had them in their bunnets!

I couldn't believe the length of that Lisbon tunnel and how cold it was, and yet the sun was scorching outside. I was at the back in the tunnel and wee Jimmy said to me, 'Have a look at them. They're like gods, all tanned, and look at their teeth.' And I said to him, 'I know, son, but can they play?' and that was that. Then we started singing and you could see the colour draining from the Inter players' faces, going up those stairs. I'll never forget that and, as a team, we sang the chorus going up the steps to the pitch. And then all of a sudden, with the encouragement from the Portuguese supporters and the Celtic supporters, it was as if we were playing at Celtic Park.

Looking back I would say we would have liked to have been presented, each and every one of us, with the European Cup in Lisbon but when we came here we went round Celtic Park on a coal lorry and there was 80,000 Celtic supporters there, and I wouldn't change that for the world.

The Vojvodina game was a bit special, particularly here when Charlie took the corner-kick and Big Billy headed it in. I thought that was a magnificent game. There was only one time where the boss got it wrong and it was against Dukla Prague. They were a good physical team and I've never seen a display of goalkeeping like Ronnie's that night. Jock always wanted to play our own style and it didn't matter whether that was home or away. He always knew how important results were but it was more important than that. He knew Celtic's reputation was at stake and he wanted us to go out and play our own style. That defensive style we played was foreign to us and he said it'd never happen again in his lifetime. For anyone to be as big as that, to apologise after getting to the final of the European Cup, was incredible. He came in and apologised to us for playing with one up front and said he'd never do it again. It was all about belief in what we could do and he apologised for doing that on that night. Amazingly, four days after that Dukla Prague game we came back to Hampden to play the Scottish Cup final against a very good Aberdeen side, and we won that 2-0.

Bobby Murdoch and I had a great balance with each other and were fortune enough to have Jock there. He worked with us in training and brought that into the team-play. But Murdy had tremendous composure, tremendous vision and there was a balance between the two of us. I ran with the ball, while he passed the ball and we played on each other's strengths and most importantly, Murdoch was always a strong player. He could tackle, he was two-footed, he could back people up and I think you need this. Like I said, we balanced each other and were encouraged to support the forwards and get into scoring positions, because that's the name of the game in football, to get goals. That's what excites supporters, people hitting the back of the net.

I honestly believe that the Lions could have played longer as a team. I remember coming down in the bus from the stadium in Lisbon and I was sitting behind Jock and Bill Shankly, and Jock said to me, 'That team will never be beaten.' I looked at him and said, 'Boss, you can't say that because everybody has an off-day, sometimes the luck doesn't go with you.' But I didn't realise what he meant. He meant that that team wouldn't be beaten because he wouldn't play it. To me, that was a shame because there was some of us getting to the thirty-mark but had tremendous experience and skill that we could have carried it that bit longer.'

LISBOA
25 DE MAIO DE
1967
CELTIC 2-1 INTER
50° ANIVERSARIO
CELTIC FC

BOBBY LENNOX

LISBOA
25 DE MAIO DE
1967
CELTIC 2-1 INTER
50º CELTIC FC
ANIVERSARIO

BOBBY LENNOX

'If I'd had Bobby Lennox in my team, I could have played forever. He was one of the best strikers I have ever seen.'

The words of Bobby Charlton, one of England's greatest ever players and a man fortunate enough to have played with some of the best players to have played the game in the 1950s and '60s, including the likes of Duncan Edwards, Denis Law, George Best, Jimmy Greaves and Geoff Hurst, offer the most succinct, but perhaps also the most accurate assessment of Bobby Lennox. That the Lisbon Lion is a Celtic legend is in no doubt. His presence in that great team which lifted the European Cup in 1967 assures him of that status. However, there is sometimes a sense, in reflecting on his career, that Bobby Lennox's contribution has been, if not under-appreciated over the years, then certainly overshadowed or eclipsed by some of his team-mates and friends.

Yet, what he did for Celtic and what he achieved in his career is nothing short of extraordinary. He played 586 times for the club. Only six men have made more appearances in the history of Celtic. He scored 277 goals during his nineteen years at Celtic Park which began in 1961 and ended in 1980. Only Jimmy McGrory scored more goals, and his tally of 446 is unlikely to ever be surpassed – and Bobby Lennox wasn't even an out-and-out striker; add in the number of goals ruled out for offside, and his tally would have been even higher. In terms of honours won, he is Celtic's most decorated player, with eleven league titles, eight Scottish Cups, five League Cups and, of course, the European Cup.

So, given the evidence, why does there still persist a sense that this needs to be proclaimed to the world and celebrated as if it's a newly-discovered fact. Perhaps it is Lennox's humble and unassuming character which has meant his exploits haven't been shouted from the rooftops. It could also be that, regardless of any self-promotion, the likes of Jimmy Johnstone and Billy McNeill would always garner more attention, while his close friend and former golf partner, Stevie Chalmers, did score the most important goal in the club's history when he steered the ball into the back of the Inter Milan net at the Estadio Nacional on May 25, 1967.

But Bobby Lennox is a bona fide Celtic legend, under any definition of the word, and those who watched him play or, like Bobby Charlton, faced him on the football field, are absolutely convinced of this football truth. The late, great Alfredo Di Stefano, another of football's aristocracy, said of the Celtic player, '... the Scotsman who gave me the most trouble was Bobby Lennox of Celtic. My testimonial at the Bernabeu was against Celtic as, of course, they were the champions of Europe in 1967 and, although I remember the Bernabeu rising to Jimmy Johnstone, I admired Lennox greatly.'

An indelible part of the fairytale story that is Celtic's 1967 European Cup triumph in Lisbon is the fact that all eleven players were born within a thirty-mile radius of Celtic Park. No European Cup-winning team before then could boast of that connection to their own stadium, nor can any side which has won it in subsequent years. Jock Stein's Celtic team were firmly rooted in their community from which the club drew much of its support, and the fact that the connection to Paradise extended as far as thirty miles away is down to Bobby Lennox. He was the 'outsider', hailing from Saltcoats in Ayrshire where he'd first honed his football talents and caught the eye of scouts, always on the lookout for players for junior and senior teams.

The teenage Bobby Lennox signed for Ardeer Recreation, a local junior side, and during that time he had gone down to England for trials with Blackpool and Chelsea. Neither opportunity appealed to him, and he continued playing for Ardeer while working in the ICI's box-making factory. Teams such as Falkirk, Morton and St Mirren showed an interest in the player, while Motherwell went so far as to offer to sign him on provisional forms. He rejected that, since it would have tied him to the club until they offered him a professional contract, and it proved to be an astute decision since, in September 1961, Celtic made an approach. This time there was no hesitation as Lennox put pen to paper on a provisional contract with the team he supported. Lennox later recalled his early Celtic connections in an interview with the *Celtic View*.

'I had a great upbringing. We weren't the richest family in the world, but I didn't want for much, although all I really wanted was a ball at my feet anyway. Ardeer Recreation was the junior team I played for and one of the Celtic scouts called Joe Connor had come to see me play, but there was a gentleman called John Murray from Saltcoats who watched the local players and he was the one that got in touch with Celtic to tell them about me. I was the only guy from out of town and the only one from Ayrshire at the club. In those days that seemed a million miles away and I had to get the bus from Kilwinning to Celtic Park, so it was a wee bit of a journey getting up to Glasgow. A lot of the guys knew each other. Wee Jimmy would know big Tommy Gemmell and he would know Bobby Murdoch and so on. So I was the kind of a shy guy and took a back seat for ages.'

The shy youngster from Saltcoats actually made his Celtic debut on March 3, 1962, a few months before he became a full-time professional at the club, though, as he explained in his autobiography, *Thirty Miles From Paradise*, it was indicative of how the club was run.

'It may seem surprising that I was selected so unexpectedly for the first-team but that was the way things were at Celtic at the time. Team selections could be a bit haphazard and there were no tactics to speak of – players were simply picked to play in certain position … As a part-timer I had had no reason to meet the first-team players previously, but if I was good enough to be in contention for the first-team, it was expected that I would be able to slot into the starting line-up immediately.'

Bobby Lennox duly did that, playing his part in a 2-1 victory for the Hoops over eventual champions, Dundee, though it was the only game he'd play that season for the first-team. The following season he made nine appearances in what proved to be another fallow campaign for Celtic. In 1963/64, he made the first of sixty-seven European appearances for the club when he played in the first round first leg Cup-Winners' Cup tie against FC Basel in Switzerland. Celtic won the match 5-1 and Lennox scored his first European goal for the club, having got off the mark with his first Celtic goal three days previously in a 4-4 draw at home to Third Lanark. It wouldn't be until the following season that he became an established first-team player and a regular in the starting XI which, given the tumultuous changes about to happen at Celtic, was good timing for the player, as he explained to the *Celtic View*.

'I had just got into the team, three or four weeks before Jock came and scored a few goals, so you wonder what's going to happen. But Jock kept me in the team and was wonderful for the side. Bertie Auld arrived at the same time as well and he moved Bobby Murdoch into a new position and we just seemed to click, although the first few months we were winning and losing. We then won the Scottish Cup, but I wouldn't say we were particularly consistent at that stage, and it was only the next season when Jock got his teeth into the job when that changed and we won the championship. We were all such a young team so achieving that was a great experience for us.

'When the gaffer arrived, I stayed through the middle for a while but when big 'Yogi' (John Hughes) got injured, he asked me to go and play outside left and I think that was the first time I had played there. Jock just made us a team. Before he came, it was just 'there is the team, now go out and play'. But he came and tinkered with things and moved players about. We got fitter and training was completely different. Now we were doing things with the ball in training so then it was not alien to us on a Saturday. From that we became more and more consistent.'

Lennox played in Jock Stein's first game in charge at Celtic – a 6-0 victory over Airdrie at Broomfield on March 10, 1965 when Bertie Auld scored five of the goals, and he would remain an ever-present for the rest of that season, scoring his first goals under the new manager ten days after that Airdrie game, in a 3-3 draw away to Dundee, following that up with another double two days later when the Hoops lost 4-2 at home to Hibernian. Celtic finished eighth in the league that season, when Kilmarnock just pipped Hearts to the title, but they had managed to book their place in the Scottish Cup final following a replay victory over Motherwell in the semi-final, when Bobby Lennox scored in both games. That set up a meeting with Stein's former club, Dunfermline Athletic in the final at Hampden, and it would prove to be a pivotal game for Celtic and what was subsequently to follow in the course of the next decade. Celtic won the game 3-2, twice coming from behind through Bertie Auld before Billy McNeill headed home a late winner. It gave the club their first piece of silverware since the 7-1 League Cup victory over Rangers back in 1957, and it was a timely boost for the players.

'All the medals I won were great,' Lennox later admitted, 'although I still say that the first one in 1965 was the best and most important. We had never won anything before, it was a big day for the Celtic supporters and for the players and it got things rolling for us. The team went from strength to strength after that game, but had we lost that day, the team might have been broken up.'

The following season, buoyed by their Scottish Cup victory, Celtic were a side transformed. Despite losing their opening League Cup sectional match 2-1 to Dundee United at Tannadice, the Hoops still managed to qualify as group winners and marched all the way to the final where they faced Rangers at Hampden on October 23. Celtic scored all three goals that day in a 2-1 victory, with John Hughes providing the two goals which won the cup, both of them coming from the penalty spot in the first-half, while Ian Young scored a late own goal to make it a nervy end to the game for Stein's side. However, they held firm and won the first piece of silverware on offer that season.

The league campaign had also started at Tannadice, but this time it was Celtic who won the game 4-0, with John Divers having the honour of scoring Celtic's first goal in what would ultimately prove to be nine league titles in a row. Bobby Lennox was now an integral part of the team, with his pace and precise finishing proving difficult for defences to handle. He scored twenty-five goals in all competitions that season, including four in the European Cup-Winners' Cup. He hit a hat-trick in Celtic's opening tie – a 6-0 victory away to Dutch side Go Ahead Deventer – and the tournament saw the Hoops progress all the way to the semi-final where they faced Liverpool. Lennox scored the only goal of the first leg at Celtic Park, six minutes after half-time, and while Celtic conceded two goals in the second leg at Anfield, it was a disallowed Lennox goal in the last minute which has remained a talking point of that tie, with the offside flag denying Celtic what would have been a decisive away goal. It wasn't the first or the last time the player would be thwarted in this way, as he later recalled.

'There are certain goals I can see clearly and know that when Bobby Murdoch or Bertie made the pass, I was never offside. Sometimes I could even see the linesman looking up and by that time I was already by someone. Put it this way, I know I should have a few extra goals to my credit! There was one game in particular when we beat

Dundee United 1-0 at Tannadice and I scored four, with three getting chopped off. On reflection, one of them was probably offside, but I should have at least had a hat-trick. I just had to keep going in there though, making the runs and not letting my head go down. I would get annoyed from time to time, but there was nothing I could do about it. I was quite crabbit on the park like anyone else, but there was no point going on about things.'

The last goal of the 1965/66 season came in the last minute of the last game, away to Motherwell, and it was Bobby Lennox who bundled the ball over the line from a Jim Craig cross to give Celtic a 1-0 victory and, more importantly, the points which secured their first league title in twelve years. It was a remarkable turnaround, going from eighth in the table the previous season to becoming champions, and it also provided the club with entry to the European Cup for the first time.

Prior to that campaign and, indeed, the whole momentous 1966/67 campaign, there were a number of important moments that laid the foundations for the success to come. The first of those was the six-week close season tour of Bermuda and North America. Celtic remained unbeaten after eleven games, winning eight and drawing three, with Bobby Lennox scoring nineteen goals in the course of the trip.

'That tour undoubtedly knitted the squad together,' Lennox said. 'It was a chance for Jock to experiment with different formations on the field, and off it we lived in each other's pockets and everyone became pals. It was exhausting. Our schedule was non-stop travelling, training, playing and then doing it all over again, and again. It would never happen today. A fifteen-day tour is a rarity for modern players, never mind the five-and-a-half weeks we were away.'

Then came a home game against Manchester United on August 3, just ten days before the start of the League Cup campaign. The Hoops won that match convincingly 4-1, with Lennox scoring the opening goal after just seven minutes. And for Bobby Lennox, later that month came a game which he has long treasured as one of his favourites – a 4-0 Glasgow Cup victory over Rangers at Ibrox on August 23, when he netted a hat-trick in front of a crowd of 80,000. He recalled that game to the Celtic View.

'We wanted to prove a point, because for a few years before that we had found it difficult to beat Rangers. But Jock arrived and we had won the Scottish Cup and the league and wanted to prove a point. I had never actually scored against Rangers before that game and it was Tommy Gemmell who played a long ball up the inside right position and I've gone after it. I then turned inside Greigy (John Greig) and hit it as sweetly as I possibly could hit it with my left and it went in off the underside of the bar to make it 2-0. It was as good a goal as I ever scored and it was up at the Celtic End and the placed went into uproar. The next goal came from a throw in, played to Charlie Gallagher. Now Charlie played this long ball over the top and I knew where it was going, so I had a wee start on Greigy and when I got to it, I knocked it by him and went on and scored. The next one came late on in the game, when wee Bertie played a pass to me and made a great run outside me. He took a couple of Rangers players with him and I cut in and just thumped it into the corner. That was almost at the finish and what a night it was, it couldn't have been better. And I'll tell you, I don't think there were 80,000 left in Ibrox at the end of it! The team played well that day, for us to win 4-0. But just scoring a hat-trick at Ibrox makes it a special one for me.'

Celtic swept all before them that season, retaining the League Cup with another victory over Rangers. This time it was Lennox who scored the only goal of the game, firing home after being set up by Joe McBride on nineteen minutes. In the league, they would only lose two games – both of them by a 3-2 margin to Dundee United, with the team scoring 111 goals and conceding just thirty-three. And in the Scottish Cup they reached the final, having to negotiate their way past Clyde in the semi-final, winning the replay 2-0, with Lennox scoring one of the goals. In the final, Willie Wallace scored both goals in a 2-0 win over Aberdeen.

Bobby Lennox scored twenty-five goals that season, along with another seven in the Glasgow Cup, hitting another hat-trick in the final against Partick Thistle. He scored twice in the European Cup campaign, a goal in both legs against French side FC Nantes in the second round. He only missed two of the nine games in that campaign – the opening match at home to FC Zurich and the home leg of the semi-final, but he was in place for the final, his tireless running stretching and straining the Inter Milan defence throughout a very hot evening for the Italians under the Portuguese sun.

May 25, 1967 was undoubtedly the pinnacle of Bobby Lennox's Celtic career, while just a couple of weeks later came that game against Real Madrid in the Bernabeu Stadium which so impressed Alfredo Di Stefano. Indeed, there were very few low points, though the experience of playing Racing Club in the World Club Championships was certainly a difficult experience, with Lennox red-carded in the last game despite not having done anything to merit such a sanction. However, for him and his team-mates, the disappointment of the 1970 European Cup, coming just three years after that triumph in Lisbon, is one that still fills them with regret. Jock Stein's team lost 2-1 to Feyenoord in Milan's San Siro Stadium, having gone into the game as favourites following their impressive semi-final victory over Leeds United, but on the night it was the Dutch side who triumphed.

'That was, without doubt, the biggest sickener in my entire football career,' Lennox later admitted. 'We had a battle to get to that final in the first place, but just didn't play well on the night. We were two minutes away from getting a replay as well, but that night was just the worst ever. We got to a European Cup final, which is a major achievement in itself, but that's been lost in the archives, simply because we did not win.'

Bobby Lennox continued to accumulate honours for Celtic and when the club won their ninth consecutive league title in 1974, it was also the ninth title for Lennox. He would also play in two further European Cup semi-finals – against Inter Milan in 1972 when the Italians won a penalty shoot-out, and then in 1974 against Atletico Madrid, when Celtic lost 2-0 on aggregate against a side who had abandoned playing football in favour of all-out assault and intimidation. That 1970 final against Feyenoord would be Lennox and Celtic's last European Cup final appearance.

Having joined the club in 1961, there was a brief parting of the ways in March 1978 when he moved to the United States, joining Houston Hurricanes. That experience lasted a few months before he returned to Celtic Park in the September of that year, answering an appeal from his former team-mate, Billy McNeill, who had taken over as Celtic manager at the start of that season. Lennox ended up staying for a couple of seasons and, in the process, was part of the famous '10 Men Win The League' side of 1979, and the Scottish Cup-winning side of the following year. He also played his last European games for the club in March 1980, in the European Cup quarter-final against Real Madrid. That emphasised a remarkable longevity, given that his first European game had been back in September 1963, but it's further evidence of Bobby Lennox's remarkable contribution to the Celtic cause.

That contribution didn't end when he eventually hung up his boots in November 1980, because he immediately moved into coaching at the club, working with the reserves for a further thirteen years, passing on the wealth of experience he had garnered over many years, and instilling in his charges a pride and a passion for the Celtic jersey that had always been evident throughout his own playing career. Even in recent years, he has been a familiar presence on a matchday at Celtic Park, regaling supporters with tales from that golden era of which he was an integral part. They sit in awe, aware that they are in the presence of one of the club's greatest ever players. Bobby Lennox would be too modest to even acknowledge such an accolade, but it is a self-evident Celtic truth. The facts speak for themselves.

IN HIS OWN WORDS...

'I don't remember at any time during the season any of the boys saying we could win the European Cup. It was just a matter of saying, 'Well that's us in another round and that's us in another round.' But when we got the draw in Prague against Dukla and got to the final, that was an incredible feeling – the final of the European Cup, and we knew we were playing one of the best teams in the world in Inter Milan. Once we got to Lisbon, however, I always thought we had a chance of winning it.

Obviously you're hoping you're going to be in the team when it gets to the final, but the gaffer just carried on the way things were, I don't think he did anything special, he just carried on. We had the Scottish Cup final coming up straight after the Dukla game and once the team got picked for that and we beat Aberdeen convincingly I think everyone knew what the team would be. I always felt we were a good team and the guys I played with were good enough to go anywhere. I could look round the dressing room and think we could win anywhere, we could go behind and we'd come back and beat teams.

We prepared for most games down at Seamill, which was a great place for us. There was a wee bit of grass where we'd come down and do all our training and we'd play five-a-sides. We'd be really light-hearted and we'd have good fun. We were out of the way, yet you're up at Celtic Park in fifty minutes. I always felt that those fifty minutes were a great preparation for the game. You'd get up to Glasgow and the boys would all start singing and it was great.

In Portugal, we stayed in this fabulous hotel in Estoril and we trained over at the stadium. The Italians watched us training and Big Jock changed everyone about. I think I played left-back and Wee Jimmy played centre-half or something, it was just a good bit of fun. There was nothing strenuous about the training once we got to Lisbon. It was good fun preparing for the European Cup final although it was a big, big game. We were all very relaxed about it and the gaffer seemed very relaxed about it and I think if the boss is relaxed, it goes right through the camp.

I can remember on the day of the final going to breakfast and out for a wee walk. Then, since it was a Holy Day of Obligation, a priest who was a friend of John Clark said Mass in the hotel for us. We came back, had a bit of lunch and then we all rested for a while. Jimmy and I went up to the room had a wee blether, sat about for a bit, then just waited to go, as it was a half-five kick-off which was quite strange at the time. If I remember rightly, the bus went the wrong way to the stadium and we were a bit late getting there. We went on to the pitch and saw the Celtic supporters, before going back in and then it was quickly time to get back on the field. Then we walked into the big long tunnel when Bertie Auld singing started *The Celtic Song.*

The Lisbon tunnel was the longest tunnel I think I've ever been in, and when we came out the Inter players were all looking great with the lovely strips. We were standing about for a few minutes and then Bertie just started singing and everybody just joined in and it was a great preparation. Had we walked out the tunnel straight on to the park it would never have happened but we were held back for a few minutes and that's why it got started. The Inter players all just looked across, probably thinking 'what's going on here?' To be fair to them, they were an experienced team and had won the European Cup a couple of times, but I think that's when they knew we were up for it.

I'm still convinced had it stayed 1-1 we would've scored three or four in extra-time because Inter had gone by the time it came the final whistle. They had really gone and it was because of our work – we worked so hard that day it was incredible, and our fitness was great. When Tommy equalised it was a great feeling and when Stevie touched the ball into the net it was incredible, and I'll never forget the final whistle. As soon as it went, I turned to the centre-circle and John Clark and Jimmy were standing next to me. John and I jumped into each other arms and he hates that – he hates a cuddle but I grabbed him and the two of us were rolling about in the grass.

It was strange in the dressing room. It was great but nobody knew where Big Billy was. The dressing room was kind of L-shaped, so we changed up with the forwards and the defenders changed together and the showers were in the middle. And Big Billy was away to get the cup. Once we got organised and on the bus we went to a restaurant in the town and waited about an hour-and-a-half for the Italians to come in. Then Billy came round with a shoe-box and handed out our winning medals. I don't think it was an anti-climax. We were the champions of Europe and we were all just young lads, I think I was twenty-three, Jimmy was twenty-two and Bobby was twenty-two. I don't think anybody could've said it was a bad night – it was just a different night. I can understand the Italians being reluctant to come along since they had lost but we were just glad to get the medal and be European champions. We had the rest of our life to think about it.

The wives and girlfriends were heading to the airport to go home while we went back to the hotel in Estoril after dropping them off at the airport, and by that time the bar was closed. Then we heard their flight had been delayed, so they came back to the hotel. People might have thought we must have had the best celebration ever, but we didn't. It was when we arrived back in Glasgow and came to Celtic Park – that was fantastic and that made up for it all.

It's been fantastic what has happened since but it takes a long time for things like that to sink in. When we played abroad at that time, people treated us with great respect because we were Celtic and we had won the European Cup and we'd been in a number of semi-finals, and the club was really successful in Europe. It was just a great period to be involved with Celtic. Worldwide, Celtic supporters were absolutely thrilled. We were a team from the East End of Glasgow and we were playing the cream of Europe. And beating them!

I am a Celtic supporter, as everybody knows, and it's great to have had such a long association with the club. It's a privilege that I really appreciate. I was only away in

The end of the Dukla Prague game and Celtic are in the European Cup final.

John Clark and Billy McNeill celebrate getting to the final.

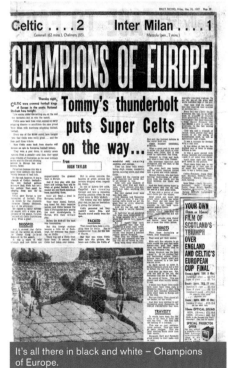

It's all there in black and white – Champions of Europe.

1

Lisbon's green and white – even the buses.

Right, let's get started.

The favourites and the underdogs line up before the game.

Jock Stein about to take the best seat in the house while Inter manager, Helenio Herrera follows up.

Former Celt Jim Kennedy with fellow fans taking to the air.

A welcome pit stop on the way to Lisbon.

A prized ticket for the big day.

Billy McNeill and Bobby Murdoch lead the Lions out at Celtic Park with the trophy.

Jock Stein receiving the 1967 BBC Sportsview Personality of the Year – Team Award, from Matt Busby.

A lap of European honour at Celtic Park – the home of the European Cup.

An exhausted Billy McNeill with Portuguese President, Americo Tomas who presented the cup.

Tommy Gemmell whips in a cross.

Jimmy Johnstone fires in one of the many Celtic shots on the Inter Milan goal.

Jock Stein and Billy McNeill lead the Celts from the dressing room.

The captains exchange pennants before the final gets underway.

A rare Inter Milan attack is about to be thwarted by Billy McNeill.

Jimmy Steele holds a hooped teddy while the Celts make their way to the tunnel.

Neilly Mochan, Jock Stein and Sean Fallon make sure the team gets the message.

The ultimate prize – a European Cup winner's medal.

From Glasgow to Lisbon by bus.

Lisbon or bust for these two supporters.

The Celts return from another continental jaunt.

Stairway to Paradise for John Clark, Billy McNeill, Bertie Auld, Willie Wallace and Stevie Chalmers.

Two lucky ground staff Bhoys parade Europe's top silverware.

America for about six months when I came back to rejoin the club and I was delighted to get the chance to come back. Like I said, it's a great honour and I am very fortunate to be associated with the club I support for so long. I have enjoyed so many good times through the club, not just as a player and a supporter, but off the park as well. I have made great friends and as people know, the Lisbon Lions are like brothers. I have been lucky enough to play in two or three different teams, with players like big Roy Aitken, Danny McGrain, Kenny Dalglish, George McCluskey and Davie Provan, I have been fortunate enough to have played with loads of good players and in four completely different Celtic teams.'

STEVIE CHALMERS

LISBOA
25 DE MAIO DE
1967
CELTIC 2-1 INTER
50º
CELTIC FC
ANIVERSARIO

STEVIE CHALMERS

It is the most important goal in Celtic's history. When Stevie Chalmers slotted the ball into the Inter Milan net on May 25, 1967, with just five minutes of the European Cup final remaining, it changed everything as far as Celtic's history was concerned. In that moment Celtic became one of the most famous names in world football; the final whistle signified that fact though, in truth, Inter Milan were a beaten team as soon as Chalmers scored. For the player, it ensured that his name would be forever synonymous with that famous triumph. He was one of eleven men who became known as the Lisbon Lions, and he wouldn't have it any other way – he was the perfect example of a team player – but scoring the winning goal has always merited a special acknowledgement in telling the story of Celtic's European Cup triumph.

Not that Stevie Chalmers would have been forgotten had he not been the one to provide the winning touch – the apt title of his autobiography, incidentally. He made 406 appearances for the club in a twelve-year period between 1959 and '71, and he is the club's fourth top goalscorer of all-time, with 231 goals. Only Jimmy McGrory (446), Bobby Lennox (277) and Henrik Larsson (242) have scored more goals for Celtic. There was also the famous hat-trick against Rangers in the 5-1 New Year's victory of 1966, and a goal in the 4-0 Scottish Cup final win over the Ibrox side in 1969, while he also hit five goals in a 10-0 victory over Hamilton in a League Cup quarter-final win – Bobby Lennox matching the feat by scoring the other five. Yet it all comes back to that day in May 1967 when he was instinctively in the right place to steer Bobby Murdoch's shot into the Inter Milan net.

Stevie Chalmers was one of the elder statesmen of the Celtic squad by that time, just a few months short of his thirty-first birthday when he won the European Cup, and while outside observers may have earmarked him as one who might potentially struggle for a place in the team when Jock Stein arrived at Celtic in March 1965, the new manager continued to use Chalmers to great effect, identifying a player of great quality who always gave everything to the team regardless of what he was tasked with in any given game. Indeed, Chalmers' professional career had started later than many of his team-mates. He was twenty-two when he joined the club from junior side, Ashfield. It was Jimmy McGrory who signed him for the club, cementing a family link that went all the way back to the early 1920s when the Celtic legend had gone on loan to Clydebank and played alongside David Chalmers, Stevie's father, who was always the most important figure in his career, as he explained to the *Celtic View*.

'My Dad was a professional footballer and he, very quietly, was always there to help me. He taught me how to kick the ball and trap the ball and I always remember that he used to take me up to Springburn Park and would place the ball and try and hit the crossbar. He was quite accurate at it and he encouraged me to practice and do the same. He played for Clydebank, back when they were more of a prominent senior team and he actually played alongside Jimmy McGrory. My Dad was a major influence on my career and I had always wanted to play football, I never really wanted to do anything else.'

Stevie Chalmers made his Celtic debut in a 2-1 league defeat at home to Airdrie on March 10, 1959. The team that day included such Celtic luminaries as Dunky MacKay, Bobby Evans and Bertie Peacock, while Bertie Auld, in his first spell with the club, was also in the line-up. That would be Chalmers' only appearance that season, though the following year, he played nineteen times for the first-team, scoring fifteen goals, including fourteen in the league campaign, though that was another forgettable one for the Hoops as they finished ninth in the table, twenty-one points behind champions, Hearts. The first of his 231 goals for Celtic came on September 19, 1959 in an away league game against Raith Rovers. Celtic were comfortable 3-0 winners that day, and after Mike Jackson had given the Hoops the lead, Chalmers weighed in with two second-half goals, the first of them coming on fifty-one minutes to get his tally up and running.

The following season, another unsuccessful one for Celtic which culminated in a Scottish Cup final replay defeat to Dunfermline Athletic, now managed by Jock Stein, Stevie Chalmers was the club's top scorer, netting an impressive twenty league goals in a campaign where the team only scored sixty-four in total, while he also scored six in both cup competitions. Those barren years for Celtic, well-documented and painfully remembered by those who suffered through them, still saw Stevie Chalmers chalk up an impressive scoring record, and he reached his century of goals for the Hoops on February 29, 1964 with the first of three goals against East Stirling in a 5-1 win, the goal coming in the first minute of the match. In just under five years, Stevie Chalmers had become only the fifteenth Celtic player at the time to score over 100 goals for the club, a mark of his quality and scoring prowess, though he was less than halfway towards reaching his final tally of goals for the club.

By that point, he had already enjoyed his first taste of European football, playing in both legs of the club's first continental matches against Valencia in Fairs Cities Cup the previous season, even having a goal disallowed in the first leg in Spain. The following season, the Hoops reached the semi-final of the Cup-Winners' Cup, with Chalmers scoring five goals in the campaign, including double in the 3-0 semi-final first leg win over MTK Budapest at Celtic Park. The second leg saw a disastrous collapse in Hungary, when Celtic lost 4-0 on the night, though six of the players who would lift the European Cup three years later played that night – McNeill, Clark, Johnstone, Murdoch, Gemmell and Chalmers.

Stevie Chalmers scored thirty-eight goals in all competitions that season, another impressive haul given that the team finished third in the league, failed to qualify from their League Cup section and only reached the fourth round of the Scottish Cup. He would score twenty-six the following season, as the Hoops finished a lowly eighth in the league, though they reached the Scottish Cup final, with Chalmers scoring one of three goals in the 3-0 semi-final replay win over Motherwell. By that time Jock Stein was in charge and Chalmers was in the team that lifted the Scottish Cup on April 24 with a 3-2 win over Dunfermline in the final.

Having won their first piece of silverware in eight years, Celtic began the following season in a confident mood, though even the most optimistic of supporters might have been happy with an improvement on the eighth place finish of the previous season and perhaps another cup success. The League Cup duly arrived in October, though Chalmers missed the 2-1 victory in the final over Rangers. However, he was in the Scottish Cup final side which lost 1-0 to their city rivals in a replay. The league campaign, however, was the clearest indication of the transformation that was happening under Jock Stein, illustrated most forcefully in the Glasgow derby on January 3, 1966.

Among the many highlights of Stevie Chalmers' Celtic career was the hat-trick he scored against Rangers in that game. The Ibrox side had actually taken the lead inside the first two minutes of the game at Celtic Park, a lead they held until half-time. However, a blistering second-half saw Jock Stein's side hit five goals without reply, Chalmers scoring the first of those in the forty-ninth minute and completing the scoring – and his hat-trick – with a goal in the last minute of the match; Charlie Gallagher and Bobby Murdoch also scored that day. The result was the most powerful indicator yet that there had been a sea-change in Scottish football. The result, and his own part in it, has always remained a career highlight for Stevie Chalmers.

'Scoring a hat-trick is great for a striker but managing it against Rangers was a wee bit special. I don't even think I was thinking about a hat-trick after I scored my second goal – you're just thinking about scoring goals and not the actual number. The last goal of the hat-trick came in the final minute of the game and it was a very slack ball, I think the keeper shut his eyes when I got close to him and I just managed a wee poke over the top of him I recall that chipping it over the keeper made it the easiest of the three goals. I came into the dressing-room after the final whistle like a dog with four wagging tails because I was so up, but somewhere along the line, Big Jock said: 'I wouldn't give you Man of the Match, big Yogi was the top man today.' That was typical of Big Jock. He was great at keeping your feet right down on the ground – but that record is still standing and there was Jock at the time playing the whole thing down.'

At the end of that season, Celtic claimed their first title in twelve years, finishing two points clear of Rangers and scoring 106 goals in the process, with Stevie Chalmers netting fifteen of them. The following season, he scored the club's first goal of the league campaign as Celtic opened up the defence of their title with a 3-0 win over Clyde at Shawfield. It would be one of thirty-six goals he'd score that season, finishing top scorer by one from Joe McBride, whose own season had finished prematurely at Christmas after he picked up a knee injury. It would take Stevie Chalmers until the last game of the season – the European Cup final – to claim the top goalscorer title, but it was a fitting game, and a significant goal with which to do so.

He scored five goals in that European campaign, including the decisive one in Lisbon. The first of those came in the first round, second leg tie away to FC Zurich, while there were goals in both legs against Nantes, and the opener against Vojvodina in the return leg at Celtic Park, which cancelled out the Yugoslavian side's 1-0 first leg lead. Perhaps his most significant contribution, outwith the winning goal against Inter Milan in the final, came in the second leg of the semi-final against Dukla Prague in Czechoslovakia. Celtic had won the first leg 3-1 and Jock Stein opted, first and foremost, to defend that lead, aware of what was at stake and perhaps also aware of what had happened against MTK Budapest just three years previously, even though he wasn't at the club.

Celtic's game-plan in Prague meant a tough shift up front for Stevie Chalmers, who ran himself into the ground, effectively playing as a lone striker, occupying the Dukla Prague backline for the entire match. Captain Billy McNeill acknowledged that effort in reflecting on the goal-less draw which put Celtic into the European Cup final.

'From the moment that Stevie stepped on to the pitch, he never stopped moving and never stopped working. He was prepared to run in behind people, he was prepared to chase things, and he was a magnificent player to have in your side. His contribution to the team was magnificent because he unsettled defences like no-one else could and his scoring record was outstanding as well. His quality as a player was there for everyone to see in Lisbon and how many other great players can say that they scored the winner in the European Cup final? He was excellent that night, but the other one performance that stands out in my mind from that season was against Dukla Prague in the second game we played against them. Stevie played up front on his own that night and was virtually the only player that we had in their half at any given time. He worked tirelessly and as I said, the amount of the effort that he put in was incredible.'

The reward was, of course, a place in the 1967 European Cup final where Inter Milan, twice winners of the competition, awaited. Once again, Stevie Chalmers' tireless running and willingness to work for the team served Celtic well, and it's unlikely the Inter Milan defence had ever been stretched so consistently and decisively in any ninety minutes before or since. Chalmers' reward came in the eighty-fifth minute when he was in the right place to direct Bobby Murdoch's shot into the net. That moment ensured Stevie Chalmers' place in Celtic history, though as part of the most famous team in the club's history, that was already guaranteed.

His friend and team-mate, Bobby Lennox, wasn't surprised to see Chalmers get on the end of that Murdoch shot, as he explained: 'Stevie scoring the winning goal in the European Cup final is my outstanding memory of him. It was the type of goal he had scored a thousand times in training, and while it might have looked as though Stevie just luckily got his toe to it, it was no surprise to any of us that Stevie had been the one to put the ball in the net. He was expert at knowing just how to get into the right spot and get that vital touch on a ball – that was the result of years of practice.'

Celtic would continue to dominate Scottish football after 1967, though they did unexpectedly exit the European Cup the following season in the first round at the hands of Dynamo Kyiv. The league title was retained, as was the League Cup, with Chalmers scoring two goals in a 5-3 victory over Dundee in the final. He would also net another famous goal against Rangers, this time in the 1969 Scottish Cup final over Rangers, when he completed the scoring in a comprehensive 4-0 victory.

The following season saw Jock Stein lead the club to another European Cup final, though Stevie Chalmers would only play in the first two games of that campaign against FC Basel. Just a few weeks after the Hoops knocked out the Swiss side, they played St Johnstone in the League Cup final. A Bertie Auld goal inside the first couple of minutes was enough to give Celtic their fifth consecutive success in the competition, but that victory was marred by the broken leg Stevie Chalmers suffered in the match. That injury ended his season and, indeed, he would only make a handful of appearances the following year in what was his last campaign for the club.

May 1, 1971 remains a poignant moment in Celtic's history because it was on this day that the Lisbon Lions appeared in a starting XI for the very last time, though Ronnie Simpson, who had effectively retired due to injury, still ran out with the rest of the team for the pre-match warm-up, but he was replaced by Evan Williams before the start of the game.

It was also the last game Bertie Auld played for the club, having been given a free transfer, and he was at his imperious best in midfield as Celtic ran out 6-1 winners Bobby Lennox scored a hat-trick that day, while Willie Wallace scored twice. It was also the last game that John Clark played for the green and white Hoops. Clyde had the audacity to score a goal of their own and it was the man who had sealed the victory in Lisbon who netted the sixth and final goal of a special Celtic afternoon, firing home with twelve minutes of the match remaining.

It turned out to be Stevie Chalmers' last goal in his last competitive game for Celtic, and it was fitting that the man whose goal had effectively created the legend of the

Lisbon Lions should score the last goal for that famous team. It was also his 231st for the club, making him, at the time, Celtic's third top goalscorer of all-time. It would only be into the twenty-first century, with Henrik Larsson's goalscoring exploits, that he would be usurped from his top-three position.

Stevie Chalmers left Celtic Park on September 9, 1971, joining Morton as player-coach alongside fellow Lisbon Lion, and he returned to Paradise nine days later as the blue and white Hoops of the Greenock side took on their more famous, and green, counterparts in a league match which the home side won 3-1, with John Clark scoring for Celtic that day, albeit an own goal.

'When Jock sent me down to Greenock to play with Morton, I was taking all the training with John Clark and we had to play as well, but I realised then I couldn't keep myself fit while I was trying to keep other people fit,' Chalmers said. 'I couldn't do the two at once and it came back on me. It seemed hard, but the hardest thing was leaving Celtic in the first place. No disrespect to Morton, but leaving Celtic Park to go to Cappielow was hard for me.'

Stevie Chalmers continued playing up until 1975, having moved from Morton to Partick Thistle in 1972, with his last year as a player under Bertie Auld, who had been appointed manager at Firhill in 1974. He subsequently became involved with Celtic Pools for many years before becoming a regular face on a matchday at Celtic Park. Bobby Lennox has enjoyed a friendship with Stevie Chalmers stretching back over fifty years that was developed in the dressing-room and on the pitch with Celtic, but was also strengthened on the golf course.

'Stevie's such a quiet and modest man and you'd never catch him talking about what he has achieved in the game,' said Lennox. 'He was a great player to play along with and when Celtic played with the two of us up front it was great, because Stevie and I could both work in the channels. He was a real selfless player, who worked his socks off and he was great in the box. If the ball went in the box and there was even half a chance, you knew that Stevie would get a goal for you. He was a great professional and during the week, he was always the first at training and he worked really hard at his job. Stevie was also the gentleman of the squad and was a really quiet guy, who loved his golf and he is still just a lovely guy.'

IN HIS OWN WORDS...

'The 1966/67 season was a very special time for all of us and, of course, we had a very good run in the European Cup. We got a good 3-1 victory over Dukla Prague in the semi-final at Celtic Park and then went over to play the return in Czechoslovakia and

I had a very specific role on the day which involved quite a bit of hard work. It just so happened that it turned out that way. I don't think Jock had planned to have defence in mind, and I don't think he ever planned it again afterwards with just one forward up the park running about doing the work. I knew that's what we had to do to win it and it doesn't matter how frustrated you are, if you're going to win the game by doing that, that's what you do.

I think it was only about two nights before the European Cup that I had an idea I'd be in the team. It was that tight. Jock had a lot of good players standing by that could've taken my place as well. I would've been absolutely gutted to miss out but I suppose that's something you have to put up with. If you were out you'd be disappointed but to get there and be successful at the game was terrific. I was delighted to be part of it, delighted. I mean, that's the ambition when you're a boy – you want to win everything you can win. We were fortunate to do everything that we had dreamed about.

We had a lot of great players at that time. Jimmy Johnstone was absolutely superb but you could also say that about the likes of Bobby Murdoch. We had Bertie Auld who was as cute as could be. On the park he was a fox and up front we had Bobby Lennox who was a terrific goalscorer. But Jock also had Joe McBride and Big Yogi, and he moved them about game by game to see how they would do and he was a master of finding out what they could do. It must've been hard luck on the players who missed out on Lisbon. All the boys would've been desperate to play.

We were fit at that time and we didn't have to do an awful lot of hard training. It was a matter of just keeping ticking over and there was a form of relaxation at the hotel, or sitting about the pool, though Jock wouldn't let you sit too long. Neilly Mochan would take you out for a walk when it was time to go and do things like that, but I think it was just a matter of building us up for that game.

It was quite a long day because there was quite a lot of excitement that day. We had been to Mass in the morning. I was rooming with Bobby Murdoch and we had a sleep in the afternoon because five o'clock was a long while to wait for the game, and it was a change of time for us. Normally a game would be later at night if it was played. I always felt the heat of the game would be a big problem and it was an awful lot hotter in that game than what people realise. I felt the heat very much a part of that game. You always got butterflies and you had to be excited. I think if you're not excited about it then you're not ready for the game. It was a great feeling to be there and knowing you were going to play.

I enjoyed the game thoroughly although I must admit I wasn't happy with my own performance. The position I was in could have been filled by anyone, it could have been Bobby Lennox or Willie Wallace just as easily as it could have been me. But that night, although I felt we were all over them, Inter showed that they were a great defending team and Jock's plan for us was based on movement. The likes of Willie, Bobby and myself would drop deep and pull the Italians into stupid positions, with our movement allowing the space for Tommy Gemmell, Jim Craig and Bertie Auld to go forward and Inter weren't expecting that. It just happened that I was further forward at the moment of the goal and just as Bobby Murdoch shot at goal, I nipped round the back of my marker to put it into the back of the net.

I always felt we could win if we got the break of the ball at all and I thought we were stronger. When Tommy Gemmell scored the first goal I was very surprised that the Italians didn't come back and try and hit us again. And the winning goal came from the training ground. That was very often worked at Barrowfield from the left wing or from the right wing – people hitting the ball hard across the goal, and two or three of the Celtic players that could've touched that ball into the net.

The highlight of my Celtic career obviously has to be scoring the winning goal against Inter Milan in the European Cup final. I don't think you can get a better highlight than that. You work every day from when you're a kid, building yourself up to that kind of challenge and it was something I had dreamed of. I am very, very lucky and I have a lot of other highlights that I can pick out as well. Just signing for Celtic was one of the greatest days in my career and there were a lot of clubs interested in signing me. The second that Celtic declared their interest, the other clubs were forgotten. It was a dream to play for Celtic

And for every player who was in the team and involved in that squad, it was a tremendous achievement to win in Lisbon. A lot of people thought that we were going there just to make up the numbers, but to go there and win, and win in the commanding style that we did win, was something to be proud of.

I'll never forget the scenes that followed the final whistle. The supporters weren't supposed to get over the moat that surrounded the pitch, but within seconds of the referee blowing his whistle, there were thousands over it. But for us the real celebrations happened when we returned to Glasgow and I will never forget the scenes and the thousands of people who gathered along the road and at the stadium to welcome us. You saw at that moment exactly what it meant to people.

That season we won five trophies and to do that with a lot of local lads, who had all grown up around the city and to beat one of the greatest teams in the world in the European final, that showed our desire and our will to win.

That goal has brought me nothing but happiness; it has had nothing other than good effects for me. It meant a lot to my family too in the immediate aftermath; my brothers and sisters would go into work and people would congratulate them on my action. My only tinge of regret is that my father never got to see it. He had passed away shortly before we got to the final in Lisbon. It would have been lovely for him to see that.

One of the greatest rewards that I have enjoyed from my playing career is the friendship I have with the rest of the lads I played with. We are very close and what I think really brought 'the Lions' together was our tour of America in 1966. We were away for five weeks together and we all lived together. Jock had a great system of shuffling people about, he never put you in with the same person. Mind you, some of the times he had to because wee Jinky and Bobby Lennox were inseparable, they were joined at the hip! But he moved the players about and you got to know each other well. When you room with somebody on these trips, you are kind of stuck with them, you don't go downstairs to meet people before the other man is ready. The two of you do everything together. I could never have imagined that I would make such great friends and their friendship means so much to me.

Everywhere I've gone people have asked me what was it like to score the winning goal in the European Cup, and it's hard to say to them because it's just the pinnacle for somebody who wanted to be a professional footballer.'

LISBOA 25 DE MAIO DE **1967** CELTIC 2-1 INTER · CELTIC FC · 50° ANIVERSARIO

JIMMY JOHNSTONE

JIMMY JOHNSTONE

He is the Greatest Ever Celt, an accolade bestowed upon him by Celtic supporters when they voted for their favourite player back in 2002. In a team full of great players, Jimmy Johnstone was the spark who, with one moment of individual skill, could change a game. He was brilliant and unpredictable, endlessly entertaining and often inspirational. He was loved by his team-mates, adored by supporters, and looked upon with almost fatherly love – and sometimes frustration – by Jock Stein, the Celtic manager well aware of the talents the diminutive red-headed winger possessed, and always determined to try and ensure that those talents were utilised for the good of the team.

Jimmy Johnstone was a wonderful player, one of the greatest to have played the beautiful game. Of that there is no doubt. His skills with a football, however, were also matched by his courage on the field of play. He had the heart of a lion – a Lisbon Lion, no less – and despite his slight stature, his bravery in standing up to the relentless physical intimidation he experienced throughout his career was remarkable to witness. That courage transferred itself to the battle he faced long after his retirement, when he was diagnosed with Motor Neurone Disease. Despite the bleak prognosis that accompanies the illness, the Celtic legend approached the fight with the same tenacity and fearlessness that had always accompanied him on to the pitch.

His passing in 2006 at the age of sixty-one was mourned by the Celtic Family who had lost one of their own, while everyone who loved football and those who play it to the highest standard also mourned the passing of a wonderful football talent. He and his team-mates had ensured their own place amongst the pantheon of footballing greats with their 1967 European Cup triumph, and within that legendary team, Jimmy Johnstone was known and revered throughout the sporting world. Known affectionately as 'Jinky', a tribute to his unique style of dribbling which, more often than not, left his opponent in knots, having been twisted and turned into bamboozlement, Jimmy Johnstone was a player who certainly owed a debt of gratitude to Jock Stein, whose timely arrival at Celtic Park in March 1965 helped to ensure that the winger became so much more than just a mercurial talent.

Brought up in the Lanarkshire town of Viewpark, Johnstone had been captivated by Stanley Matthews' wing wizardry in the 1953 FA Cup as the veteran England winger, at the age of thirty-eight, inspired Blackpool to a 4-3 victory over Bolton Wanderers. It was a pivotal moment in young Jimmy's life. From then on, he wanted to be like Stanley Matthews, as he explained to the *Celtic View* in what was his last interview with the club magazine.

'I read in Stanley Matthews' book about just how much time, effort and training he put into his game and I realised talent like that just didn't come automatically. I also remember seeing the old black and white clips of that famous FA Cup final and I knew right way that's what I wanted to do. After reading his book I knew what I had to do to get there. I took everything on board and took up the mantle by spending as much time as I could just training and playing football. The book was a massive help to me and that's when I started training by dribbling around milk bottles.

'I lived it to the full and knew what I had to do, so I would play for five or six hours a day – *every* day. I played before school, after school and during school but the main thing was that I really enjoyed playing football as well and I wanted to be as good as I could be. The enjoyment grew as, thanks to the training, when it came to playing in games and kick-abouts, I realised I could do things that no-one else on the pitch could. That was when I knew the training was working and it was all self-taught. In those days there were no coaches telling me what to do.'

Johnstone's talents, God-given but already being brought to the fore through all those hours of dedicated practice, were soon being noticed by football scouts, and Manchester United showed interest in the player. However, his heart always lay at Paradise, and when Celtic moved in to see off the interest from England, Johnstone was delighted to join *his* team.

'Back when I was a ballboy at Celtic Park, I think even then Celtic were keeping an eye on me and at that age I suppose that was the first step to becoming a player at the club,' Johnstone explained. 'Then Manchester United had me down there for a youth tournament and their scouts were watching me but Celtic got the gist of what was going on and I signed for them.'

He signed for Celtic in November 1961, though it would be nearly two years later before he made his first-team debut, having initially been farmed out to Blantyre Celtic. His first-team debut for Celtic came in less than auspicious circumstances as the Hoops lost 6-0 against Kilmarnock at Rugby Park in March 1963. Also making their debuts that night were defender John Cushley and goalkeeper Dick Madden; that was Madden's one and only appearance for Celtic. Jimmy Johnstone made a total of five appearances that season, including one in the Scottish Cup final against Rangers at Hampden. The game finished 1-1, and Johnstone, then only eighteen-years-old, had acquitted himself well. However, he was left out of the replay, which Celtic lost 3-0, just one example of many team selections during that time at the club which seemed inexplicable, and were evidence that control of such a fundamental thing as team selection did not rest solely with the manager, Jimmy McGrory.

Johnstone also scored his first goal for the club in a 4-3 defeat against Hearts at Tynecastle that same season. However, he quickly found himself a regular in the first-team the following season, and he also netted his first European goals for the club in their Cup-Winners' Cup campaign, against FC Basel in the first round and then in the first leg of the semi-final against MTK Budapest. He also netted in the return leg, as did John Hughes, but both goals were ruled out for offside and Celtic saw a 3-0 first-leg lead overturned as the Hungarians won 4-0 to progress to the final. The following season followed a similar pattern for player and club, with the league campaign in particular less than impressive, the team ultimately finishing eighth in the table, though they ended the campaign with a new manager, as Jock Stein took over from Jimmy McGrory in March 1965.

Throughout Jimmy Johnstone's time at Celtic, there were many examples of Jock Stein's influence on the player ensuring that the team got the best out of him; Stein did say of Johnstone that 'no player has caused me more headaches since I went to Celtic and on no-one has more time been spent to sort out his troubles,' though he knew that all the effort was worth it for what could, and often was, produced on the pitch. Indeed, Stein's impact could be seen even before he returned to Celtic Park as manager. Just twenty-four hours before he officially took over at Celtic, Stein was at Easter Road to watch a reserve watch between Hibernian and Celtic. Jimmy Johnstone was playing for the Hoops and at half-time he encountered Stein in the gents' toilet. The manager asked the player why, with his talents, he was languishing in the reserves. Johnstone later explained: 'That was a real boost for me and I went out and scored a hat-trick in the second half.'

Celtic would go on to win the Scottish Cup at the end of that season under their new manager, although Jimmy Johnstone was not selected for the final against Dunfermline Athletic. Indeed, when Jock Stein had returned to the club, he wasn't convinced that the winger had a future at Celtic, though the astute Sean Fallon persuaded the new manager that this was a player worth persevering with. How right the Irishman was. The following season, Stein's first full campaign in charge, Johnstone was an integral part of the manager's plans and he played in fifty-four of Celtic's fixtures that season across four competitions, including the League Cup final win over Rangers. He also played in seven of the eight European Cup-Winners' Cup ties the team played that season, the only one he missed being the second leg of the semi-final against Liverpool at Anfield. In 1966/67 he would start every one of Celtic's nine European Cup ties, up to and including the final in Lisbon.

By then, Celtic had swept all before them, winning the three major domestic honours as well as the Glasgow Cup. The League Cup was retained with a 1-0 victory in the final against Rangers, while Aberdeen were defeated 2-0 in the Scottish Cup final, with Stein's decision to play Johnstone through the middle alongside Willie Wallace – who scored both of Celtic's goals that day – rather than on his more familiar right-wing position, proving to be a masterstroke which unsettled the Aberdeen team. A week after lifting the Scottish Cup, Celtic travelled to Ibrox knowing that if they avoided defeat they would retain their league title.

Glasgow had been lashed with overnight rain, making the Ibrox pitch heavy underfoot, but it did not deter the Hoops who, in front of the watching Inter Milan manager, Helenio Herrera, duly gained the necessary point to confirm themselves as champions again. Rangers had actually taken the lead on the fortieth minute through Sandy Jardine, but that lead lasted all of sixty seconds before Jimmy Johnstone bundled the ball home to equalise. With just over fifteen minutes of the match remaining, Johnstone scored a glorious second goal for Celtic, cutting in from the right flank and unleashing an unstoppable shot into the roof of the net to put the Hoops ahead. And even though Rangers managed to grab an equaliser, Celtic saw out the game to clinch the first domestic treble in the club's history. Now, all that was left was the small matter of the European Cup.

That day in Lisbon, as was so often the way in big matches, Jimmy Johnstone rose to the occasion, causing Inter Milan problems from first minute 'til last. He may not have got on the scoresheet, but he was one of Celtic's main attacking threats as Jock Stein's side won the game and the biggest club trophy in the game by playing 'pure, beautiful inventive football', and Jimmy Johnstone was at the heart of that, twisting and turning the Inter defenders who had surely never faced a talent like that before.

If Celtic reached the pinnacle of the game with that victory over Inter Milan on May 25, 1967, they offered further proof of their supremacy just a couple of weeks later when they faced Real Madrid in a testimonial for Madrid legend Alfredo Di Stefano at the Bernabeu Stadium. The Hoops outclassed the Spanish giants, with Jinky setting up Bobby Lennox's goal in a 1-0 win. Johnstone was outstanding that night. By the end, the Real Madrid fans greeted his every touch with 'Ole! Ole!' At time up, he lifted the ball to the sky as he was given a standing ovation. Bobby Lennox later said: 'Jimmy was at the top of his game and Madrid must have tried to sign him after that match, they must have.' We'll never know for sure, but Jimmy Johnstone was definitely remembered in Madrid, and at his funeral in 2006, Alfredo Di Stefano sent a telegram paying tribute to him.

After that game in the Spanish capital, the Celtic players were heading home to enjoy a well-earned break following the unprecedented success of the 1966/67 season. Jimmy Johnstone and his wife, Agnes, were going on holiday to Benidorm straight from Madrid, which was just an hour's flight. However, Johnstone's legendary reluctance to get on a plane meant that he took a taxi to the holiday resort instead – a journey of some 300 miles! That fear of flying had materialised as he returned home early from the club's close-season tour of Bermuda and North America summer 1966 in order to get married. Somewhere over the Atlantic Ocean, the aircraft hit heavy turbulence, with people thrown into the aisles, and various objects thrown about the plane. From then on, Johnstone had a genuine terror of getting on a plane, though he had to suppress it as Celtic's European adventures continued and increased.

However, Jock Stein's legendary man-management skills came into play when the team faced Red Star Belgrade in the second round of the European Cup in 1968. The first leg at Celtic Park was tied 1-1 at half-time when legend has it that Stein took Johnstone aside for a quiet word, promising the winger that he wouldn't have to fly to Yugoslavia if Celtic won the game by at least four clear goals. Duly motivated, Johnstone produced a stunning second-half performance, scoring twice and inspiring the team to a 5-1 win, appearing in his own area to clear any danger when he wasn't creating it at the other end. Stein was true to his word and Johnstone didn't travel for the second-leg, which finished 1-1.

The 1969/70 season was another impressive one for Celtic on the European stage, with Jock Stein leading his charges all the way to the final. The semi-final clash with Leeds United, billed predictably as a 'Battle of Britain' saw the English champions approach the match full of confidence. That lasted all of forty-five seconds before George Connelly scored at Elland Road, and in both that game and the return leg – played at Hampden to cope with the demand from fans for tickets – Jimmy Johnstone was in sublime form. The crowd of 136,505 which packed into Scotland's national stadium saw Billy Bremner score early in the first-half to cancel out Celtic's first-leg lead, but John Hughes equalised just after half-time and then Bobby Murdoch fired home Celtic's second after he was set up by Johnstone, who was too much for the experienced Leeds defenders to cope with in either leg. Indeed, the player himself believed that the game at Elland Road was one of his finest in the Hoops.

The high of that tumultuous semi-final win was followed by the bitter disappointment of losing the final to Feyenoord after extra-time. It was to be the closest that Celtic would come to repeating their success of 1967. Domestic dominance continued, while a semi-final clash with old foes, Inter Milan, saw the Italians triumph this time following a penalty shoot-out at Celtic Park after both legs had finished goal-less. And in 1974, Celtic, and Jimmy Johnstone, won their ninth consecutive league title, a 1-1 draw against Falkirk at Brockville securing the historic success. Johnstone wasn't always a regular feature in the starting XI for the team at that point, and he made fifteen appearances in the league that season. However, he remained a potent weapon for Jock Stein as, once again, Celtic advanced to the semi-final of the European Cup.

If the game against Real Madrid in June 1967 had been a footballing highlight for Celtic and Jimmy Johnstone, showcasing the talents of the player and his team-mates who were now the Kings of Europe, then a game against Real's city rivals, Atletico Madrid, eight years later, was an example of the dark side of football, though it also provided evidence, if any was still needed, of Jimmy Johnstone's bravery and courage in the face of almost overwhelming physical intimidation. Atletico Madrid had three players sent off and eight booked in a goal-less European Cup semi-final first leg at Celtic Park on a night when they shamed football. Jimmy Johnstone had been identified, naturally enough, as a danger-man for Celtic, and so he was singled out for particularly brutal treatment that should have merited criminal charges over and above whatever ineffectual sanctions the referee was able to issue.

That the Celtic player refused to bow to the intimidation, but got up and went back for more says much about Jimmy Johnstone, and it was to the shame of the football authorities that the Spanish side were not expelled from the tournament. The return leg in Madrid, which was precipitated by death threats issued to both Jock Stein and Jimmy Johnstone, saw Celtic lose 2-0 after conceding two late goals. It remains, to date, the last time the club has reached the semi-final of the competition. The only silver lining, such as it was, was that Atletico were beaten in a replay of the final by Bayern Munich.

A year later, Jimmy Johnstone would leave Celtic, much to the dismay of the support, who had not imagined a Celtic squad without his presence. It was a sad day, too, for the player himself. Jimmy Johnstone won 19 major honours during his fourteen years with the club. He lifted nine league championships, four Scottish Cups and five League Cups. He was at his inspirational best as Celtic beat Inter Milan in the final of the 1967 European Cup. He created countless goals during the club's most productive era but he also scored his fair share and that's what sets him apart. For a winger, his record of 130 goals in 515 games is exceptional. Not only that, he scored in big games – derbies, league deciders, cup finals and huge European ties.

It was little surprise that the Celtic supporters voted Jimmy Johnstone the Greatest Ever Celt in 2002. They had always loved his unique talent when he had worn the green and white Hoops, while there was recognition that he was one of their own, appreciative of the fact that he had been lucky enough to play for the club he, and they, had always supported. And the appreciation was mutual, as Johnstone later explained

'I was always aware I was an entertainer. The crowd provided the expectation, the hairs on the back of my neck would go up and I loved the applause. The pitch was my stage. The whistle meant it was show-time. That's why I admired Stanley Matthews. The way he took people on and beat them, that was entertainment to me and that is all I wanted to do. Without the fans, you are nothing and what I am most thankful of is that I got a chance to realise my talent at Celtic, because it is a special club, supported by special people.'

Having been diagnosed with Motor Neurone Disease, Jimmy Johnstone passed away on March 13, 2006. Just a few days later, Celtic faced Dunfermline Athletic in the final of the League Cup, and that game at Hampden saw the Celtic team all wear the No.7 on their shirts as a special tribute to a special player. Just as fittingly, they won the game and lifted the trophy.

His friend and fellow Lisbon Lion, Jim Craig, was able to appreciate the talents of Jimmy Johnstone at close quarters, playing right-back with Jinky ahead of him on the right wing. He's in no doubt as to the scale of his team-mate's footballing talent, as he told the *Celtic View*.

'Wee Jimmy never paid the slightest bit of attention to Jock's team talks. He'd be picking his nails and looking out the window and didn't have the foggiest idea of what we were meant to be doing. His attitude was, 'just give me the ball and I'll beat ten players' and that night he was fantastic. I don't think that any player, with the exception of Lionel Messi, has played like Jimmy Johnstone, beating a man and putting the fear of God into a defence. I still remember the great moment in the game against Leeds when Jack Charlton shouted across to Terry Cooper, 'For God's sake, just tackle him' and he shouted back, 'You do it, I can't get near him'. When he was at the height of his powers he could really get a defence worried, he was just a colossal player. I had the best seat in the house, playing behind him and there was a game when we played Dundee United at Celtic Park in 1969 when we won 7-2 and he ran riot. He went on a run on one occasion, beat four or five, raced to the byline, beat another, overran the ball, ran behind the goal, beat two ball boys behind the goal and ran out the other side of the goal before flicking the ball into the goalkeeper's hands and running back to outside right. The crowd rose to a man and at the end of the game, former Rangers player, Davie Wilson of Dundee United, was waiting for him. He lifted Wee Jimmy aloft and carried him off, saying that it was the finest performance he had ever seen.'

A statue of Jimmy Johnstone stands outside the front of Celtic Park, alongside those of Jock Stein and Celtic's founder, Brother Walfrid, while at the beginning of the Celtic Way, Billy McNeill's statue holds aloft the European Cup. All of those statues stand as permanent tributes and a reminder to future generations of the contribution made to the Celtic cause.

Perhaps the final word is best left to Jock Stein, who summed up the importance of Jimmy Johnstone to Celtic, and how much the player meant to him when he said, 'People might say I will be best remembered for being in charge of the first British club to win the European Cup or leading Celtic to nine league championships in a row, but I would like to be remembered for keeping the wee man, Jimmy Johnstone, in the game five years longer than he might have been. That is my greatest achievement.'

IN HIS OWN WORDS...

'We had watched videos of Inter Milan – this was the best team in the world twice over. They must've been thinking that we were just turning up to make up the numbers and that's the kind of impression that we got. We were standing in the tunnel and the Italians were standing next to us, all tanned and with the hair gelled back, and they were all looking at us. I had my teeth out, Ronnie had his full set in his bunnet. That's the reason why he used to be quite good down his right-hand side – because he kept his teeth in his bunnet there!

The heat was tremendous. It was eighty degrees or something like that and it felt like it was burning a hole in your head. But that was something we overcame as well because even in the last five minutes we were still taking the game to them.

I was asking Facchetti for his jersey as we walked out on to the pitch because he was *the* player in the side at the time and the Italian national side at the time and I thought it would be good to get his jersey. I had met him before then when were up training and they appeared and I had a photo taken with him and he said in broken English – 'You get the jersey after the match.'

Then the game began, and in the first-half I said to myself, 'When is this team going to start playing?' We made so many chances we couldn't believe it, and before we came out for the second-half, Big Jock said, 'Right, let's go. We're going to win here.' And we all had that same feeling.

It was a tremendous performance, although it wasn't one of the best games that I had ever played or the forward boys like Bobby Lennox and Stevie Chalmers, though Stevie did score a goal. But I think the ones who really excelled themselves were the midfielders and the people at the back, including the two full-backs. But possibly we made it for them because we were taking people into positions and we were leaving that open. But the midfield was tremendous that day – the balls that Bertie and Bobby Murdoch were hitting and playing, they completely controlled it.

Although we were 1-0 down, we knew because of the type of player in the team that we could win. Big Tam and Jim Craig, and the midfield, revelled in it because Inter just fell back and I had a man-to-man situation with Burgnich and Bobby Lennox was with Facchetti and we pushed them more or less back to their eighteen-yard line.

The Celtic fans were amazing. Some of them got mortgaged right up to the hilt or sold anything they had so they could go to the final. But that's Celtic people. They are the greatest people in the world and I'm not just saying that for the sake of saying it. I'm saying it because I mean it, because I love them and they loved us. I believe that there were some of them who never came back. On my fiftieth birthday, I got a postcard from Lisbon and it was from a Celtic fan and he said, 'Jimmy, some of us are still here!' That is the Gospel truth. The rapport that we've got with them is incredible and they love the sincerity that we've got and always will have because they look at that Lisbon Lion team and the fact we took Celtic to the top of the world as a football club.

Even after it we didn't really realise what we had done – we'd won the European Cup and we were the best team in Europe.

I remember feeling numb when the final whistle sounded and all hell broke loose around me. It wasn't the feeling I had expected. Sure, all the boys jumped around and the fans flooded on to the pitch as we raced for the dressing-rooms. But even after I had the cup in my hands, it did not sink in that we were the best in Europe. Throughout the post-match banquet and the flight home I was in a daze. When we touched down in Glasgow I thought there had been a nuclear holocaust. The streets were deserted. But when we hit London Road I could see why. Every Glaswegian seemed to be packed into that little pocket of the city – 60,000 men, women and children were waiting at Parkhead to salute the champions of Europe and we paraded the cup to the people who matter most, the punters.

Alfredo Di Stefano came to watch us in the final and asked if the winners of the game would play in his benefit match and that was outstanding. It was the whole occasion and the whole atmosphere. There were 130,000 in the Bernabeu and we were playing Real Madrid, who were a class act. We literally tore them apart. There were a lot of great individual displays on the night, such as John Fallon. If somebody had seen John that night they would've paid a million pounds for him. He was outstanding. Willie O'Neill fitted in at left-back. He was a great player, very under-rated.

We got a standing ovation at the end of the game. I played out of my skin that night and that will always be in my mind as the best game I've ever played in. Everything just seemed to happen for us, it was great.

After the game we were at the banquet and Di Stefano was up on the stage with Puskas and Gento and Santa Maria and he asked me to come up on to the stage with them. That was a great honour. He was more or less saying that I was sort of in their class and that was an honour because you're talking about some great players there.'

WILLIE WALLACE

LISBOA
25 DE MAIO DE
1967
CELTIC 2-1 INTER
50° CELTIC FC
ANIVERSARIO

WILLIE WALLACE

Even within Celtic's extraordinary 1966/67 season, Willie Wallace's story has an air of fantasy about it. Indeed, there were probably moments at the time when the player must have thought it was all just a dream and that at any moment someone was going to wake up him and drag him back to reality. There are probably moments now when he still feels the same when reflecting on that period in his life.

He was, in effect, the last piece of the Lisbon jigsaw, though when he joined Celtic from Hearts on December 6, 1966, neither he nor his new team-mates would have allowed themselves to dream the impossible dream – that of a European Cup triumph, though they were on the verge of booking their place in the quarter-final of the tournament with the second leg of their second round tie against French side, Nantes, taking place at Celtic Park the night after Wallace's signing. Yet, within six months, the player had won a Scottish Cup medal – scoring both of Celtic's goals in the final – had secured his first league winner's medal, and become a European Cup winner. He was also part of the Celtic team which then beat Real Madrid 1-0 in the Bernabeu Stadium, in Alfredo Di Stefano's testimonial. For good measure, he was also part of the Scotland team which beat the reigning world champions, England, 3-2 at Wembley in April 1967.

It's no wonder then that the player, known to his team-mates as Wispy, said of that time, 'I was hopeful that things would pan out and I would be quite successful at Celtic. But if they said to me that, in my six years here, I would win six league titles, I wouldn't have believed them! It was the pinnacle of my career. I look back on those first six months with joy and happiness. Nothing else. There is no way you can explain it. Once I was involved in football, obviously my aim was to win what I could, but to think I had won every honour I could in Scottish football, well, that's not a bad career.'

While Wallace had missed out on Celtic's League Cup triumph that season, when they'd defeated Rangers 1-0 at Hampden in October 1966 courtesy of a Bobby Lennox goal, he was already in possession of a winner's medal from that competition, having been part of the Hearts team which lifted the trophy in 1962 with a 1-0 victory over Kilmarnock in the final. His contribution to the rest of Celtic's all-conquering season, however, was significant, with the two goals he scored in the European Cup semi-final first leg win over Dukla Prague as important as his Scottish Cup final double.

From his debut on December 10, 1966, in a 4-2 home win over Motherwell in the league, he would go on to play a total of thirty games that season, scoring twenty-one goals across the league, Scottish Cup and European Cup tournaments. It had proved to be a shrewd acquisition by Jock Stein, buying a player of proven ability and with plenty of experience already garnered at Stenhousemuir, Raith Rovers and Hearts.

His professional career had begun at Stenhousemuir, whom he joined in 1958 from junior side Kilsyth Rangers, and within eighteen months he had moved to Raith Rovers. He scored his first goal against Celtic in a Scottish Cup third round tie at Stark's Park on February 25, 1961, but it was a mere consolation as the Hoops won 4-1 on their way to reaching the final that season, though they would lost to Raith's Fife rivals, Dunfermline Athletic, 2-0 in a replay, with Jock Stein in charge of the Pars. Before the end of that season, however, Wallace had left for Tynecastle, and in his first clash with Celtic in the maroon of Hearts, he scored in a 2-1 home win for his new side in October 1961. Perhaps his most notable scoring feat against Celtic, and certainly one which would have emphasised his ability to Jock Stein, by then in charge of the Hoops, came in a league match on January 29, 1966, when he scored twice in a 3-2 win for Hearts at Tynecastle. It was one of only four league defeats that Celtic would suffer that season as they clinched their first title in twelve years, while Hearts finished a distant seventh. Stein had already worked with the player during his time with the Scotland national squad prior to that.

Wallace played three times against the Hoops the following season – twice in the League Cup sectional stage, and once in the league, with Celtic winning all three matches – but it was just ten days after the last of those games, a 3-0 Celtic home win on November 26, that Jock Stein signed him for £30,000. The player wasn't happy at Hearts, and had been looking for a move away from Tynecastle. There had been interest from clubs in England, most notably Stoke City and Newcastle United, while there were also rumours of interest from Rangers, but it was the Scottish champions who swooped and he made the move from east to west. That transfer also started a debate which has continued over the intervening years amongst Celtic supporters – who, if anyone, was Willie Wallace bought to replace? There is no definitive answer, in the same way that it is impossible to say what the starting XI in Lisbon would have been had Joe McBride stayed fit for the remainder of that season.

Of course, there is the butterfly effect of such speculation; imagine Joe McBride back in the team for the second half of the campaign, and it has an impact on absolutely everything else that happens that season. For Willie Wallace, it's never been a question of his arrival signalling the departure of anyone else. It was simply a shrewd move by Jock Stein to add to an already potent attacking force already at Celtic Park, as he told the *Celtic View*.

'I was never bought to replace anybody. It was never indicated to me that I was coming in to replace anybody. They were just adding to the pool of players. People say they already had Joe McBride, Stevie Chalmers, John Hughes – even Bobby Lennox could play through the middle. Jock bought me because I was an experienced professional and he was just strengthening the squad. Every department of the team scored. I remember we were playing a game in Europe, I think it was in Belgrade, and somebody had written in a newspaper that this was a team that you felt even the goalkeeper might score, which was just about true. It didn't take me long to settle in at Celtic. It was so easy to come and play with good players, and I was part and parcel of the team within a month.'

Wallace made his debut for Celtic on December 10, four days after joining the club, and the Hoops won 4-2, with Stevie Chalmers netting a hat-trick. His first goal for Celtic came in a 6-2 home win over Partick Thistle a week later, when he scored two of the goals. The line-up that day also included Stevie Chalmers, who also scored twice, and Joe McBride, and the three strikers were also in the team which faced Aberdeen on Christmas Eve, though it was Bobby Lennox who scored Celtic's goal in a 1-1 draw. That was also the last game before McBride suffered the knee injury which would effectively rule him out for the remainder of the season, though it wouldn't be until January 14, 1967 that the starting XI that would soon become known as the Lisbon Lions lined up for the first time, beating St Johnstone 4-0 at Muirton Park.

He missed the 3-1 home win over Nantes in the second round of the European Cup, which had taken place just twenty-fours after he joined the club, while bureaucratic red tape meant he wasn't eligible for the quarter-final clash with Vojvodina Novi Sad. He watched the second leg of that tie in the stand at Celtic Park, and the atmosphere in the stadium as Celtic overturned a 1-0 deficit from the first leg in Yugoslavia to win 2-0 on the night, with the winning goal coming in the dying seconds of the match from the head of Billy McNeill, was as thrilling to the new Celtic striker as it was to the estimated 75,000 supporters packed into Paradise, as he later explained in his autobiography, *Heart of a Lion*:

'I had been sitting beside the injured Joe McBride in the stand at Celtic Park to witness the astounding quarter-final against Vojvodina and I thought 'Wispy, this is the place for you'. I wanted a slice of that, believe me. I know all the lads would say the same thing, but the atmosphere generated by our support on those occasions was just breathtaking – quite staggering really.'

It wouldn't be too long before he got to savour that atmosphere himself, when Dukla Prague came calling in the first leg of the semi-final on April 12. He had already gained European experience with Hearts, having played in three Fairs-Cities Cup campaigns, and scored four goals in that time. He quickly got off the mark for Celtic, scoring twice in a 3-1 win over the Czech champions. Those goals proved vital in a game where the teams had traded goals in the first-half – Jimmy Johnstone putting Celtic ahead on the half-hour mark before Dukla equalised on the stroke of half-time through Stanislav Strunc. The first of Wallace's goals came after sixty minutes. A right-footed clearance from Tommy Gemmell on the halfway line deceived the Dukla defence, and from eight yards out, Wallace volleyed the ball into the back of the net to restore Celtic's lead. Just five minutes later, he made it 3-1, though the goal owed much the impudence and ingenuity of Bertie Auld. The Hoops were awarded a free-kick about twenty-three yards from the Dukla goal after a desperate handball from Jan Zlocha. Auld ran up as if he was going to take shot but then, at the last minute, stopped and leant over like he was going to readjust the position of the ball. Instead, he passed it forward into the path of Wallace who, from the edge of the 'D', smashed home an unstoppable shot beyond Ivo Viktor in the Dukla goal. And Wallace could even have grabbed a hat-trick when he steered a Stevie Chalmers cross goalwards from six yards out, but the ball spun up into the air and came back off the crossbar. However, Celtic had a vital two-goal lead and Willie Wallace had scored his first European goals for the club.

Before the second leg in Prague, however, Wallace, along with Celtic team-mates, Ronnie Simpson, Tommy Gemmell and Bobby Lennox, had international commitments to contend with and a game with the Auld Enemy, England, at Wembley on April 15. Alf Ramsay's side were the reigning world champions, having won the World Cup the previous year with a 4-2 extra-time victory over West Germany, at Wembley, and that might well have acted as an extra incentive to the Scottish players, over and above the normal desire to beat their international rivals. Scotland won the game, the 3-2 scoreline perhaps not telling the full story of a dominant display by the Scottish team, with Bobby Lennox among the scorers.

April continued at a hectic pace for Willie Wallace and Celtic, with a hard-fought goal-less draw in Prague sealing a place in the European Cup final. It was an incredible achievement for the club, and one that the player could barely believe had happened within months of his arrival. Celebrations would have been tempered within the squad, however, as they returned home to face a Scottish Cup final on April 29 against Aberdeen. A crowd of 126,102 packed into Hampden for the game, which Celtic dominated. Wallace opened the scoring for the Hoops three minutes before half-time, steering home a Bobby Lennox cross from the edge of the six-yard box. Just four minutes after the break it was 2-0, and once again it was Wallace who scored. This time it was Jimmy Johnstone who was the provider, cutting it back from the byline for Wallace to fire home from eight yards out. It gave Celtic a 2-0 victory and the third piece of silverware that season, added to the League Cup and Glasgow Cup.

Just four days later, Celtic suffered only their second league defeat of the campaign when they lost 3-2 at home to Dundee United for the second time that season. Wallace scored Celtic's second goal of the game, but United returned to Tayside with all three points. The Hoops couldn't afford to wallow in self-pity, however, as they faced a Glasgow derby at Ibrox on May 6. Jock Stein's side knew that a point from the game would secure a second consecutive title. On a pitch made heavy by the overnight deluge of rain which drenched Glasgow, two Jimmy Johnstone goals gave Celtic a 2-2 draw and the point they required. Jock Stein's side were once again the champions and Willie Wallace now had a full set of major domestic honours. The focus for the Celtic squad could turn to May 25 and the impending meeting with Inter Milan in the European Cup final at the Estadio Nacional in Lisbon.

Willie Wallace made his third European appearance for Celtic in the Portuguese capital, and it proved to be a momentous day for both him and the club as they defeated the European aristocrats of Inter Milan 2-1 to lift the European Cup. In the space of six months, since signing for Celtic on December 6, 1966, Wallace had won a league title, the Scottish Cup and the European Cup to go with the League Cup winner's medal he'd previously won with Hearts. It was the most remarkable season for him on a personal basis, in a year when Celtic achieved hitherto unimaginable success.

It was always going to be difficult, if not impossible, to replicate the success of 1966/67, though the following season the team did retain their title, while the League Cup was won again following a 5-3 victory in the final over Dundee, with Wallace scoring the fifth and final goal. Season 1968/69 saw Celtic secure their second domestic treble, although they fell at the quarter-final stage of the European Cup to AC Milan, but the following season the Hoops once again made it all the way to the final of the competition. And in both of those seasons, Willie Wallace was the club's top goalscorer. He played in eight of the nine games on the road to Milan and a meeting with Feyenoord in the San Siro, scoring two goals – against Benfica and Fiorentina respectively, with his goal against the Italian side also his 100th for Celtic. The only game he missed was the second leg of the semi-final against Leeds United at Hampden, having picked up an injury in training ahead of the match, which relegated him to the bench for the tie that was played in front of a European Cup-record crowd of 136,505. His team-mates still completed the job against the English champions, however, but there was to be no repeat of the success they had enjoyed three years previously in the final, as Wallace recalled:

'We'd had to beat Leeds United, who were the English champions at the time, in the European Cup semi-final. I didn't play the game at Hampden – I was on the bench – but I played at Elland Road and they were never in the game. After about five minutes we knew we were never going to lose because we were playing with so much confidence, and we were used to the physical challenge that a team like Leeds would give you. We were beaten in the final by a good side in Feyenoord, but when you lose you don't think about it much afterwards – if we'd got a replay, it would have been a different ball game. I always think the second-best achievement for the club was in getting to the 1970 final, and to do that we had to beat some of the best teams in Europe to get there.'

The following season would be Willie Wallace's last full season with Celtic and he continued to win more medals, with a league and Scottish Cup double procured, although the Hoops fell at the quarter-final stage of the European Cup, this time eliminated by Ajax. He scored twenty-eight goals that season across all competitions, which included a hat-trick against Waterford in the second round of the European Cup.

Europe also provided the platform for Willie Wallace's last goal for Celtic and it came just over a month before he left the club for Crystal Palace in a transfer that also saw John 'Yogi' Hughes move to Selhurst Park. It was the first round, second leg tie against BK 1903 Copenhagen, and the Danish side had shocked Celtic, along with the rest of Europe, by winning the first match 2-1. Natural order was restored in the return game, however, with a 3-0 victory for Celtic courtesy of two Willie Wallace goals and one from Tommy Callaghan.

Wallace opened the scoring on twenty-three minutes, but it was not until eleven minutes from time that Callaghan added a second. The final goal of the night, which would also be Wallace's last for the Hoops, came five minutes from time to ensure that it would be Celtic in the next round of the competition. They would go on to reach the last four that season before losing out on penalties to Inter Milan after both ties finished goalless, but by then Wallace was plying his trade in England.

His last game for Celtic had come on October 2, 1971 in a home league match against St Johnstone, and it wasn't the best way for him to bow out as Celtic lost the match 1-0. Whether Wallace realised at the time that it would be his last game for the club is debatable, and certainly the 38,000 fans who came along to Celtic Park that day would have given the player a rousing farewell in appreciation for his contribution to the cause. He moved to Crystal Palace but returned to Scotland a year later, joining Dumbarton where, in the twilight of his career, he played alongside a youngster who would go on to forge an impressive career of his own in the Hoops – Murdo MacLeod.

Willie Wallace had proved to be a superb signing for Celtic, scoring 134 goals in 232 games, and he joined his fellow Celts at the time – Lennox, Chalmers, Hughes, Johnstone and Murdoch – in surpassing 100 goals in the Hoops. He is the club's twelfth top goalscorer of all-time and can rightly be regarded as a Celtic great.

IN HIS OWN WORDS...

'My move to Celtic came at a time when I was having a lot of problems at Hearts. I was still playing every week but I hadn't been happy there for two years and joining Celtic was the luckiest thing that ever happened to me. I don't think anybody knew what was in front of us. Within six months I had won everything that I could possibly win. Within a couple of weeks of joining Celtic, it was as if I had been there for years. I knew most of the boys and had played with a few of them for Scotland. I actually played alongside Stevie Chalmers with Kirkintilloch Rob Roy in one game back in 1956/57.

The Scottish Cup final against Aberdeen was memorable for me. I was still the new boy on the block, so to score the two goals which won the cup was great, and it was the first time I'd won the Scottish Cup, although I'd scored two in the European Cup semi-final against Dukla Prague. The Dukla Prague game was my first game in the European Cup for Celtic. I had played a lot of games with Hearts in Europe, but in the Fair-Cities or the Cup-Winners' Cup, so playing in Europe wasn't something new for me, but scoring those two goals took a lot of weight off my shoulders and the fact that I'd contributed to get to the final of the European Cup was important.

We went to Lisbon not knowing who was playing, and we didn't know until a couple of days before the game. Everybody went there hoping they'd be playing but once you were in, it was something different. It was unique going on that field, walking beside all these big handsome Italians and there was us. Some people were saying that we were just there for the ride, but I think that was one of the best games we played that year. I don't think we had played much better at any other time in the season

Inter Milan were all experienced European players, but the likes of Facchetti, the left-back, just couldn't handle Jinky. That day we outplayed them in every department and I think the Inter players would even say the same. It was a shock for them because, after the game, they couldn't believe that they'd been beaten. It was a victory for football and even the Italian press thought the same. They had watched this stereotypical football for so long and they were happy to get a change from that, but it was the best thing for football, particularly with a team like Inter Milan who won the European Cup twice before then by playing that style of football, but the success of Celtic that night changed football for the better.

I'm glad to say that I had a hand, quite literally, in Big Tommy's equaliser in Lisbon. I took the throw-in that moved the ball around the field before finishing past the redoubtable Sarti. I recall I was going to throw it into the penalty box but their giant defender Giacinto Facchetti blocked my view. Big Jock used to hammer it into us to play the ball into the opposing team's box because you couldn't be offside at a throw-in. But Facchetti prevented that and I actually threw it back to Big Tommy. I thought if nothing else, it would be better to keep possession and from that came our leveller.

I felt the team were very relaxed and confident during our warm-up before the kick-off. When the referee called together Armando Picchi and Billy McNeill, the team captains, for the coin toss, I experienced a bit of nervous tension but was ready to go. Then I had my first touch of the ball and the tensions disappeared – no fumbles or mistakes – and, along with the rest of the team, I settled down quickly. What did surprise me was the apparent lack of real urgency from the opposition. Inter Milan appeared to be waiting for something to happen.

We were playing well and mounted a few good attacks on the Inter goal. Jinky Johnstone headed the ball at goal, which was unusual for him, and Tommy Gemmell had a strong shot which just cleared the crossbar. I had what I thought was a good, strong shot but Inter's goalkeeper Sarti plucked it from just below the bar as if it was a back-pass.

In the first few minutes, we had most of the play and were creating chances but, in one of the few attacks by Inter, Jim Craig brought down Renato Cappellini. Inter were awarded a penalty kick and Sandro Mazzola scored. This was gut-wrenching but the team pulled together strongly and were soon attacking again, in the fashion which was Celtic's trademark at that time. However, Inter's goal kept them in front right up to half-time.

The half-time team talk from the Boss was short and simple: Keep playing as we were and we would certainly score. Our plan up front was to push Inter's back four into their own box and create chances from outside the box for Bertie Auld and Bobby Murdoch.

The longer the second half went, the Inter players seemed to be tiring and they were finding it difficult to cross the halfway line or even get out of their own penalty box. There was one incident midway through the second half where I chased the ball to just outside the goalpost, almost on the dead-ball line, beat Sarti and another Inter defender and slipped the ball between them.

I was just about to roll the ball into the net when Sarti grabbed both of my legs and held on to them, pulling me down. To my amazement, the referee waved 'play on'. I questioned his decision and he replied that he hadn't had a clear view so he couldn't give a penalty!

Looking at replays of the game, it was a 'dead cert' penalty and if the referee or his linesman couldn't have seen that, then white sticks should have been issued as part of their gear. The incident was extremely disheartening – but I realised there and then that we would have to score goals that couldn't possibly be disputed.

As things turned out, it wasn't long until we scored a goal that was not only indisputable but was one of the best goals I saw throughout my career. Tommy Gemmell ran on to a good cut-back from Jim Craig just outside the box and hit it hard and sweetly into the top right-hand corner of Sarti's net. What a feeling! Now we had them and the Inter players were looking dejected and their heads had dropped. Not long after Tommy's goal, Stevie Chalmers glided home a shot and made the score 2–1 in our favour.

The initial shot was from outside the box, so the Boss's tactics worked to a tee. After that, we went on to change the play a bit by keeping the ball as much as possible. The minutes dragged out like hours until, finally, the referee blew the full-time whistle.

After the game it was chaotic. I didn't know much about what was going on because I was surrounded by guys who were trying to get my shorts, shirt and socks, so all I wanted to do was really get somewhere I felt safe. When I finished up in the dressing-room, I had no idea that Billy had gone to get the cup. It would've been nice to go and get the presentation of the cup but the fact of winning it alone was something that was unimaginable for me nine months before so it wasn't too much of a disappointment.

If somebody had told me when I was a wee boy in Kirkintilloch in the early 1940s that I was going to do what I did in 1967, I'd have thought they were joking. It still gives me a bit of awe to think about the life I've had and what I've done. Those forty-three days were special but it had me taken a lot of years and a lot of hard work to get there. And then, in June we played in Alfredo Di Stefano's testimonial and I was glad to play in that game because Di Stefano was my hero. So to play in his benefit match was the climax of everything that had happened in those forty-three days. And Real Madrid really wanted to beat us that night because we were the champions of Europe.

To play in two European Cup finals is something that still makes me proud, and we achieved a lot of things at Celtic over a good few seasons. I never played a season here when we didn't win the league, which is quite a good record, and there are a lot of the boys who are in the same position. The attitude at the club was that we didn't worry about other teams. We were only concerned with how we played and if we took care of that, then we'd win our matches. And there was a great camaraderie amongst all the players. It was a phenomenal time here and it shows how good we were when you look at our achievements. The eleven players from that night will never be forgotten. The Lisbon Lions will be around forever because of the way it happened – all Scots, all born within a thirty-mile radius of Celtic Park, and the way we won it, playing attacking football, which was a breath of fresh air after all the defensive football that had gone on before.'

JOHN FALLON

JOHN FALLON

The famed Celtic support wrapped in green and white in the stands and on the terraces of football grounds throughout Scotland and Europe have become synonymous with the men adorned in green and white on the pitch, so much so that they are the archetypal twelfth man so oft revered and written about in the annals of the club's history. And, it could be argued, that in the evening of the club's biggest ever game, that legendary twelfth man would be needed in vocal support as he had never been needed before. But Celtic had another twelfth man that glorious evening as in the pre-substitute days, a back-up goalkeeper was allowed on the bench for the first time in a European Cup final, and as the twelfth man term has become one and the same as the devoted and unfaltering backing of the men on the pitch, it's more than appropriate that the man on the bench that night would bleed green and white if you cut him.

John Fallon was Celtic's twelfth man that historic night in Lisbon and if John Fallon had been in the employ of any other club in 1967, he would still have been in Lisbon waving a Celtic scarf rather than on the bench wearing a goalkeeper's top. When John Fallon joined Celtic on December 11, 1958, he fulfilled a lifelong dream, signing for the club he had supported passionately as a boy. He joined as an eighteen-year-old and was farmed out to Fauldhouse United and made the breakthrough from Jock Stein's coaching system when regular keeper Frank Haffey was injured at work.

Fallon made his debut for the first team in a league game against Clyde at Celtic Park on September, 26, 1959 shortly after his nineteenth birthday. Following that, he made fleeting appearances while Haffey held the gloves but by November, 1963 he had made the No.1 spot his own until the arrival of Ronnie Simpson. The Blantyre-born goalkeeper was understudy to Ronnie Simpson in the all-conquering season of 1966/67 and was one of the first on the pitch at Lisbon to celebrate when the final whistle sounded. Fallon later took over from Simpson and went on to play 184 first-team games, in many ways epitomising the passion and enthusiasm of the Celtic support.

Among his greatest performances was an inspirational display in a 0-0 draw with AC Milan at the San Siro in 1969 amid a heavy blizzard and also in the victory over Real Madrid in Alfredo Di Stefano's Testimonial two years previously. Fallon is also credited with a leading role in the 1969 League Cup final win over St Johnstone, with some commentators stating that his two saves near the end of the game effectively handed

Celtic the cup. However, on May 25, 1967, if an injury to Ronnie Simpson meant he was called into the fray, he wouldn't have been thrown in at the deep end as he had previously garnered European experience playing as the last man behind the Hoops.

Indeed, he was involved when Celtic dipped their toes into continental waters for the very first time but he travelled to Valencia for the Hoops' game in Spain as no more than a tourist – or so he thought. Celtic travelled out for the game in the last week of September, 1962 with players and supports alike presuming that Frank Haffey would be between the sticks, as Jimmy McGrory's No.1 had played in all ten league and League Cup games prior to the club's first game in European history. He had also played in every game from September two years previously apart from six League Cup ties and two league games in which Frank Connor stepped up to the mark. All of this meant John Fallon hadn't played a first-team game for two years almost to the day, his last being a 0-0 draw at home against Aberdeen on September 24, 1960. That was part of a seven-game run while Haffey was injured and that came eight months after he ended his initial eleven-game run following his debut in 1959. From lazing by the pool and thinking about cooling off, he literally was thrown in at the deep end when he expected it the least.

The man himself later recalled: 'A couple of hours before the game I didn't even know I was playing. I was sitting at the side of the pool enjoying myself and wee Doc Fitzsimmons came and said to me 'What you doing here? You're playing tonight'. I was told that big Frank Haffey had taken an asthma attack or had a stomach bug and that I was in the team. That was the first I heard of it. I got thrown in again. Quite a few times, I got thrown in at the last minute but that was just part and parcel of being a professional footballer. Your mind has got to be set there and then and be ready for anything thrown up in front of you. But the best thing is you wear the Celtic strip and run out in front of the supporters. It's the greatest feeling in the world.'

Quite literally, John Fallon did wear the Celtic strip as he always wore the Hoops beneath his goalie's top so, therefore would technically be the first keeper to wear the Hoops since Davie Adams, who was the No.1 when the rule insisting that keepers wear a different coloured shirt to the rest of the team was introduced in season 1909/10.

'I always put the Hoops first before I put the goalkeeper's top on," Fallon said. 'I always wanted to play in the all-green every game. If you see some of the old photos, you will see that I had the green strip, green shorts and sometimes, green socks. I was one of the first Celtic goalkeepers to start it. I said to Bob Rooney one day to give me the green strip and it seemed to stick if I was playing. Ronnie Simpson would maybe wear the yellow but I would always wear the green. After I left Celtic I was playing for Motherwell against Rangers and I was wearing a green jersey, yellow shorts and white socks, so you could imagine the abuse I was getting from both sets of fans!'

So it was John Fallon who stepped in behind Dunky MacKay as the captain led the Celts out for their first European clash but after the 4-2 defeat, it was Haffey who was back in goal for the visit to Raith Rovers the following Saturday, the return leg against Valencia, and, indeed, the rest of the season. In fact, it wasn't until November 16, 1963 and a 1-1 draw with Hibernian at Easter Road, with Ronnie Simpson in goal for the Edinburgh side, that Fallon became the No.1 automatic choice, a position he held until, ironically, an away European match in Spain when he was replaced by recent signing, Ronnie Simpson.

On the European front, in 1963/64, Fallon played against Dinamo Zagreb, Slovan Bratislava and MTK Budapest in the European Cup-Winners' Cup and played in Portugal the following season when he took part in both legs of the Inter-Cities Fairs Cup against Leixoes before being ousted for the Barcelona games. So, Fallon wasn't without European experience, a two-legged semi-final included, when he was the only Celt on the bench for the biggest and most important game of the club's history. Today, thanks also to his place on the bench for the 1970 European Cup final against Feyenoord in Milan, he is the only Celtic keeper to be involved in two European finals.

He said, after being a guest at the 2002 UEFA Champions League Cup final at Hampden when Real Madrid beat Bayer Leverkusen 2-1: 'That was the first European Cup final I had seen live in the flesh, apart from the two that I was involved in. I missed the famous final at Hampden in 1960 when Real Madrid beat Eintracht Frankfurt 7-3 because I was on a boat going over to Ireland with Celtic. I didn't know the score until we berthed in Belfast the following morning.'

So, his first experience of a European Cup final was on the bench in Lisbon and the manager ensured that Fallon played a part in a piece of typical Jock Stein one-upmanship regarding that bench. These days a European bench holds enough to rival the crowd at a typical Albion Rovers game, but back in 1967, Fallon was the only player on the bench and although he wasn't part of the action, he did play a vital role in Celtic's first victory of the day – before the first whistle blew.

He said: 'I can remember Lisbon as if it was yesterday and I actually slept alright the night before, me and Ronnie were rooming as keepers and both of us slept alright. I don't know about the supporters though, I don't think they slept at all but there were a few in the team like that as well. Wee Jinky, wee Bobby and big Murdy, they were all hyped up but I think Ronnie and I were different, we just relaxed and conked out. What I remember is that when we came out of the tunnel Big Jock said to me, 'Go and get that bench.' He wanted it because it was nearer the halfway line and I ran up and just sat in the middle of the bench. Of course the Inter Milan boys were all trying to muscle in and I said, politely, 'Naw, naw, naw it's ours,' and the police came and moved them away up to the other side. So we were 1-0 up already, it was a wee bit of brinkmanship from Big Jock and that was my first duty.'

As for the actual game, he had one of the best views in the house and in-your-ear match analysis from none other than Jock Stein himself. Fallon recalled: 'The game went quickly. You don't realise until you see the film how much we were on top or the pressure that we were putting on them. I remember some of the great saves that Sarti made and I was sure he'd never play like that again. When you really count the saves, we should have won by about five or six and, as the film shows, I don't think we would have worried about extra-time. They were down, they were all pointing at each other and we were really up for it so we controlled the proceedings.

'Near the end of the game Big Jock got up from the bench and set off down the track. I think he was just getting away out of the road as the presentation was supposed to take place in the stand opposite from we were sitting and I think everybody will tell you that was our biggest disappointment – not being presented with the trophy because of the fans' exuberance. What was that moat all about? There wasn't even any water in it – if they put water in it then they might have had a chance.

'At the final whistle I just jumped. We all jumped, I remember seeing it in the film, I just ran. I think there's a photo with Bob Rooney running in front of me, I think that was the quickest Bob ever moved. We all started hugging each other and then the invasion started and that was it. After that we all got into the dressing room and we sat waiting to see what was happening, it was a long wait and we were all looking at each other. Then Billy came in with the cup and just put it down on the table. It was a big anti-climax, and then at night what made it worse was that Inter turned up late. I think they were refusing to turn up and we were being messed about, the presentation was a shambles because nobody got a medal. They called big Billy up and, I'll never forget this, they gave him a brown cardboard box, he got his medal and he went round the table handing everybody else one.

'In '67 the arrangements were a bit more low-key than they are now. After the banquet we got back to the hotel and the wives were leaving that night to fly back so we went to the airport and waved cheerio, and then headed back to the hotel to relax. But we got a phone call and Big Jock came in and said right get the boys up, the wives' plane has broken down. So the wives had to be picked up and we had to vacate the rooms so that the wives could use them, so I remember sitting at the poolside with Alex Boden just watching all the champagne corks floating about in the pool. There was champagne everywhere, it was one of those nights. Thinking about it, it was great to win but I think everything went wrong following the final whistle and we didn't get the real feeling.

'We actually felt it more when we got back to Celtic Park. If you watch wee Jinky's video he says he can't remember the supporters until we got to the park but I remember when we hit Glasgow the streets were lined right along all the way. We came along the Gallowgate and then when we go to the park there must have been about 40,000 outside and 60,000 inside and that was a great night.'

When John Fallon left Celtic he didn't move far at all, first Motherwell then Morton and there wasn't much hope of watching champagne corks bobbing about in swimming pools at Fir Park or in Greenock. He would, however, taste champagne on numerous occasions as a fan as he is still as committed a Celtic supporter as he ever has been – and that's saying something.

LISBOA
25 DE MAIO DE
1967
CELTIC 2-1 INTER
50º CELTIC FC
ANIVERSARIO

JOE McBRIDE

JOE McBRIDE

The season of Lisbon was a season of success and one thing in the world of football delivers more success than anything else – goals, and lots of them. Skill is another vital, not to mention tasty ingredient of the recipe for success, but how many times have we seen a skilful team control a game over less imaginative opponents only to see the spoils grasped from their hands by a solitary strike from their seemingly unworthy combatants?

This is the reason why strikers are worth their weight in gold and when a natural born goal-scorer is added to a side already overflowing with skill, not to mention a more than worthy record of bulging the net in any case, that is when the firecrackers of success start popping with abandon. The team that Jock Stein inherited was awash with goal-scoring potential but, with seventy-six league goals scored in their eighth place finish in season 1964/65, there was definite room for improvement.

Still, with Kilmarnock snatching the championship on the last day on goal average over Hearts, the Ayrshire side did put forward the case that their defence played as important a part as the strikers in lifting the title that year. Although Kilmarnock had scored only sixty-two goals (all of the seven teams below them, including Celtic, had scored more goals; Hearts scored ninety), they had lost only thirty-three goals in thirty-four games. Stein would also have to work on tightening up the Celtic defence that shipped fifty-seven league goals that term but the new manager believed that the games thrived on supporters and Celtic supporters, more than most, craved entertainment.

However, all the entertainment in the world would mean little if there was no-one up front to convert that skill into goals but, and this was a big but, where was Stein going to find this magical fountain of the end product? The most likely sources of goals in the then current team were John Hughes, Stevie Chalmers and Bobby Lennox but Stein wanted more, he needed an insurance policy of a proven goal-scorer to add to the attacking options already at his disposal. In the 1960s, that invariably meant scouring Scotland and that's exactly what happened.

With Rangers presumably off the shopping list, Stein also marked off the twelve other teams who had scored more league goals than fourteenth-placed Motherwell and he homed in on their top scorer, Joseph McBride. He had started his goal-scoring spree with St Gerard's Secondary School in his local Govan and, after turning out at Amateur and Junior level, he took his first senior steps with Kilmarnock in season 1956/67 just after his eighteenth birthday and scored twenty-four league goals in fifty-seven games for the Rugby Park club before being tempted south by Wolves.

The striker was only at Molineaux for a short time before moving to Luton Town, but in 1960 he returned to Glasgow and Partick Thistle where his league goal-scoring average upped to over a goal every two games with thirty-one in fifty-nine games. Following Firhill, Fir Park was where he improved even further, scoring fifty-one goals in eighty-eight games. Could he even improve on that? Jock Stein decided that the striker might have a better chance of that in the green and white Hoops of Celtic and, on June 5, 1965, McBride became the new manager's first signing.

Stein had hit the nail right on the head as McBride's prowess in front of goal was the highlight of the season in which Celtic returned to league domination with their first title in twelve long years, indeed he rivalled the legendary and record-breaking Jimmy McGrory in his ratio of more goals than games in the league, McBride scored thirty-three goals in only thirty-one games. In fact, he struck forty-three times in all competitions and that included four hat-tricks (two of them in successive home league games against Falkirk and Dundee) and, rather importantly, two goals in successive European Cup-Winners' Cup games. The reason for the importance of that continental experience was that the club were entering the European Cup for the first time ever as McBride added a 1965/66 title medal to the League Cup gong he had won earlier that season.

Not only was he Celtic's top goal-scorer that term, but he shared the country's top league scoring with a certain Alex Ferguson of Dunfermline Athletic who also hit thirty-one of his side's ninety-four league goals. Although the Fife side were second in the goal-scoring stakes, they were fourth in the league and it was Jock Stein's gentle tweaking of both defence and attack that delivered Celtic's first title since 1954, with a player that he sold from Hibernian and a player he would later sell to Hibernian, helping make the difference.

Ronnie Simpson was the arrival from Easter Road in goal and when Celtic lost fifty-seven goals the previous season he barely played while, in season 1965/66 he helped keep goals against down to thirty – beating previous title-holders Kilmarnock's tally of thirty-three. In 1964/65, Celtic scored seventy-six league goals while in Joe McBride's first term they hit 106. So McBride's thirty-one goals were basically the difference between seventy-six and 106 – or the difference between finishing eighth and finishing champions!

Now came the big season, could the club improve on the league and League Cup tally of the previous season? Could McBride and the team as a whole improve on the forty-three and 166 goals respectively? However, the big question was – how far would the club have to go in the European Cup for it to be an improvement on narrowly missing out to Liverpool in the semi-final of the 1965/66 Cup-Winners' Cup? Would Stein add to the team? Would he need to? The early signs provided a negative answer to both questions as Joe McBride and his Celtic team-mates returned from their North American trip on the front foot and McBride scored Celtic's first goal of their greatest ever season.

Indeed, he scored both goals in the 2-0 away win over Hearts in the League Cup on August 13, 1966 and would score an amazing thirteen in the six sectional games played before the league season kicked-off (the thirteen goals actually arrived in five games as the away game against St Mirren was the only one in which he didn't score). McBride also scored in Celtic's first league game as champions, a 3-0 win over Clyde at Shawfield in a month that would start with a League Cup win, carry on with three opening league wins and end with the club's first ever European Cup tie.

That game came against FC Zurich was played at Celtic Park on September 28 and while the honour of scoring the Hoops' first European Cup goal fell to Tommy Gemmell, it was Joe McBride who tied the knot on Celtic's first victory with the second goal in the sixty-ninth minute. A few days later he scored Celtic's last two goals in a 6-1 win over St Johnstone (while failing to convert a penalty) but Jock Stein rested him for the away tie against Zurich on October 5, although McBride returned with four goals against Hibernian just three days later.

Those goals were the first of seventeen scored before Celtic's next European tie on November 30 against Nantes in France. No fewer than fourteen of those goals came on league duty – one of them a dramatic eighty-ninth-minute penalty to give Celtic an amazing 5-4 win over Dunfermline at East End Park. It was the sort of goal-scoring sequence and form that had Celtic's greatest ever goal-scorer, Jimmy McGrory choose McBride as the best Hoops striker he had ever seen, saying: 'It was due to injuries that Joe only had a few seasons at Celtic. If he had been allowed a full career I am sure he would have become one of the all-time great goal-scorers. He was a tremendous header of the ball and could take a half-chance on the ground. And his heart was in the right place.'

Joe McBride said: 'It was a fantastic compliment, particularly from someone like Mr McGrory. He obviously scored more goals than anyone else in the club's history and I'm proud to say that, in goals to games, I'm second only to him. My record's better even than Henrik Larsson's and what a player he was!'

McBride's other pre-Nantes goals included one in the 2-0 League Cup semi-final against Airdrie and two in the 4-0 win over Queen's Park at the same stage of the

Glasgow Cup, and McBride picked up two more winner's medals in the finals of both competitions as Celtic marked up trophies number one and two in their clean sweep to beat all clean sweeps. Back on the European front, Nantes opened the scoring in the sixteenth minute but McBride's twenty-fourth-minute equaliser took the wind out of their sails and the Hoops went on to win 3-1 on the night and 6-2 on aggregate with the striker missing the home tie because of a knee injury. Little did Joe McBride know that the game in France would be his last European action of the campaign.

Returning home, McBride played in a 0-0 draw at Rugby Park and then missed both the Nantes return game and the following 4-2 win over Motherwell. He returned, and scored, in a 6-2 home win over Partick Thistle but, sadly, that would prove to be his last goal of the season and his last game at Celtic Park that term. Joe McBride played in a thrilling 1-1 draw with Aberdeen at Pittodrie on Christmas Eve and was then listed as part of a fully fit squad for the visit to Dundee United on Hogmanay.

However, a knee injury in training saw him drop out, to be replaced by John Hughes who was making his first appearance in two months. On the final day of the year, a 3-2 defeat at Tannadice gave Celtic their first defeat of the season, but sidelined Joe McBride would feature no more that term. He recalled of the injury: 'It's the biggest regret of my career. It was a serious injury and I suppose that I can count myself lucky that I did eventually recover from it and had another five or six years playing after the operation. I now know the severity of the operation and if the surgeon, Professor Barnes, had not carried it out it could have turned cancerous.

'He was the man who found a very slight piece of bone that had come out of my kneecap and who also bored five holes into the back of the kneecap in the hope that the bones would grow over the holes. That happened, but it took a whole year at the very highest point of my career. It was as if I had been stopped dead in my tracks, right at the pinnacle. But if he hadn't done what he did, I would never have played again. It was as if my knee was locking and felt as though someone had stuck a knife in my leg and, like I said, it could have had even greater repercussions.'

Despite playing his last game on Christmas Eve, McBride had scored eighteen goals in fourteen league games, fifteen goals in ten League Cup game and two European Cup goals in two games for a McGrory-like record of more than a goal-a-game with thirty-five in twenty-six games. Incredibly, as Celtic took to the field for their final game of the season five months later, McBride was still top of the Celtic scoring charts, head-to-head with Stevie Chalmers on that thirty-five-goal tally.

However, Joe McBride cheered as loudly as any Celtic supporter when Chalmers scored the club's last goal of the season and took his personal tally to thirty-six with the winner in the 2-1 European Cup victory over Inter Milan in Lisbon. Celtic played as a team, won as a team and lost as a team so when Joe McBride cheered that Stevie Chalmers goal in Lisbon he was also cheering every single one of the vital goals he himself had scored in Celtic's most important and greatest ever season.

Speaking of Lisbon he once said: 'Everyone remembers the '66/67 season when I was injured in December, missed the rest of the season, and still finished with all those goals. In the end, those goals were vital because, although that was a fantastic Celtic team, we only won the league by three points. Had it not been for my injury, God knows what I would have finished up on that season. But what people sometimes forget is that, the season before, I scored forty-three goals and the next guy behind me was Stevie Chalmers on thirty-seven. Again, it was tight that season – we only won the league by two points over Rangers – so I feel proud that it was my goals that got us into the European Cup for the '67 season in the first place.'

McBride fought back from the injury and returned to the side but never fully reclaimed his automatic first-team spot and Jock Stein sold him to Hibernian before the striker moved on to Dunfermline and, finally Clyde where he retired in 1972, but the manager fully admitted to the striker years later that he sold him too soon. He still, though, wouldn't have been able to play in Lisbon due to his injury but who would Stein have played up front if McBride was still fit? The myth grew that Willie Wallace was bought because McBride was injured but the Hearts man came in before the latter was out.

So, would Jock Stein have gone for Wallace and McBride up front at the expense of Stevie Chalmers – the man who scored the winning and most famous goal in Celtic's history? McBride, of course, missed out on the final but said of that season: 'I enjoyed it, but after the European Cup final I was sitting crying and, although half of it was joy that we'd won, the other half was absolute sorrow that I hadn't been playing. I knew that I'd done enough to be worthy of a place in that team and it broke my heart not to be involved. But it's typical of Celtic folklore that I've never been forgotten by the fans. The way it is with this club is that grandfathers tell fathers and then fathers tell sons and, because of that, I get so many young people who can't have been alive to see me play coming up and speaking to me. That's fantastic.'

Joe McBride sadly passed away on July 11, 2012 at the age of seventy-four and he was right, Celtic supporters don't forget. And maybe Jock Stein was right as well, and he did sell Joe McBride too soon, but that could only have changed Celtic's history after 1968. It would not have changed what happened in Lisbon on May 25, 1967.

JOHN HUGHES

LISBOA
25 DE MAIO DE
1967
CELTIC 2-1 INTER
50° CELTIC FC
ANIVERSARIO

JOHN HUGHES

Perhaps out of all the 'squad' members of the Lisbon Lions, the men who didn't actually play in the final, it is John Hughes who can feel the most despondent about missing out on being on the Estadio Nacional turf on that sun-kissed evening of May 25, 1967. That's not just because he himself has stated his dejection at missing out on many occasions, but the facts state that he should have been in the running for a place in the final had he been fit.

Of the others, if we look at them logically, there are reasons why it would have been a surprise bonus that they would be in the side. The position of goalkeeper is unique and it was only going to be one or the other so unless Ronnie Simpson was injured, John Fallon would be on the bench. At the other end of the pitch, Joe McBride was definitely out due to his long-term injury while, in other areas of the pitch, Willie O'Neill had breached the thirty-game mark but all had been played before the New Year and Charlie Gallagher had played only seventeen games dotted throughout the season.

Hughes, meanwhile, had also crossed the thirty-game mark but had only missed a handful of games since the start of the year and with five European Cup games, he had made the most continental appearances of the 'squad' players. Added to that, the history books tell us that Hughes was the more 'complete' Celt of the five, and easily eclipsed the others in career appearances both before and after the summit of Lisbon. Indeed, post-Lisbon he also made more Celtic appearances than some of the Lions – Ronnie Simpson, John Clark, Bertie Auld and Stevie Chalmers.

He was one of the quintessential Celts of the 1960s and '70s and it would have been a tough decision to leave him out of the Lisbon side. It was, however, a decision that Jock Stein didn't have to make as injury ensured that John Hughes wouldn't play in Lisbon, indeed, club doctor and former Celtic player, John Fitzsimons advised that he didn't even travel to Portugal. However, Hughes was a dyed-in-the-green-and-white-wool Celtic supporter as well as a player and there was no way on earth he was going to miss the match.

A Coatbridge Bhoy, born on April 3, 1943, Hughes starred for St Augustine's School before blazing a trail with Kirkshaw Amateurs and Junior side, Shotts Bon Accord. It was from there that he made the move to the team had always supported and joined

Celtic on October 3, 1959 at the age of just sixteen. It wouldn't take this towering striker long to make the step up to the first team. Still only seventeen-years-old, he got the call-up on August 13 for the opening game of the 1960/61 season, a League Cup tie against Third Lanark at Celtic Park and the 25,000 crowd saw him open the scoring in the fiftieth minute before Neilly Mochan tied up the 2-0 win.

Although he would later become a valued member of Lisbon squad, Billy McNeill and Stevie Chalmers were the only other Lions on the field that day. A week later, the teenager ran Rangers ragged in the same competition at Ibrox and scored what proved to be the winner in a 3-2 victory for the Hoops, watched by a crowd of 60,000.

He later recalled: 'The funny thing was that I didn't feel any responsibility. I remember we went to Ibrox and they had just signed Dougie Baillie. I gave him a roasting and basically finished his career, although that certainly wasn't intentional. I didn't feel anything. It's only when you start playing you might think this is an important game, but when I was younger, I just felt I was good enough to do anything so it didn't bother me.'

He was to go on and score nearly 200 goals in over 400 appearances but it was his goal tally that told of a career of two halves, as between his first and 100th goals for Celtic, he won no major honours for the club. Between his 100th goal and final strike, his 189th, he won six league titles – all in a row, one Scottish Cup – the 1965 win that kick-started the glorious trophy trail – and four League Cups, the first three successively and the first of those featured two John Hughes penalties in a 2-1 victory over Rangers, watched by a crowd of 107,600.

Celtic were in the midst of a golden era and Hughes was right in the thick of it. From the years of 1965 to 1971, when the forward left the club, Stein's Celtic were unstoppable and Hughes played more often than not. To add to that tally of medals, the Hoops, of course, played in two European Cup finals just three years apart during that time, and he had the misfortune of playing in the one that was lost and being sidelined for the biggest ninety minutes of the club's history.

He was, though, a fixture during the Celtic's golden European years and they were among the highlights of a long Hoops career. He said: 'I loved the European nights, we all did. Half-an-hour before our games kicked off there were 70,000 people in the stadium, all of them singing. The atmosphere on European nights was phenomenal. Then, when we went away from home, it was an adventure. We were all just young boys from Coatbridge and Bellshill and we were all heading off together. The furthest we had been before then was Saltcoats for our holidays! We were just a big bunch of raw laddies. They were the games you looked forward to and loved to play in. Looking back, I enjoyed almost every one of them, especially the ones we won.'

As far as individual performances go, though, there was his glancing header to put Celtic back in the driving seat on aggregate against Leeds United in the 1970 European Cup semi-final at Hampden as 136,505 looked on. However, in domestic terms, the red letter day was a performance against Aberdeen on January 30, 1965 when he borrowed Billy McNeill's sandshoes to play on the icy rock-hard surface and he scored five goals in the 8-0 win.

Hughes was a versatile player able to operate through the middle or on the wing with equal effectiveness and he recalled: 'I actually preferred playing wide because you were getting the ball half-turned a lot of the time. In the middle, your back was to the goals a lot of the time and that didn't suit me either. But early in my career I scored thirty goals in what wasn't the best Celtic team, playing at centre-forward. What people are surprised about is that I am the sixth or seventh highest goal-scorer in Celtic's history. People don't really equate a lot of goals to me, although I got my fair share. But I certainly preferred playing wide as you are side-on and getting the ball all the time, rather than having your back to goal. I was a big guy and so it wasn't easy to turn a lot of the time. So I did prefer playing wide.'

It doesn't, however, rankle with Hughes that the first 100 of his goals for the Hoops delivered nothing in the way of silverware. He said: 'It didn't frustrate me as we didn't really know anything else at that time. When I came in, the team wasn't good anyway, but we could have reached a European final quite easily. We beat MTK Budapest here 3-0 in the European Cup-Winners' Cup semi-final and Bob Kelly told us that we would beat them over there. We beat them here, and then we went out there and played like amateurs. We could have been in a European final in a team that was considered not to be very good. I didn't really think much about it because at that time, that was just what Celtic were. You had no comparisons, if you know what I mean.'

The experience of not one, but two close-run European semi-finals inside a short space of time was clearly eclipsed by the events of season 1966/67 and for Hughes that meant playing in the first nineteen straight matches which included the two European Cup ties against FC Zurich, seven successive league victories with twenty-six goals scored and only six against and all ten League Cup ties, that last of which being the October 29 final against Rangers at Hampden when Bobby Lennox scored the only goal of the game to deliver the first trophy of the season.

However, Hughes was injured at the start of the second half and that led to Stevie Chalmers being the first substitute used in a domestic cup final. Hughes wouldn't be back on the pitch until the last game of 1966 against Dundee United at Tannadice when he replaced fellow Lions 'squad' member, Joe McBride who had succumbed to the injury that would make him miss Lisbon.

Another three league games were missed by Hughes before he made a more realistic return from injury and he was then a regular in the side for ten straight league matches, three Scottish Cup games and both of the European Cup quarter-final legs against Vojvodina, but it was the middle game in the Scottish Cup trio that would see him ruled out of two upcoming finals. It was the Scottish Cup semi-final against a high-flying Clyde side at Hampden which finished 0-0 and nothing of note, apart from Celtic being denied a penalty four minutes from time, seemed to happen. It was on April Fool's Day of all days in that Clyde match that John Hughes took an innocuous kick to the ankle that deprived him of even thinking about a starting berth in Lisbon, or Hampden for that matter. The severity of his ankle knock wasn't immediately obvious, though, and he would feature again that season – most significantly coming on as substitute in the Hampden replay against Clyde and playing in the first leg of the European Cup semi-final, the 3-1 win over Dukla Prague, to help his team-mates get to both of the finals he wouldn't play in.

Ironically, the game that was supposed to mark his original comeback and the game in which he kicked a ball for the final time that term were both against Dundee United and both featured Celtic's only domestic defeats that season, two 3-2 reverses to the Tannadice side. That defeat against United came just days after Celtic had lifted the Scottish Cup, with Willie Wallace scoring both goals in the 2-0 win over Aberdeen watch by 126,102. The problem for Hughes was that he was among the six-figure crowd watching the final.

Time was running out in his bid not to be part of the crowd in Lisbon but, knowing there was no way he'd be risked in the side for what turned out to be the league decider against Rangers, the 2-2 draw at Ibrox, there was only one more chance available – the domestic finale against Kilmarnock on Monday, May 15, the start of the ten-day countdown to Lisbon. However, prior to the visit of the Ayrshire side, the club doctor uttered the words he was dreading to hear. In his own words, Hughes recalled: 'A couple of days before that encounter, Dr Fitzsimons delivered his calamitous news. 'I'm sorry Yogi, there's no way you can play.' Those words will live with me forever.'

He had to keep it secret, though. There was no way Jock Stein was going to give Inter Milan manager, Helenio Herrera, one single clue as to what the Celtic team would, or could be. Even the transfer of back-up centre-half, John Cushley to West Ham was kept under wraps. John Hughes travelled to Lisbon as one of only a handful of people who knew he would be a spectator and not a player for the club's finest hour. Fate decreed that he would play in a European Cup final for Celtic but after the 2-1 extra-time defeat to Feyenoord at the San Siro in 1970, Hughes inwardly felt that Jock Stein secretly blamed him for the defeat having missed a chance to score in extra-time when the game was still poised at 1-1, but, just as the Lions won as a team, the 1970 version lost as a team as well.

Fate also decided that his last game for Celtic was also in the European Cup. It was against BK 1903 Copenhagen in the European Cup on September 29, 1971, with the Hoops 2-1 down from the first leg. Willie Wallace had levelled the tie on aggregate by the time Hughes replaced Bobby Lennox at half-time. Roared on by a 53,000 crowd, Celtic took the game thanks to Tommy Callaghan finding the net and another counter from Wallace for a 4-2 aggregate win.

Both he and fellow Celt, Willie Wallace, moved south to Crystal Palace on the same day, October 19, 1971 and then Hughes teamed up with younger brother, Billy, at Sunderland. He had moved to Roker Park in January of 1973 but was freed at the end of that season and retired from the playing side of the game in October of that year.

His heart was always at Celtic, though, and looking back to those days, he said: 'I don't think that there is another group of players in Celtic's history that get that special attention as well. It perhaps helps that we were all Scots and were born and brought up so close to the stadium. I think, with the finances and the way the game has gone today, that it would take an absolute miracle for that to happen again. We loved the club and the supporters as well, we had a special rapport with the supporters, mainly because we were supporters ourselves.'

LISBOA
25 DE MAIO DE
1967
CELTIC 2-1 INTER
CELTIC FC
50° ANIVERSARIO

CHARLIE GALLAGHER

LISBOA
25 DE MAIO DE
1967
CELTIC 2-1 INTER
50° CELTIC FC
ANIVERSARIO

CHARLIE GALLAGHER

Of the many images and highpoints from Celtic's road to glory when Jock Stein took up the managerial reins, there are two that stand out like shimmering diamonds set in gold amid the gleaming silver that was so evocative of the era. They are, of course, the subject of this very book, lifting the European Cup in 1967 and, maybe not quite so obvious but stated by the players themselves as the seed from which everything else grew, the 3-2 Scottish Cup final win in 1965 over Dunfermline that kick-started the trophy-laden era.

Both of those roads were signposted by Charlie Gallagher and, if it weren't for his input in teaming up with Billy McNeill at crucial points in vital games, the Lisbon, or the Scottish Cup win and, therefore everything that followed, may not have happened at all. We don't know that for sure, of course, but although it could be argued that Charlie Gallagher's Celtic career was winding down while the club itself was in an upward spiral, the Irish internationalist was certainly worth his weight in silver as his pinpoint crosses were as good as an 'Open Sesame' to Jock Stein's hopefuls.

The first came in that Scottish Cup final, a game he nearly never played in because Stein felt that he and Bertie Auld were too similar to play in the same team, especially in such an important game, but both players were to play crucial roles in a match that changed Celtic's history. Jock Stein had steered Celtic through the semi-final and replay against Motherwell, going into the tie knowing that progression would mean meeting one of his former teams in the final as both Hibernian and Dunfermline clashed in the other semi-final. Indeed, the Big Man's last act as manager of Hibs was to put out Rangers in the quarter-final.

Therefore, it was Jimmy McGrory who took Celtic to the semi-final and trophies under the management of the club's greatest ever scorer were, sadly, few and far between. Indeed, the last trophy won by Celtic was the eulogised 7-1 League Cup final victory over Rangers in October 1957 when Charlie Gallagher was a mere sixteen-years-old and still a couple of years away from being a fully-fledged Celt.

He was, along with his cousin, Pat Crerand, part of the Celtic side that lost the Scottish Cup final to Jock Stein's Dunfermline in 1961, so four years later in 1965, was Stein going to deprive him of another winner's medal in the same competition by not selecting him on the day? However, Gallagher did play in the game and although the

Fife side took the lead twice, it was Bertie Auld who equalised twice, the first from a header after a stunning Gallagher twenty-five-yarder came off the bar.

So, as the game progressed and went into the final ten minutes, Celtic minds harked back to 1962 and the last final against Dunfermline which finished all-square and went to a losing replay. Then, in the eighty-first minute, Celtic were awarded a corner when putting the ball over the line was all Jimmy Thomson could do to halt a marauding Bobby Lennox run down the left. It was Gallagher who took the corner. Lennox must have got a shout because he ducked as Billy McNeill came careering in and headed the winning goal that took the Scottish Cup back to Celtic Park for the eighteenth time.

It was, however, the first of no fewer than twenty-three top class medals for McNeill and we can only wonder how many that would have been had Gallagher not sent over such a precise corner kick. Gallagher, like his cousin Crerand, was born into the Irish stronghold of the Gorbals. Like many brought up in that area of Glasgow, he dreamed of one day wearing the Hoops and he had been a Celt for over six years before he won that first trophy.

He added a championship medal and a League Cup gong before the start of the majestic 1966/67 season but he would only make fleeting appearances throughout the term, indeed, his only League Cup appearance was in the very last sectional game against St Mirren, a statistic he shared with fellow Lisbon Lion, Jim Craig. Gallagher did make a small piece of history in Celtic's very first competitive game of the term as, although he wasn't used, he was listed as Celtic's very first substitute in line with the new rule brought in that season, and the game he watched from the bench instead of the stand was the Hoops' 2-0 League Cup win over Hearts at Tynecastle on August 13.

The majority of his eleven league appearances that term came when Bertie Auld was out of the side injured while he would also deputise for John Hughes and Bobby Lennox, and his first appearance of the campaign was a 3-0 home win over Airdrie on October 15. However, despite scoring in consecutive home matches just four days apart against Dundee and Clyde in January, it was probably one of his three Scottish Cup appearances that gave him the most joy – well, domestically at least.

The reason was, he had become the first Scottish-born player to be chosen to play for the Republic of Ireland. The Irish chose him for their game against Turkey in Ankara and, to celebrate the fact, four days before Gallagher's Irish debut, Jock Stein made him captain for the visit of Elgin City in the Scottish Cup and he led the Celts out of the tunnel to a 7-0 win.

He recalled: 'That was one of the nice things Jock did, letting me lead the team out. It must be a big, big honour to be a Celtic captain, but just to lead them out once was nice. One of my proudest moments was when I was capped by the Republic in 1967. I was the first Scottish-born player to play for Ireland. Big Jock made me captain of Celtic the same week and I led the team on to the park that day.

'I particularly enjoyed my second cap which was in Dublin against the team that was running riot in Europe, Czechoslovakia. They were one of the top teams in the world at the time. To do that and be reminded every time I get introduced that I was the first Scots-born player to play for the Republic is something I am quite happy with. Both my parents were Irish and everyone in my family were Irish, so I was quite happy with that.'

Gallagher's only other Scottish Cup appearance that season was in the semi-final replay against Clyde when he helped Celtic to a 2-0 win that meant a possible clean sweep of all five trophies was still on. In the league, he played only five times after the Elgin game, taking his tally to eleven games in which he scored two goals, the aforementioned consecutive games against Dundee and Clyde.

However, it was in the European Cup that Gallagher made the biggest impact in the season to beat all seasons, though he played in only two games throughout the campaign. Even if he had missed the first game and made only one appearance, his bearing on the season, and even the club's history, is unquantifiable. Celtic had already got past the first hurdle of FC Zurich and were protecting a first-leg 3-1 lead over Nantes thanks to goals from Joe McBride, Bobby Lennox and Jimmy Johnstone over in France.

A knee injury to Joe McBride, one that was to recur and have far more serious repercussions for the striker, kept him out of the home tie against Nantes and Charlie Gallagher was drafted in for his first European Cup game. It was not, however, his first foray into European football as he had played in Celtic's very first European ties home and away against Valencia in the precursor of the UEFA Cup and Europa League, the Fairs Cities Cup. He also played in both legs of Celtic's European Cup-Winners' Cup semi final against MTK Budapest the following season.

It was a scenario that irked the player with the club chairman's involvement in team selection and it was a low point of Gallagher's career. He said: 'The most disappointing thing was the time we were 3-0 up against MTK Budapest in the semi-final of the Cup-Winners' Cup, and we went away to Hungary and Bob Kelly wouldn't change the team to make it a more defensive and we lost 4-0. That was a big disappointment at the time as it would have been our first European final and we would have had a chance to win it. That was my biggest regret. We went to Hungary, put out an attacking team and never changed the defence. A lot of Celtic supporters have forgotten about it but some of us who were involved still talk about it. Okay, we won the European Cup and were unlucky in the final of another one but that would have been the first.'

He had also faced the likes of Barcelona in the Fairs Cities Cup of 1964/65 and Dynamo Kyiv in the '65/66 European Cup-Winners' Cup. For his first European Cup outing he came in at inside-right against Nantes but it was outside-right, Jimmy Johnstone who opened the scoring in the thirteenth minute to put Celtic 4-1 ahead on aggregate but the French visitors were not for lying down and Gerard Georgin equalised on the night less than ten minutes before the break. However, Jinky was in inspirational form and created two very similar goals for Stevie Chalmers and Bobby Lennox in the fifty-sixth and seventy-eighth minutes respectively.

The club's next European jaunt was on the other side of the New Year when the Hoops travelled to play the Yugoslavian champions, Vojvodina in Novi Sad which is now part of Serbia. Gallagher, though, wasn't in the side that lost 1-0 on March 1, with the goal from Milan Stanic coming in the sixty-ninth minute – only Celtic's second defeat of the season in all competitions. Both Vojvodina games were played only a week apart and, in between times, the Hoops travelled to Paisley to take on St Mirren, the only side that had left Celtic Park so far that season with anything other than a defeat, thanks to a 1-1 draw on November 5.

With Stevie Chalmers nursing an injury from the game in Yugoslavia three days previously, Gallagher was drafted in and although Celtic won no fewer than nine corners in the first 15 minutes, and partly due to an excellent performance from future Celt, Denis Connaghan in the Love Street goal, it wasn't until the half-hour mark that the Hoops went ahead through Willie Wallace and 1-0 was the half-time score. However, another four goals were added to Celtic's tally, including what is thought to be the first spot-kick taken by new penalty-taker, Tommy Gemmell, and although Bertie Auld came off injured two minutes from the end, Jock Stein, who was never an initial fan of the new substitute rule, kept substitute Jimmy Johnstone on the bench.

And so it was that 75,000, the same number that took in the game in Novi Sad, clicked through the turnstiles on March 8 but this time the vast majority of them were roaring on the Celts. Gallagher remained in the side who wore their all-green change strip for the occasion and in the days running up to the match, Jock Stein had called on the support to make their presence felt for to visit of the Yugoslav side. Added to the obvious skilful threat coming from Vojvodina, there was a psychological barrier of sorts to overcome – Celtic had yet to win a European game at Celtic Park after losing the first leg away.

They had tried and failed against Valencia and Barcelona previously when draws earned at Celtic Park were not enough to earn progress. This would be the same.

Nothing but a win of more than one goal would do for Celtic as a 1-0 victory would see the teams level on aggregate and a play-off in Rotterdam was pencilled in for that eventuality.

Celtic also went into their make-or-break European game, which was refereed by a one-handed Swede, knowing that twenty-four hours earlier, Rangers had sneaked into first place in the league on goal average thanks to a 1-0 win over Airdrie; the Hoops did have a game in hand, though. The match would be a battle of wits between two master tacticians in Jock Stein and Vujadin Boskov and there was one almighty scare in the fifth minute when striker, Vasa Pusibrk missed a great chance from only six yards out and for the remainder of the first half, Celtic battered at the Vojvodina goal relentlessly but to no avail.

After the turnaround, Stein switched the play and just before the hour mark, Miodrag Pantelic, who was a legend in goal, fumbled a Tommy Gemmell cross and Stevie Chalmers was there to score and make it 1-1 on aggregate. For the next half-hour, wave after wave of Celtic attacks bore down on Pantelic's goal but nothing was forthcoming, and nobody really expected anything different when Jimmy Johnstone won a corner in the last minute.

Gallagher took up position just off-field and was about to place a short corner to Johnstone, until he saw two markers being drawn out of the area. In an instant, a split second that forever changed the history of Celtic Football Club, he changed his mind and sent a beautiful delivery into the box and once again, just like two years earlier against Dunfermline at Hampden, Billy McNeill avoided the crowd in the area and rose to head home another winner – this time past the stranded Pantelic.

While Pantelic's team-mates surrounded the referee, his opposite number, Ronnie Simpson, was doing cartwheels in the Celtic penalty area. Just seconds later, as the ball was replaced for kick-off, the final whistle blew. Prague instead of Rotterdam would be Celtic's next European destination on the road to Lisbon.

Gallagher recalled: 'I suppose a goal I am always associated with is the one we scored against Vojvodina. When I go to supporters' clubs now and it's a Question and Answer session, they always say they remember me famously for taking the corner kick in the cup final against Dunfermline and also against Vojvodina when Billy McNeill scored the header. That goal led to the club winning the European Cup and a new era for Celtic.'

He also revealed that Jock Stein actually didn't spend a lot of time rehearsing corner-kicks. Gallagher said: 'There wasn't so much done on corner-kicks, but he worked hard on tactics. One of his favourite ones in training was the midfielders getting the ball inside the full-back and to the winger to hit it hard across. That was one of his favourite things in training, playing without defenders. I bet there is not a record of how many goals Chalmers, Lennox and McBride scored from close in. When Jock Stein came and told us all these things, it was simple. They were simple tactics but they worked. And those two goals are always bought up. When I was playing I never thought about it when the goals went in. It just seems to come up in every conversation, particularly when there is a game against Dunfermline in a cup tie. It's nice to have your name mentioned in the paper on a regular basis, through that and other things, and it keeps my grandchildren amused to see my name in the paper every so often.'

Charlie Gallagher's Celtic appearances wound down over the next few seasons and he moved to Dumbarton n 1970 before retiring from the playing side of the game in 1973. He didn't leave the club without playing his part in yet another piece of Celtic history, though. He didn't know it at the time but his last game was against Hamilton Accies in the League Cup quarter-final second leg of September 25, 1968.

Jock Stein was able to field a fringe team thanks to the cushion of a 10-0 first leg score, courtesy of five goals apiece from Stevie Chalmers and Bobby Lennox. The game was won 4-2 for a 14-2 aggregate and in the second half, Jock Stein made a decision that would end one Celtic career and start another. Charlie Gallagher walked off the field for the last time as a Celt, while shaking his hand and walking on for the first time ever was a seventeen-year-old kid named Kenny Dalglish.

LISBOA
25 DE MAIO DE
1967
CELTIC 2-1 INTER
50° CELTIC FC
ANIVERSARIO

WILLIE O'NEILL

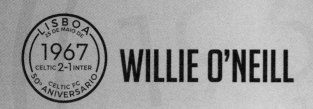

Had Willie O'Neill played in any other era of the club's history, his eighty-two appearances may have gone, not unnoticed, of course, but, unremarked upon in any great detail if not for three vital claims to fame for the dyed-in-the-wool Celtic supporter. They say timing is everything and apart from being a full-back of some repute. Willie O'Neill's time in the Hoops arrived at a period of great change in the game in general and Celtic in particular, and three completely different facets delivered a hat-trick of mementos for the defender – two of them unique among his peers.

One is obvious, and evident by his inclusion in this book that he is a member of the most valued squad in Celtic's entire history and his status as a Lisbon Lion is secured. Even in the capacity of being a squad member who didn't actually play in the final, he is joined by John Fallon, Charlie Gallacher, Joe McBride and John Hughes who all have their own chapters in the club's greatest story. He is one of a group of players from the Lions and beyond who were at the club when Jock Stein took up the managerial reins for more than a decade to deliver the most trophy-laden period in the club's history.

However, Willie O'Neill was also one the band of men who experienced the days before Stein when gentleman Jimmy McGrory didn't rule with a fist of steel when it came to team selection, with the board in general and Robert Kelly in particular having a say in team matters, often at the last minute. So, timing played its part in the first of Willie O'Neill's highpoints as he made his Celtic debut in not just any old game, but in a Scottish Cup final.

He was also playing for the Hoops at a time when the first ever substitutes were allowed, with the introduction of one player on the bench arriving in season 1966/67. Jock Stein was wary of such new changes and would use a substitute only when there was absolutely no chance of an injured player returning to the fray, and it was under those circumstances that Willie O'Neill became the first ever Celtic substitute in a competitive match. That, however, was all still to come when European football, never mind glory, seemed a long way off for the club and possibly nothing more than a pipedream as Willie realised his Bhoyhood ambition when he joined Celtic from St Anthony's on October 12, 1959.

He joined as a left-half after first developing his football skills just down the road from Celtic Park at Sacred Heart School in Bridgeton while also playing for Our Lady of

Fatima Boys' Guild before donning the green and white hoops at St Anthony's. He signed on as an eighteen-year-old at Moorpark but the big Hoops at Celtic weren't slow off the mark when they became aware of his talents and he was still eighteen-years-old when he was snapped up by the only team he ever wanted to play for. There was to be no quick first-team debut for Willie, however, as Bertie Peacock was still starring in the left-half position for the club and although he could also play left-back, Neilly Mochan and later, Jim Kennedy, held down that slot.

However, after converting to full-back, it took him a couple of years to break through into the first team and he was to go on and feature in those remarkable 'firsts' in the Hoops. Not many players make their debuts in a cup final but that's exactly what happened to the twenty-year-old when he was thrust into the cauldron of a Scottish Cup final on April, 26, 1961. The game was, in fact, the replay following a 0-0 draw four days earlier with 113,328 watching, and he replaced Jim Kennedy and took to the field in the Hoops for the first time in front of a crowd of 87,866. Celtic lost that replay 2-0, though the debut Bhoy never let anyone down in that match, but it was to a Dunfermline Athletic side managed by Jock Stein and once the Big Man returned to Celtic Park, he would be instrumental in Willie O'Neill racking up another couple of Celtic firsts.

However, before that, aside from playing in the final two league games following that Hampden debut, Willie O'Neill dropped back into the reserves until season 1962/63 when he played in sixteen games but that would be his highest seasonal tally until the glory campaign of 1966/67 when he took part in thirty-two games. That tally would only have been thirty-one had it not been for another of those 'firsts', for it was on September 3, 1966 in a League Cup sectional 1-0 win over St Mirren at Love Street, that Willie O'Neill became Celtic's first ever substitute.

Bobby Murdoch had put Celtic ahead in the fifty-third minute but in the sixth-fifth minute Jimmy Johnstone suffered slight concussion and had to be talked into coming off by Neilly Mochan. Jock Stein moved Tommy Gemmell up to the attack on the left wing and Willie O'Neill replaced his great friend, Jinky, indirectly by moving into the left-back berth vacated by Gemmell. Charlie Gallacher was actually the first named but unused sub a few weeks earlier in another League Cup tie against Hearts but Jock Stein had reacted to the new rule by saying: 'We will certainly be prepared to carry on with ten men for a short period in certain circumstances. We have got to make allowance for the possibility of a player making a good and quick recovery from injury. If I have selected one of my first-team pool to do a particular job in a certain match, he is No.1 for the task – the substitute is only second best. So we shall try to have an injured first-choice back on the field as soon as possible. Remember that one substitute only is allowed.'

The day after that St Mirren game, Jock Stein flew out to Switzerland to spy on FC Zurich and that led to another first for O'Neill when he was named in the starting XI for

Celtic first ever European Cup tie. That first sub appearance also ensured that O'Neill played in every single one of Celtic's League Cup games that season, which included his pivotal part in the final against Rangers on October 29. He appeared from nowhere to clear a sure-fire Rangers 'goal' off the line in the final that Celtic won 1-0. So his clearance was crucial in lifting the first trophy of Celtic's clean-sweep that season, and a week later he played in another winning final as the second of the five trophies, the Glasgow Cup, was lifted.

Following his appearance in Celtic's opening European Cup game, the 2-0 home win over Swiss side, FC Zurich, Willie also played in the 3-0 return leg win in Switzerland for the 5-0 aggregate victory. He also played in the two legs against French side Nantes in the next round, taking his European tally for that season to four games to add to his earlier continental matches – both games against Valencia in season 1962/63 and the home 0-0 draw with Barcelona in 1964/65. Following the Nantes games, Willie played in the four remaining league games of that calendar year as the Celts beat Motherwell 4-2 at home, Partick Thistle 6-2 away, then drew 1-1 with Aberdeen at Pittodrie before experiencing their first defeat of the season – a 3-2 loss to Dundee United at Tannadice on the very last day of 1966.

However, there would be no more European football for Willie O'Neill as, by the turn of the year, following the Hogmanay defeat to Dundee United, Jock Stein had decided on the full-back pairing of Tommy Gemmell and Jim Craig and, indeed, O'Neill would play only once more that season in a 3-2 home league win over Dunfermline on March 18 when Jim Craig dropped out through injury. Tommy Gemmell moved to right-back, with O'Neill slotting into his usual left-back berth as the 41,000 who took in the game meant that Celtic Park had broken the one-million spectator barrier for that season.

Two days later, though, when Celtic hosted Falkirk on a Monday night, Jim Craig was back in the side. At the start of the season, Stein had been ruminating over tweaking the defence and ahead of a League Cup tie against Clyde in August, he said: 'Bobby Lennox will be back in the side tonight and somebody else can have a well-deserved rest. I think we shall give Jim Craig his first game in the big team this season at right-back and switch Tommy Gemmell to left-back in place of Willie O'Neill.'

As it happened, the backline remained the same for that 3-1 win at Shawfield. However, a few days later Tommy Gemmell was at left-back while Jim Craig came in at right-back for the first time that season, although O'Neill would still have a say in twenty-five minutes of the match, for that was the September 3 game at Love Street when he became the club's first ever substitute. The full-back berths were up for grabs at the start of that season as, while Tommy Gemmell's performances over the past few seasons made him a stick-on at either left or right sides the field, Jock Stein hadn't yet decide on who was his preferred option to play opposite him.

Ian Young had held the right-back berth for the best part of two seasons but Jim Craig was beginning to edge him out while Willie O'Neill hadn't featured at all during season 1965/66. However, Craig had opted out of the close-season tour of North America that did so much to bond the Lions to concentrate on his progress as a dental student at Glasgow University. Young and O'Neill were on the tour, though, and it was on the first game of the trip, a 10-1 win over Bermuda that being a substitute, although this time in a non-competitive capacity, was to have a bearing on the career of Willie O'Neill.

Despite only leaving from Abottsinch Airport the previous day, Celtic sauntered to the double-figures win on May 12 and even had Tommy Gemmell playing at centre-forward in the match as an 'experiment' – he managed to score two of the goals. For the second half, though, O'Neill, who hadn't played a first-team game since April of the previous year, replaced Young who had started the match. Young would start only one more game on the tour and, for the start of the 1966/67 season, Jock Stein had decided on his full-back pairing of Tommy Gemmell and Willie O'Neill.

Jim Craig had gambled on fighting back to regain his place after opting out of the summer tour, a slot in the team he may have thought was reasonably safe as, even though Gemmell slotted into the role seamlessly, there was no doubt that he was even more formidable on the left flank, but Jock Stein had decided to do what future Scotland managers would similarly do years later with Danny McGrain, and that was switch one full-back to accommodate somebody else. And so, Gemmell started the season at right-back while Willie O'Neill slotted in to his natural left-back position and Celtic's unbeaten run began.

That run started on August 13 with the 2-0 League Cup opener against Hearts and took in ten games in that tournament (all wins), three in the Glasgow Cup (all wins), four in the European Cup (all wins) and sixteen in the league (three drawn games) and Willie O'Neill played in all thirty-three games. He also played in that aforementioned last game of the calendar year which was Celtic's first defeat of the season and their first league defeat for ten months since a freak 1-0 loss at Stirling Albion in February.

Whether it was that Tannadice result which prompted Jock Stein to make the change or whether it had been in his mind for some time regardless of that score, we will never know. But what we do know is that in Celtic's next game, a 5-1 home win over Dundee on January 7, Tommy Gemmell moved back to his preferred left-back berth in his ninety-eight consecutive game for the Hoops and Jim Craig was back in at right-back. And that, barring that one game on March 18, was the way it would remain until May 25 in Lisbon and beyond.

Willie, or 'Pumper' as he was known, reverted to being a squad player once more, a much-valued squad player. He got his nickname because he sat beside and worked the pump in the team bath and he was a vital cog in the fantastic team spirit that prevailed in the Celtic dressing room, none more so than when he was keeping Jimmy Johnstone's mind occupied during Jinky's dreaded flying trips with Celtic. Their close friendship got stronger over the years as did O'Neill's standing with the fans when he played mine host at Baird's Bar, but he sadly passed away on April 28, 2011. In all, he played eighty-two games for Celtic before joining Carlisle United in 1969 where injury forced him to retire in 1971, but there is no doubt where his heart lay and he will be forever known as Willie O'Neill of Celtic – Lisbon Lion.

LISBOA
25 DE MAIO DE
1967
CELTIC 2-1 INTER
CELTIC FC
50º ANIVERSARIO

JOCK STEIN

JOCK STEIN

The course of Celtic's history has been shaped by many people, both on and off the field, and there is a litany of players whose contribution to the many successes enjoyed down through the years continues to be treasured and celebrated. Some enjoy an elevated status amongst supporters due to their achievements, and rightly so – there is a special group revered and remembered within the pages of this very book, after all – although every player who has ever had the good fortune to pull on a Celtic jersey is worthy of appreciation. However, there have also been a few key characters without whose influence the Celtic story would undoubtedly have been very different and the fabric and fortunes of the club unrecognisable from the worldwide institution that is Celtic Football Club today.

Brother Walfrid, as our founding father, is one such figure. His was the first statue to be erected outside the front of Celtic Park in recognition of his vision in wanting to form a football club in late nineteenth century Glasgow as a means of tackling the abject poverty suffered by his parishioners, and of his drive, determination and focus in ensuring not only that this happened, but that his club would take root and thrive in the East End of the city. In this regard, Willie Maley was a key figure in establishing the club as the premier football force in the country; David Potter's excellent biography declares Maley as 'the man who made Celtic', and there would be few who could argue with that assertion. He was a towering figure at the club in the first fifty years of its existence, moulding successive Celtic teams into ones that won leagues and cups; he did, as the fans now celebrate in song, 'bring some great names to the game'. Celtic's reputation as a club who played attacking football, and who aimed to develop young players through its own ranks, was forged by Willie Maley.

In modern times, where would Celtic be without Fergus McCann? Having moved from Scotland to North America, where he made his fortune as a successful businessman, he returned home in March 1994, stepping in to save the club when it was perilously close to financial Armageddon which would have seen it go out of business. From the moment he took over, ending a near perfect line of familial control of the club amongst a select few going back to the early days of Celtic, McCann began the process of re-establishing Celtic as the pre-eminent force in Scottish football and restoring its reputation on the European stage. That has been achieved, with the 60,000-capacity all-seater stadium subsequently built following the successful takeover in '94 a monument to Fergus McCann's impact on the club and his vision for its future.

Joining these Celtic giants, and standing shoulder to shoulder with them in terms of influence and importance to the club, is Jock Stein. He had an impact on the team when he joined as a player in December 1951, particularly during the 1953/54 season when, following the surprise success in winning the Coronation Cup, the club went on to win the league and Scottish Cup double at the end of that season. There were players in that Celtic team with more ability – the likes of Charlie Tully, Willie Fernie and Bobby Collins – but few possessed more leadership qualities than Stein, something that his team-mate, Sean Fallon, immediately identified, suggesting that Stein step into the captain's role when he suffered an injury midway through the previous campaign. The respective roles would later be reversed when the Irishman was Stein's assistant in the dugout at Celtic Park, a partnership as successful as any in football.

Jock Stein's playing career began in 1938 as a sixteen-year-old with junior side, Blantyre Vics – Billy McNeill would later be farmed out there after he signed for Celtic in 1957, while chairman Robert Kelly had also previously played for the club – but within four years, Stein had joined Albion Rovers, and he was part of the Rovers side which gained promotion to the top flight of Scottish football for the 1948/49 season. It was a short-lived sojourn, with the Coatbridge side relegated at the end of that season, having gained just eight points from thirty games. One of those points came at Cliftonhill in their first meeting of the campaign against Celtic. The match ended 3-3, with Rovers scoring twice in the last ten minutes to gain a point. After one more season with the club, Stein was on his way to Wales, responding to an advert by Llanelli which stated that the club was looking for 'players of proven ability. Transfer fees no detriment...only top players need apply.'

Throughout his career in Scotland, Stein had combined his football career with that of his job as a miner, and although he was switching to non-league football in the mining heartland of Wales, he was still paid enough to be able to give up mining and become a full-time footballer. However, while he and his family stayed in Llanelli, they'd kept up the rent on their council house back in Hamilton, and news reached them of a burglary at the house. A second break-in was too much for his wife, Jean, so Stein started to think about moving back to Scotland. The legend goes that Stein turned up to impart the bad news to his chairman that he wanted to go back home when the Welshman stopped the player in his tracks to tell him that Celtic wanted him.

This was by no means a dream move, though. Celtic needed short-term cover in defence as well as an old head to influence the younger players in the reserve side. Celtic assistant trainer Jimmy Gribben remembered 'something' about Stein and for the princely sum of £1,300, the Hoops believed they'd secured a temporary defensive stop-gap, while the player himself hoped his security problem at home would be over. By then twenty-nine, Stein was originally a fourth-choice centre-half, but when Jimmy Mallan, Alec Boden and Johnny McGrory were all sidelined with injury, he stepped into the Celtic first-team and never really left it again.

On August 31, 1955, however, Jock Stein would pick up an ankle injury that was to effectively end his playing career. It was ten minutes from half-time in a League Cup sectional match at Celtic Park against Rangers. In that pre-substitutes era, he was forced to go to outside-right, with Bobby Evans slotting into the centre-half role, and Celtic suffered a dismal 4-0 defeat, with three of those goals coming in the second-half. By now, Stein was also coaching and he became the club's reserve coach, which put him into contact with some of the talented young players coming through the ranks at the club, including the likes of Bertie Auld, Billy McNeill, John Clark and Bobby Murdoch. Crucially, he also persuaded Celtic to purchase Barrowfield, former home of junior club Bridgeton Waverley, as a training ground, and it would be there that he would later mould a team to conquer Europe.

That injury was naturally a pivotal moment in Stein's own career, and perhaps pushed him into a more prominent coaching role than he would otherwise have contemplated, and another event in 1955 would leave an indelible mark on him and influence his managerial style and his demands on being invited to return to Celtic Park ten years later as manager. The 1955 Scottish Cup final – the first ever to be televised live – saw Celtic take on Clyde at Hampden in front of a crowd of over 106,000. Willie Fernie gave the Hoops a first-half lead and they should have gone on to lift the cup. However, Clyde equalised with just three minutes of the match remaining, and a replay was scheduled for five days later. Despite dominating the first game, Celtic, inexplicably, made a series of changes to the line-up, most notably by dropping Bobby Collins, who had been outstanding in the first game.

It was thought that the physical and competitive nature of his play had not pleased Celtic chairman, Bob Kelly, who selected the team for the replay, with a number of players also played out of position. Clyde won the replay 1-0, and Stein, who had been in the team for both games, noted the negative impact of such boardroom interference; it was something he would never countenance throughout his own managerial career. At the end of that season, the James Kelly Blantyre Celtic Supporters' Club selected Stein as their Player of the Year, in recognition of his contribution and value to the team, while he also acknowledged the deepening bond between player and club in a message to the Celtic Supporters' Association that year, when he stated that, 'I cannot, like other Celts, claim that Celtic was my first love, but I know it will be my last and most enduring…'

The young players at the club – dubbed the 'Kelly Kids' by a local press eager to find the Scottish equivalent of the famed 'Busby Babes' of Manchester United – benefited from working with their new coach, and in particular some of his methods which appeared revolutionary at the time as he got his charges to do most of their training with a football; traditionally, it was only on a matchday that players got to see a ball! And he won his first trophy as a coach/manager in 1958 when Celtic thrashed Rangers 8-2 on aggregate to lift the Reserve Cup, winning the reserve league a year later. However, Stein was keen to forge his own path in football management, and he was appointed boss of Dunfermline Athletic in March 1960, a side who would finish thirteenth in the league that season, four places and four points behind Celtic.

Billy McNeill recalls those early days under the tutelage of the man who would later deliver unprecedented success to Celtic. He said: 'We were all Lanarkshire boys so we used to go and get the bus up at the Gallowgate just round from Parkhead Cross after training because we were all part-time in those days and we trained Tuesdays and Thursdays. We used to walk up the road with Big Jock – he went on the Burnbank bus and the rest of us went on buses that went to Motherwell and to Wishaw, and we weren't allowed to get on a bus unless his came first. We always had to wait with him! I remember Celtic got him a car at that time so we then got a lift from him, and it was good because, not only did we get the benefit of his football knowledge, we got to know him a lot better and we became very friendly with him, so it was a great dismay to me that later on he went to Dunfermline.'

There wouldn't be much of an upturn in the Fife side's league fortunes the following season under their new manager – they finished twelfth in the table – but Stein did manage to steer the club to the Scottish Cup final for the first time in their history. Awaiting them in the final at Hampden on April 22, 1961 was Celtic. That game, in front of a crowd of 113,328, finished goal-less, and four days later the teams met in a replay, this time in front of a crowd of 87,866. Two second-half goals consigned Celtic to yet another major disappointment, while Jock Stein and Dunfermline celebrated their first ever major honour.

The triumph saw an upsurge in the club's confidence, with a fourth-place finish in 1961/62, three points behind the Hoops in third place, while they reached the quarter-final of the European Cup-Winners' Cup before losing 5-3 on aggregate to Ujpest Dozsa of Hungary. The following season, Dunfermline were in the Fairs-Cities Cup, and faced Valencia in the second round of the competition. The Spaniards had seen off Celtic in the first round, beating the Hoops 6-4 on aggregate, but their game against the Pars ended 6-6 on aggregate – Dunfermline had won the home leg 6-2 but lost 4-0 in Spain – and the tie was decided in Valencia's favour when they won a play-off 1-0. While Celtic were taking their first steps into European football, Jock Stein was also garnering valuable experience on that front.

In April 1964, he moved to Easter Road, taking up the managerial position with Hibernian and quickly winning the Summer Cup, but it would be a short-lived tenure as, just eleven months later, he swapped the green and white of the Edinburgh side for the green and white Hoops of Celtic. Jock Stein was back where he belonged. It had appeared that the natural succession line at Celtic would be Sean Fallon to replace Jimmy McGrory, and certainly Jock Stein wouldn't have countenanced either a junior role to his former team-mate, or even a join managerial partnership. He was the boss; that was the case at East End Park and Easter Road, and Celtic Park wouldn't be any different if the club wanted him to take over. There were a couple of hurdles for Celtic chairman, Bob Kelly, to overcome in order for the appointment to be made. One was the fact the club would be appointing its first non-Catholic manager in its history.

Given that there had only ever been three men previously in charge, with Willie Maley accounting for over fifty of the eight-five years, meant that the position wasn't dictated by religion, while both Jimmy McStay and Jimmy McGrory were former players of note. The club was Irish and Catholic in its roots but, unlike others, had always operated an open signing policy since its inception, with Jock Stein just one of many, many examples of non-Catholic players that Celtic signed and who were admired and revered by supporters. Stein, as an ex-player, ticked that box while his religion, ultimately, was not an issue. As Willie Maley himself had famously once said of any Celt, 'It is not his creed, nor his nationality which counts – it's the man himself.'

By far the bigger issue for the Celtic board, and for Robert Kelly in particular, was that Jock Stein would be in total control of all team matters. He had seen first-hand the detrimental effect boardroom interference had had on team matters during his own playing days at the club, and he was not going to accept the status quo if he was in charge. Once that had been agreed upon, Stein's appointment was announced January 31, with the new manager due to take over in the middle of March.

Bertie Auld, who had himself only rejoined Celtic from Birmingham City in January of that year, recalled the significance of the appointment, saying, 'We had a tremendous run in the Scottish Cup before Jock came. He came in for the semi-final (having led Hibs to a quarter-final win over Rangers) when we beat Motherwell and that was the first cup-tie after he'd had taken over. But Jock's first game in charge of Celtic was away to Airdrie on a Wednesday night and we beat them 6-0 and I scored five. His first cup final that he took charge of Celtic was the Scottish Cup final of 1965 when we beat Dunfermline 3-2. I scored two and Billy scored one. After that, Disney couldn't have made a film about it. The most important thing about each and every one of us – Jock brought Celtic supporters into the dressing room. He knew what the Celtic supporters should have had long before and he wanted to give them what they deserved – trophies and entertainment. That's all he kept saying going out of the tunnel – 'Entertain these people. You have the ability or else you wouldn't be there at Celtic Park'. And that's what happened.'

That 1965 Scottish Cup final success has been cited by all the players from that era as being the pivotal moment in changing the fortunes of the club for the better. The victory, too, gave the players a long overdue sense of what it felt like to be winners, while it was very early evidence that they now had a manager able to deliver success in the form of silverware, something which hadn't happened at Celtic since 1957.

Jock Stein later said of his appointment: 'The chance to come to Celtic did arise which naturally is a big, big call to anyone, I had played here, the club wasn't going very well and I just thought – if I can achieve for Celtic what I achieved for Hibs I would be doing a good job for them. I could have gone to England; the reason for me coming here was at that particular time I had a good offer to go to England and I discussed it with the chairman at Celtic at the time and he said out of the blue, 'How would you like to come back?' I didn't think it would work because Celtic had never, I don't think, ever worked with a manager having full control. What I wanted to do was to prove to people I was capable of taking full control, and I came on that basis.

'I was possibly more fortunate than anyone else. I came here when Celtic were in the semi-final of the cup against Motherwell. The team had been in quite a number of finals and semi-finals before that, but we got the breakthrough of winning something, beating Dunfermline in the final. I think that was the key moment when we won the cup that day. On that particular occasion it broke a barrier for lots of players like Stevie Chalmers, Billy McNeill, John Clark, Bertie Auld and Bobby Murdoch. They all had losers' medals, and they possibly felt that once they had reached this peak and got over the peak of winning something, there were other things to be won.'

Suitably buoyed by the Scottish Cup success, Celtic began the 1965/66 season in confident mood, and qualified from their League Cup section, finishing ahead of Motherwell, Dundee and Dundee United. Having finished a lowly eighth in the league the previous season, the aim at the club was for a big improvement, and the first two games saw the Hoops beat Dundee United (4-0) and Clyde (2-1), though their third league fixture was a game at Ibrox, which the home side won 2-1. However, that would be one of only four league defeats that Stein's side would suffer on their way to a first league title in twelve years, scoring 106 goals and conceding just thirty in thirty-four games along the way.

One of the most pivotal games in that title-winning season came at Celtic Park on January 3, 1966, in the second derby of the season. Rangers took the lead inside the first couple of minutes, a lead they maintained up until half-time. However, the second forty-five minutes was the clearest indication yet that the balance of power in Scottish football had well and truly shifted to the East End of Glasgow. Stein's side scored five goals without reply, including a Stevie Chalmers hat-trick, to inflict a comprehensive 5-1 defeat on their city rivals. The race for the title was neck-and-neck for the remainder of the season, with Celtic finally confirming their position as Scottish champions in the last minute of the final match of the season, when Bobby Lennox scored to give the Hoops a 1-0 win over Motherwell at Fir Park.

Celtic finished two points clear at the top of the table, a remarkable turnaround for a side which the previous season had been a distant eighth, while for good measure they also lifted the League Cup, beating Rangers 2-1 in the final courtesy of two John Hughes penalties. The league triumph, however, not only signifying that Celtic were back in their rightful place as Scotland's best team, also secured qualification for the 1966/67 European Cup competition, and having steered his side to the semi-final of the Cup-Winners' Cup that season, only losing narrowly to Liverpool, Jock Stein approached the new campaign intent upon building on the success his side had already enjoyed in his short time at the club.

At the end of that season, Stein took his players on a tour of Bermuda and North America, the squad remaining unbeaten after eleven games – winning eight of them. More than the games, however, which were important in their own right, was the sense of team unity which was forged during those six weeks. It was something that the players clearly felt was beneficial, and Celtic's domestic dominance was asserted throughout that milestone season, with League Cup and Scottish Cup final triumphs secured against Rangers and Aberdeen respectively. The league campaign was a phenomenal one for Celtic, as they only lost two fixtures out of thirty-four – both of them 3-2 defeats to Dundee United – while they scored an impressive 111 goals, conceding just thirty-three.

It was in Europe, however, that Stein's side were to make the greatest impact. Celtic's first ever European Cup tie was against Swiss champions, FC Zurich, and a comfortable 5-0 aggregate win was secured, Tommy Gemmell having the honour of scoring the club's first goal of that campaign. The victory set up a second round clash with French side, Nantes, and 3-1 victories for the Hoops home and away saw them progress to the quarter-final.

Vojvodina Novi Sad stood between Celtic and a place in the last four of the competition, and the first leg in Yugoslavia resulted in the Hoops' only defeat in that European Cup campaign, Stanislav Stanic scoring the only goal of the game. The return leg at Celtic Park was as dramatic a night of European football that Paradise has ever seen. Stevie Chalmers scored on the hour mark to level the tie, and it was heading towards a play-off in Rotterdam when Billy McNeill rose high in the penalty area to head home a Charlie Gallagher corner. It was an incredible result for Stein's side, one that they thoroughly merited, and it put Celtic into the semi-final of the European Cup. The dramatic upturn in the club's fortunes was almost too incredible to comprehend, although many Celtic supporters had started to believe that the season was going to end up in Lisbon on May 25 for the European Cup final.

The champions of Czechoslovakia, Dukla Prague, had other ideas, of course, but a 3-1 first leg victory, courtesy of goals from Jimmy Johnstone and a Willie Wallace double, put the Hoops in a strong position for the second leg in the Czech capital. Celtic defended resolutely throughout the tie, however, and the game in Prague finished 0-0. And as the referee's whistle signalled the end of the match, there were celebrations amongst the Celtic players, who had achieved something extraordinary. They didn't know yet who they would face in the final – Inter Milan and CSKA Sofia were still to battle it out for that privilege – but it was enough that, to paraphrase the famous Glen Daly song, the Glasgow Celtic would be there.

Celtic's style of play in that game in Prague was more defensive than had been characteristic up to that point, or would be in future. With so much at stake, it was perhaps not surprising that a degree of caution was adopted and, indeed, Jock Stein said after the game, 'I'll never resort to tactics like these again – never.' However, the way the game unfolded was due, in the main, to the determination of the Dukla Prague team to try and get back into the tie and the quality of the players in the Czech team, and it was to the credit of the Celtic players that they were able to withstand such an intense onslaught. Several of them subsequently stated that there had been no pre-match instructions to defend, and that it was circumstances during the match which dictated those actions. The ultimate outcome, of course, was success for the Hoops, and a date with destiny on May 25 in Lisbon's Estadio Nacional.

Before then, Celtic sealed another league title and the Scottish Cup, for a domestic clean sweep of the three major honours up for grabs. However, it was on Thursday, May 25, 1967, in Portugal's capital city, that Jock Stein's reputation as a world-class manager was signed, sealed and delivered. The final against Inter Milan, who had seen off CSKA in a play-off victory, was more than just a match between two sides determined to win club football's top prize. It also represented two competing football philosophies; Helenio Herrera had made Inter, arguably, the best team in the world in the first half of the decade with a pragmatic style of play built on a defensive system that appeared, at times, to be impregnable. The system was called 'Catenaccio', and it had won Inter Milan two European Cups and two World Club Championships, as well as numerous domestic honours.

The success that Celtic had already enjoyed since Jock Stein joined the club in March 1965 was the antithesis of Herrera's philosophy. While having a solid defensive foundation, Stein's Celtic side placed the onus on attack, and they'd hit over a century of league goals in both the 1965/66 and 1966/67 seasons, winning six domestic trophies in that short period of time and also reaching the European Cup final just twelve months after they'd advanced as far as the semi-final of the Cup-Winners' Cup. The clash with Inter Milan, however, was undoubtedly their biggest test against their toughest opponents to date.

While the Celtic players, led by Bertie Auld, were bursting into song in the Lisbon tunnel, Stein and his backroom staff were already pitch-side and making their way towards to the benches laid out on one of the touchlines. And as his team walked across the pitch to line up in the centre, they witnessed their manager winning the first psychological battle of the afternoon, insisting upon the removal of the Inter Milan managerial team who had attempted to commandeer the Celtic bench. It was only a small incident in a day full of momentous events, but it signalled to the Hoops players that they were here to win and past reputations counted for nothing; they would take that lesson from their manager and display it in abundance over the course of the next ninety minutes.

That the final scoreline from that game read 2-1 in Celtic's favour was flattering, in one respect, to the Italian side, given the complete dominance by Stein's side, as the match statistics illustrate

	CELTIC	INTER MILAN
Total shots	45	3
On Target	16	3
Corners:	10	0
Successful passes:	310	224
Attacking crosses:	40	4
Passbacks:	7	20
Possession:	64%	36%

However, the only statistic which ultimately matters in any game is the scoreline and the one from Lisbon's Estadio Nacional confirmed that Celtic were the champions of Europe. Despite going behind after just seven minutes through a Sandro Mazzola penalty, Stein's side continued to play a thrilling brand of attacking football that was eventually rewarded, first with an equaliser from Tommy Gemmell just after the hour mark and then, five minutes from time, with a winner scored by Stevie Chalmers. The legend of the Lisbon Lions was born.

Jock Stein's Lions were in no doubt as to his importance, not only to their own careers, but to Celtic Football Club as a whole. Stein's captain, Billy McNeill, who succeeded him as manager at the club in 1978, said of his mentor, 'Big Jock came in March 1965 and the whole thing changed – the dreams that we once dreamt about all came true. Training became very demanding. He really looked for hard training. He liked fit teams and he liked fit players. He wanted his players to be supremely fit but with it came an enjoyment. The ball appeared more often than not. For years at Celtic Park you used to run around the big track – that was basically all you did. The only time you saw a ball was on Saturday and at times you wondered if you knew what to do with the bloody thing. But when Jock came back, everything changed. Then obviously we won the Scottish Cup at the end of that season and that transformed everything.'

Bobby Lennox added, 'Jock was a great manager and he helped every one of the players that worked under him, but I don't know if any of us got to know him really well as a man. Billy was maybe closer to him. The year he arrived, in 1965, I was in the first-team and the year he left, in 1978, I was in the first-team, so he must've known something about football to have me in the team! I'm proud of that record as well, that I played the whole time he was there.'

And Jim Craig stated, 'Without Jock none of it would have been possible. He was extremely good at what he did and never lost track of the idea that the game was about scoring goals at one end and not losing them at the other. People talk about 3-5-2, 4-5-1 and Christmas Trees today, but it's all just a way of making sure that you score at one end and don't concede at the other. Jock never forgot that and he always insisted that everyone put in a shift. You just cannot under-estimate his value to Celtic.'

The domestic dominance that had already been established would be enforced over the next ten years as Celtic proved to be far too good for any of their rivals, winning nine league titles in a row. It overtook the previous record that had been set by Willie Maley's side back in the first decade of the twentieth century when they won six-in-a-row. However, another European Cup eluded the Hoops. There were semi-final disappointments in 1972 against Inter Milan and two years later when the thuggery of Atletico Madrid, sadly, won out. However, it was 1970 which was the biggest disappointment of all.

Celtic had made it all the way to the final, a journey which included an epic 3-1 aggregate victory over English champions, Leeds United, with a European record attendance of 136,505 established after the second leg of that clash at Hampden. That semi-final against Don Revie's side was seen, in clichéd terms, as 'the final before the final', and the winners of that tie were expected to go on and lift the trophy in Milan's San Siro stadium. The opposition in that final were the Dutch champions, Feyenoord, and it was to be their name which would be engraved on the trophy after one hundred and twenty minutes of action in the Italian city.

Tommy Gemmell opened the scoring for Celtic on the half-hour mark with a blistering free-kick from the edge of the area, becoming one of a select band of players to score in more than one European Cup final, but that lead lasted all of two minutes before the Dutch side equalised. There was to be no further scoring in the game until late in extra-time when, with just four minutes remaining, Ove Kindvall, scored what proved to be the winner. It was a major disappointment to the Hoops and their manager, on a night when they did not perform to their usual high standard. Seven of the team which had won in Lisbon were in the starting XI for the game against Feyenoord, and the accepted wisdom of that occasion is that, if Celtic had managed to see out the game and take it to a replay, the outcome would have been different if they'd been given a second chance. That game on May 6, 1970 remains, up to now, the closest that Celtic have come to winning the European Cup again.

Stein's other major disappointment had come three years previously, in that otherwise momentous year of 1967 when his side faced Racing Club of Argentina in the World Club Championship. The first leg at Hampden saw Celtic win 1-0, courtesy of a Billy McNeill goal in the second-half. The return game in Buenos Aires finished 2-1 in Racing Club's favour, with Celtic forced to change goalkeepers before the start of the game when Ronnie Simpson was hit on the head by a missile thrown from the crowd behind his goal. The two games had shown the worst elements of Racing Club's character, and there was a debate within the Celtic camp as to whether they should travel on to Uruguay for a third match to decide the outcome of the contest. In the end, they did, but the resulting match in Montevideo, which Racing Club won 1-0, descended into a farce, not helped by an abysmal Paraguayan referee, with several players sent off, including, erroneously, Bobby Lennox, while Bertie Auld refused to leave the field. The subsequent castigation of his team by the English-based BBC angered Stein, as did the fact he lost the chance to proclaim his team as world champions, though there's no doubt that had Celtic been allowed to play football, they would have won.

Jim Craig later reflected on the game, telling the *Celtic View*, 'The games against Racing Club were a regret for me. To reach the final of the World Club Championship and then blow it, which we did do, was hard to take. We didn't play particularly well and what was worse, we reacted to their style of play. It's easy to sit at a distance and some people say that you shouldn't react to things, but I often wonder how they would react if someone walked up, unprovoked and slapped them in the face. In the first game at Hampden there was a fair bit of illegal tactics, elbowing and obstructions, but when we went out to South America, the spitting started and that was hard to cope with. But at the same time, there is this feeling that we blew it.'

Season 1973/74 was a momentous one for Celtic and Jock Stein as the club secured its ninth league title in a row, finishing four points clear of second-placed Hibernian, while the Scottish Cup was secured with a comfortable 3-0 victory over Dundee United in the final at Hampden. The Hoops also reached the semi-final of the European Cup, but lost 2-0 on aggregate to an Atletico Madrid side whose tactics were reminiscent of Racing Club seven years previously. The following season, while both domestic cup trophies were won, saw Celtic finally relinquish ownership of the league championship trophy when they finished third in the table, bringing to an end a remarkable run of success for the club. Indeed, throughout the nine-in-a-row success, season 1967/68 was the only one that Celtic did not reach both domestic cup finals and thus have a chance of securing a domestic treble.

In July 1975, while returning home from holiday, Jock Stein was involved a serious car crash that left him critically ill. Thankfully, he survived, though he was absent for most of the 1975/76 season, which was a trophyless one for the club, with his assistant, Sean Fallon, taking charge of team matters. And though he returned to the helm for what proved to be a double-winning 1976/77 campaign, it was said that he was not the same person as before. One more trophyless season followed before, in May 1978, he stepped down as Celtic manager. He had delivered a golden era for the club, with ten league titles, eight Scottish Cups, six League Cups and, of course, the European Cup to his name. It had been an extraordinary period in Celtic's history, setting a benchmark that all subsequent managers have strived, with varying degrees of success, to try and equal or at least come close to.

It was his captain, Billy McNeill, who took over the helm at Celtic Park, returning to Paradise from Aberdeen, and as he later explained to the *Celtic View*, 'It was difficult, because Big Jock had been there for an incredible period of time and all of a sudden everything had to change, almost from top to bottom. I felt that the club was slow in seeing the changes in football during both my spells as manager. The change was coming and most clubs had sorted out their long-term plans. From that point of view we had some fantastic experiences, but maybe not enough.'

Jock Stein briefly dabbled in club management later that year, becoming Leeds United manager for all of forty-four days before he took over as boss of the Scotland national side. That was a position he would hold until that fateful night of September 10, 1985 when, towards the end of a vital World Cup qualifier at Cardiff's Ninian Park, he suffered a heart attack and died shortly afterwards in the stadium's medical room. He was only sixty-four. It was a tragedy that was felt by the whole of Scottish football, and beyond, but nowhere more so than at Celtic, and amongst its supporters, who had admired him as a player, revered him as a manager and loved him as a fellow Celt.

Thursday May 25, 1967 was his crowning glory, when the group of players born within a thirty-mile radius of Celtic Park that he moulded into an exciting and attacking team, defeated Inter Milan 2-1 in Lisbon's Estadio Nacional to lift the European Cup, doing so by playing pure, beautiful, inventive football. A statue of Jock Stein stands outside the front of Celtic Park, the legendary Hoops boss holding the 'Big Cup' that he and his team won back in '67. It's a permanent reminder for future generations of one of the most important figures in the history of Celtic Football Club, and a tribute to one of the greatest managers that the beautiful game has ever seen.

SEAN FALLON

SEAN FALLON

Sean Fallon was Celtic's assistant manager throughout the golden era of the 1960s and '70s, Jock Stein's right-hand man, the two former Celtic team-mates reuniting a decade after they'd played together for the club, helping the Hoops to some of the few honours they managed to win in the 1950s. When Stein had joined the club as a player back in December 1951, he did so originally as a fourth-choice centre-half, but events, mainly injuries to other players, transpired to catapult him into the first-team, and there he more or less remained until injury called time on his career. His leadership qualities were evident for all to see, including Sean Fallon, and when the Irishman suffered an injury during the 1952/53 season, his recommendation was that Stein take over the captaincy from him. It was an inspired decision, and cemented a friendship and respect between the two men that was to last a lifetime

However, in reflecting on the Lisbon triumph and, indeed, Jock Stein's managerial reign, to simply label Sean Fallon as assistant manager would be to do the Irishman a disservice and massively underplay his influence in the club at that time and his importance in delivering the success enjoyed both in Scotland and throughout Europe. Those who had played for Celtic during that period knew what Fallon did for the club, but it was only with the publication of Stephen Sullivan's exceptional biography, *Sean Fallon: Celtic's Iron Man*, that the true extent of his contribution to 'the Celtic Football Club' that he loved and devoted a lifetime of service to became known.

Many of those players who would acknowledge Fallon's influence behind the scenes at Celtic Park also owed their Celtic careers to the Irishman, whose genial and gentle demeanour off the pitch was in stark contrast to the fiercely competitive nature he displayed when he wore the green and white Hoops as a player. He was a man whose focus was always on what was best for the club – best reflected in the fact that he remained with the club when Jock Stein was appointed manager, a position that Fallon would have coveted and, at one time, looked as though would be his when it came time for Jimmy McGrory to step aside. His loyalty to Stein was unquestioned, however, and the contrast between the two men in terms of personality and demeanour worked well within the dressing-room, the Irishman often the Paradise peacemaker as well as being the conduit between players and manager. There was always genuine affection for Sean Fallon, reflected in the glowing and heartfelt tributes paid to him when he passed away in January 2013 at the age of ninety.

Bobby Lennox said, 'Sean will be remembered as one of the four guys who ran the club. Big Jock was the gaffer and Sean was the second in charge, with Neilly and Bob Rooney. We couldn't have done what we did without those four guys. He was also involved in bringing a lot of the Quality Street Gang through and deserves a lot of credit for that, and he was so happy the night we won the European Cup.'

Sean Fallon's talents were many, both on and off the pitch, chief among them his ability to spot a player of talent, and the number of players he brought to Celtic Park reads like a who's who of Hoops legends; Kenny Dalglish, Danny McGrain, Lou Macari, George Connelly, Davie Hay, Pat Bonner, Paul McStay and many, many others. More than that, he was influential, if not instrumental in ensuring that the eleven men who would become the Lisbon Lions all signed for Celtic, with the exception of Willie Wallace, who joined the club in December 1966.

The Sligo man was almost twenty-eight when he joined Celtic in March 1950 from Glenavon, and perhaps there was part of him which had thought the chance of fulfilling a long-held dream had passed him by, but once he got to Paradise, he never wanted to leave.

He later reflected on his Celtic connections; 'I was working in a bakery in Lurgan and we played against a team called Glenavon, which is about 20 miles from Belfast. I was an amateur playing for Sligo Rovers at the time and we played them in a friendly in Sligo. After the game, I was approached by the Glenavon directors to see if I wanted to go and play with them, which meant I would be based there. I thought this was a step in the right direction because in my mind, all that time from when I was a boy, I thought about Celtic. My dad was in the 1914-18 war and he received a shoulder wound. He got hit with one of those dum-dums and was hospitalised to Glasgow, and during a series of operations, he used to come here to watch Celtic.

'In fact, later on, I met a chap called Liam McMenemy. His father had been a famous Celt, the Napoleon of Scottish football, Jimmy McMenemy. Well, I met his son in Sligo. At that time, a lot of Scottish boys used to go there on holiday. I had three sisters and they were in the lake that day and one of them were in difficulty and the Glasgow boys were also on the lake, and this boy, Joe McMenemy, dived in and saved her. Of course, my mum invited all the Glasgow boys over to her home to entertain them and thank them properly, and he started to talk about Celtic and he sent me *The Story of Celtic* by Willie Maley. I read that from front to back. I was only a kid at the time but my dad got me a green and white jersey and I ran about in that Celtic jersey, little realising that I was going to realise that dream, which I did. That was my aim in life and I achieved that and was very fortunate indeed.

'When I pulled on that jersey it meant everything I had dreamed about was happening. And I was fortunate to sign a lot of boys who had that same dream. I think that is of the utmost importance: when you pull on a Celtic jersey that you want to give 100 percent, if not more. There were a lot of boys like that. Some may have wanted to play for other clubs but once they came here, they never wanted to leave.'

Sean Fallon wasn't called the Iron Man for nothing, and he brought a physicality and incredible desire to win every ball and every game into a Celtic team which had toiled since the end of the Second World War, even flirting with relegation in the 1947/48 season. Within a year of joining his beloved Celtic, however, Fallon had won his first major honour, being part of the side which beat Motherwell 1-0 in the 1951 Scottish Cup final. He missed out on the 1953 Coronation Cup success through injury, but started the new season in the team until he broke his collarbone in a home game against Hearts in October 1953. It saw him miss most of the championship-winning season, with Jock Stein stepping up from his vice-captain's role to skipper the side. However, the Irishman was back playing by the time that the Hoops faced Aberdeen at Hampden on April 24, 1954 in the Scottish Cup final, and he not only won his second Scottish Cup medal, he also provided the winning goal, scoring just after the hour mark to give Celtic a 2-1 victory.

Success for Celtic was a rare commodity throughout the 1950s, though Sean Fallon was usually at the heart of whatever triumphs the club did enjoy. He helped the Hoops win their first ever League Cup trophy in October 1956 as they defeated Partick Thistle 3-0 at Hampden in a replay, and a year later, on October 19, 1957, he played his part in one of Celtic's most famous ever results as they retained the League Cup with an incredible 7-1 victory over Rangers in the final.

By this time, Jock Stein was coaching the reserves at the club, having been forced to call time on his playing career due to injury, but by then the friendship between Stein and Fallon, which would develop into an unrivalled managerial partnership in the next decade, had already been cemented. Reflecting on that time, Fallon said, 'I always remember some of the players saying, 'Imagine bringing in an old player like that,' especially Charlie Tully, who was saying, 'He's very old for coming here'. And little did Charlie realise that I was five months older than Jock. The old assistant trainer here, Jimmy Gribben, recommended him and brought him up for the centre-half position as we needed a good centre-half at that time. Jock walked into the position and he took it from there as he was a tremendous player with great knowledge of the game and could read situations. We used to have great chats – Bertie Peacock, Jock, Bobby Evans and myself. We used to go to Ferrari's every day after training for a bite of lunch, and we used to sit there and discuss the game, which was a good thing really as we got to know each other and, more importantly, we got to know each other's game. Jock was a one-off, before his time.'

Sean Fallon's own retirement as a player came in August 1958, after 254 appearances and fourteen goals. And having worked so hard to get to Paradise, Fallon remained at the club, becoming coach and then assistant manager. It was during this period that his ability as a talent spotter first started to come to the fore, and he was already working with most of the Lisbon Lions before Jock Stein arrived at the club in March 1965. Whatever other suggestions might have been put to Stein – a role as assistant to Fallon, or a joint managerial role – were dismissed by the former Celtic defender. If he was going to return to the club, it would only be as manager, and with absolute control over all team matters. When Stein left Celtic, he may well have thought that it would be Sean Fallon who'd be Jimmy McGrory's successor as manager. In the event, he took over from the man he always referred to as 'The Boss', while it was the Irishman who became assistant. A Celtic man to his very core, whatever personal ambitions Fallon might have harboured as a manager were submerged by his desire to serve his club. That it was in the role of assistant manager did not lessen the absolute commitment he gave, and that partnership between Stein and Fallon, forged when they were team-mates the previous decade, was integral to the success that Celtic would enjoy over the next ten years.

Without Jock Stein's arrival as Celtic manager, it's highly unlikely that the club would have achieved even a modicum of the success they did achieve under him. Without Sean Fallon in the dugout alongside him – a man he could, and did, completely trust, would Celtic and Stein have been so dominant? The two men complemented each other, and it says much about Fallon's character that he accepted Stein's appointment without rancour.

He explained in his biography about when he and Jimmy McGrory were informed by Robert Kelly of Jock Stein's impending arrival as Celtic manager, 'I won't lie to you and say I didn't want the job. By that stage, being Celtic manager had become an ambition of mine. I had fulfilled a dream by playing for Celtic and captaining the club, and to have been made manager would have capped it all. And I believed in myself; believed that I could improve things and do a good job. But as soon as Jock went out to Dunfermline and did so well, I knew in myself what was going to happen. Even then, I knew he would be back. And, honestly, I wasn't too disappointed. After all, I knew Jock and I knew he'd do a good job. There was never any doubt in my mind that he'd be a success. The chairman was worried I would be annoyed. He thought I would feel that I had done my time in the background with Jimmy McGrory, and would think I was entitled to the job. Actually, I felt Jock was entitled to it. He had gone out into management and proved himself; I'd stayed with Celtic and things hadn't really improved. I wasn't annoyed: not at the club, not at Jock and especially not at Bob Kelly – because I would have made exactly the same decision had I been in his shoes. It was never about me anyway. All I wanted was for Celtic to be successful, and I could see Jock was the man the club needed.'

Robert Kelly described Sean Fallon as the most 'faithful, reliable Celtic servant,' and those words certainly sum up the character of the Irishman, who always put the club before any personal ambitions. But though Fallon believed that the appointment of Jock Stein as manager was the correct one, even he couldn't have envisaged just how successful Celtic would become overnight. The Scottish Cup triumph of 1965 heralded a period of domestic dominance, with nine consecutive league titles following, along with seven Scottish Cups and six League Cups. Then there was the European Cup, won within two years of Jock Stein's appointment. The two men had plotted Celtic's success in Scotland and steered their way through the uncharted waters of the European Cup, arriving in the final on May 25, 1967 and sinking the aristocrats of Inter Milan.

Reflecting on the European Cup triumph many years later, in his biography, Fallon said, 'I just remember looking around the stadium, feeling so happy for the supporters. They were the best around, the Celtic fans, and we hadn't always repaid them as we should have. For that reason, I actually think the part of the European Cup win I enjoyed the most wasn't Lisbon, but bringing the cup home to Glasgow and seeing the joy it had brought to so many people. That journey back to Celtic Park, with the streets packed and the stadium overflowing, will stay with me forever.'

Having been alongside Jock Stein throughout the historic nine-in-a-row triumph, Sean Fallon would also enjoy a short period as Celtic manager, taking over for the 1975/76 season when Stein was seriously injured in a car crash. The previous season had been the first in a decade that the Hoops hadn't won the title, and the following campaign was to prove as equally disappointing. And while Fallon was ostensibly the manager, Jock Stein still exerted a degree of influence and control even before he returned to work. In 1976, Fallon was moved to the role of chief scout, with former Partick Thistle manager, Davie McParland, taking over as assistant manager. It was an obvious demotion although, characteristically, the Irishman did not rock the boat by complaining or leaving, though his departure from Celtic Park came two years later at the same time as Jock Stein vacated the managerial position. A short period at Dumbarton followed, before Sean Fallon retired, though he would later hold board positions at Dumbarton and then Clyde.

At the start of the 2012/13 season, Sean Fallon was invited to unfurl the championship flag at Celtic Park as the club celebrated another league title triumph. The Irishman, who was ninety-years-old, was delighted to do so, and the reception he received from the Celtic supporters was an indication of the esteem in which he was held by his fellow fans. Six months later, on January 18, 2013, he passed away, mourned by all who knew him, and also by many, many more who did not but who still appreciated what he had given to the club.

The final, modest words, however, must go to Sean Fallon, who said of his time with Celtic: 'I was just an ordinary player with only a big heart and a fighting spirit to recommend me... I can never find words to express my feelings at becoming a member of the Celtic Football Club.'

LISBOA
25 DE MAIO DE
1967
CELTIC **2-1** INTER
50° CELTIC FC
ANIVERSARIO

THE BACKROOM BHOYS

LISBOA
25 DE MAIO DE
1967
CELTIC 2-1 INTER
50° CELTIC FC
ANIVERSARIO

THE BACKROOM BHOYS

If there was another team off the park on Lisbon that sunny evening, the team behind the team as it were and the trio that allowed Jock Stein and Sean Fallon the time and leeway to concentrate on what they did best, it was Neilly Mochan, Bob Rooney and Jimmy Steele. The labels attributed to them respectively were trainer, physio and masseur but, they were worth much more than their individual titles such was their flexibility and they played a vital role in not only their job descriptions but in creating the team spirit in the dressing room and on the training field in what was the most crucial of seasons.

In a season that should have been fraught with nervousness, stress and mental fatigue as much as the more normal physical bumps and bruises in the daily course of a footballer's life, it's remarkable how many of the Lions declared that they went into each game expecting to win, seemingly without a care in the world. Much of that was down to the Mochan, Rooney and Steele triple act, each with their own brand of humour that was part of the overall story but, on a more serious note, another thing the Lions unanimously agree upon was their fitness. That, too, could be attributed to the Backroom Bhoys.

Jock Stein was a manager in the days when the role was exactly that. Not just the manager of eleven men, but manager of a team, manager of a club, manager of a business, manager of a building and he managed everything that was going on in that building without the army of working professionals that every big team now has. Football clubs now have more departments than they had actual staff back then, and each of these departments will have more staff than actually ran the whole of Celtic Park in 1967.

So Jock Stein would have been at the ticket window of Celtic Park selling briefs for the next sell-out European tie had he not been dutifully employed elsewhere in the stadium with some other equally important matter. Everybody mucked in and none more so than the Backroom Bhoys when it came to the most important job of all – preparing eleven Celts for each and every game. That all came to a head in Lisbon.

There is a famous photograph taken with a minute to go in the Estadio Nacional and most observers would have us believe that this was the moment when Jock Stein couldn't take the pressure anymore and moved away from the dugout. Bob Rooney is still intently watching the action and Jimmy Steele is focusing on the photographer while, what presumably is a UEFA/Portuguese official, wonders why the Celtic manager is disappearing into the horizon. According to both Sean Fallon and Neilly Mochan, though, Jock Stein knew the game was Celtic's and he was moving around to the presentation area while rubbing his hands with glee at the imminent prospect of winning the European Cup; a cup that was won by the eleven men on the park, and the men behind the scenes who prepared the players. That preparation went into every single game, not just the European Cup final in Lisbon and not just every game that season. It went right back to their individual debuts as Bobby Lennox pointed out when talking about his first Celtic game.

'I didn't really know many of the players," he said. 'I was the wee boy in the corner. They all came over and introduced themselves but you could picture them, thinking, 'Who is this'. I remember Jimmy Steele giving me a laugh and getting me settled down. He was the best person the dressing room at that time. He came in, wound all the guys up and gave everyone a laugh. I found out later that Stevie Chalmers had the flu and that was the reason I was called in. I didn't really have time to think about it. After about ten or fifteen minutes into the game, big Ian Ure hit the ball off me. It hit off my chest, bounced past him and then I put it into the net, but the referee gave handball. It was one of those decisions that go against you. I could have cried. Frank Brogan equalised for us and then Billy scored the winner as he did in so many games, out-jumping everyone to head the ball into the net. Billy was a great help for me coming into the team. He always had a few words to say to me before the games.'

Captain Billy McNeill was merely carrying on Steely's pre-match manner beyond the debut day for the young Lennox, but for years after that bow the masseur with the magic hands and even more charismatic words was helping quell any nerves down at Seamill before any of the big games. Lennox said: 'One of the big events down there was the putting competition on the front lawn on the Friday and wee Steely had the blackboard out, giving odds on everybody.'

For the Lions it seemed as if Jimmy Steele had always been at Celtic Park and, indeed, by the time he packed up his massage bag for the last time, he had spent nigh on half-a-century as masseur for not only Celtic, but also Scotland. Among his other clients was world light heavyweight boxing champion and actor, Freddie Mills as their paths had crossed while Steely was on National Service, and it was in the forces that he learned his trade as a masseur. His real 'day job' was his draper's shop in Larkhall, where the strips for Celtic's first game wearing numbers on the shorts, the 5-1 friendly win over Sparta Rotterdam in 1960, supposedly were supplied from, and in all of the years he worked for Celtic, he never took a single penny in pay. That is an amazing fact when you consider how important he was in conditioning the players that won so many trophies in the second half of the last century. He was also honoured by UEFA in the late 1990s for his lifetime service to football.

It wasn't only the Lions who benefitted from the foresight of Jimmy Steele as Danny McGrain pointed out when, considering the odds on it happening, no-one in the Celtic party dared to even contemplate preparing for a celebration on May 3, 1986 when Celtic travelled to play St Mirren needing a win while hoping Hearts would lose to Dundee on the day the title would be decided. No-one that is except Jimmy Steele, who still had the winning mentality of the Lions ingrained in him. Danny McGrain recalled: 'I will never forget wee Steely at the final whistle. He had been with Celtic for donkey's years, Mr Stein had brought him to the club and he was a great, great guy. Steely had brought a bottle of champagne with him that day, one bottle of champagne for the whole dressing room. I think it got sprayed everywhere and we all got one sip from it, but to Steely's credit, he believed in us and he brought that champagne with him. He liked a wee bet from time to time and had a few bob on us as well. I think Mr Stein recognised how important a person he was. He was always on everybody's mind, he was great, just so, so funny. He had this great laugh, a wee titter that just made you laugh as well and he would laugh at anything.

'If you got smacked on the nose, he'd be standing there laughing and you'd end up giggling as well! He had a fantastic personality and was admired and loved by everyone. He was a great friend to Mr Stein and was great with the players as well. His room was always full of people, laughing and talking, and whenever you went in to see him you ended up coming out covered in talcum powder! He was a jolly old man, he always had a twinkle in his eye and he kept everyone happy. He helped to relax us and whenever you went to see him you always got a sweetie as well. Mr Stein knew he could trust him and every manager that followed Mr Stein knew just how important he was.'

Working closely with Steely was physio, Bob Rooney and he, too, was respected and revered by the Lions even if his humour was a little more laconic and gruff compared to Messrs Steele and Mochan. Jim Craig recalled an occasion when he had to approach Rooney regarding one of the physio's other duties, providing boots for the players as the full-back's pair had seen better days.

He said: 'Bob was a good pal to all the boys but was feeling a bit miffed with me because of an incident the previous week, but I told him I had burst one of my boots. 'What foot?' he asked and I was quite taken aback as boots do come in pairs. I told him it was the left and he said: 'Well, that's all right, then. You don't use that one very often. We'll just tape it.' However, when he saw the boot in question even he realised the damage was beyond repair. 'I'd better get you a new pair,' he muttered, making his way to the boot cupboard. Then, he turned back to me and raised his voice, 'and take more care of this pair!'

One of Bob Rooney's matchday duties was to run the bath and one Lion in particular rued the fact that he didn't pay more attention to the physio's timetable. The case in point was the game against Dundee United at Celtic Park in October 1968 when, a bit miffed at being subbed, Jimmy Johnstone took off his jersey and threw it at the dugout, where it hit Jock Stein. The manager jumped up immediately and his incandescent rage didn't dissipate any when he thumped his head off the old brick dugout roof as he rose. Jinky, sensing what was about to happen, sped off down the tunnel with the manager hot on his heels cursing, and the winger very quickly running out of hiding places.

Once in the dressing room he had the marvellous idea of jumping, boots, kit and all, into the bath as he knew the manager wouldn't follow him in there. The ploy worked, except in one respect, and that was that Bob Rooney was in the habit of running the bath not long after half-time so that it would be ready at the perfect temperature at the end of the 90 minutes. Jinky's 'early-bath' was a little too early for that and in mid-flight he realised the water would be scalding hot! His skin turned as red as his hair, not to mention the colour of Jock Stein's face, but the winger thought it was better to remain suffering where he was, rather than figuratively 'feel' the wrath of his manager.

Rooney's son, Benny, was also at Celtic Park at the tail-end of 1950s and on to 1963 but not getting beyond the reserve side, mainly because he was trying to break into a defence marshalled expertly by Billy McNeill, although those two youngsters were to become lifelong friends. It was with St Johnstone that Benny would find his feet and he captained them in their first European campaign in the 1971 UEFA Cup which they qualified for after finishing third in the league behind Celtic and Aberdeen. It was two years before that when Bob Rooney's heart must have been swelling with pride, not to mention a slight wavering of loyalties, as the captains who shook hands on the Hampden centre-spot prior to the 1969 League Cup final were none other than Billy McNeill and Benny Rooney. We don't know if Rooney Senior was in a win-win/lose-lose scenario but the end product was a Celtic win thanks to a solitary Bertie Auld goal after only two minutes in a tight game.

Auld recalled: 'Benny, being an ex-Celtic man, was always a hard man to play against. And I don't mean that he was hard and vicious. He was always a competitor and a leader. That's what he showed any time you played against him.'

Benny Rooney would also follow in his father's footsteps by becoming a Backroom Bhoy at Celtic when, alongside Lisbon Lion, Bobby Lennox, he coached the reserve side during Billy McNeill's second spell as manager and on into the mid-'90s. Still a Backroom Bhoy when Benny Rooney joined the tracksuit team at Celtic Park was one of his father's buddies, the inimitable Neilly Mochan.

Mochan was not only the obvious connection between the 7-1 game in '57 and Lisbon in '67, thanks to playing in one and being on the staff at the other, but he was one of the most loved and respected Celts in over forty years at the only club he ever wanted to be at. He joined as a player from Middlesbrough in 1953 and helped lift the Coronation Cup almost immediately before also picking up medals for the championship and Scottish Cup double in 1953/54 and the League Cups of 1956/57 and '57/58, scoring the historic seventh goal against Rangers in the latter. In 1960 he joined Dundee United and also played for Raith Rovers before returning to Celtic Park as a coach in 1964, and he directly influenced the careers of many Celts from several different generations.

Among the lucky few who had the benefit of Neilly Mochan's expertise at putting players at ease as both a team-mate and as a coach was Bertie Auld who joined the club in 1955, becoming a rival to Mochan for the outside-left position. Auld found himself working alongside a player who not only strived to improve his own game but who was also happy to help others as well, even if he knew they were vying for his place in the team.

'He was the perfect professional for a young player to come in and learn from,' admitted Auld. 'We had a lot of experienced players at Celtic Park at that time, and Neilly was one of them, but the most important thing was that he was always there to speak to you and give you a bit of advice. He would always encourage you on the park. I was hitting shots as a young player – and he'd come up just right after it and say, 'Listen son, that's twice you've shot and both times you've hit the near post. Looking at the angle that you're hitting it from, always hit the back post because if you don't score then at least the goalkeeper will have to save it or parry it and somebody else will get the chance to put it in.'

Both players would leave the club only to return, but this time Auld was being fully coached by Mochan. 'Neilly was a fitness fanatic as well,' he said. 'He was a tremendous trainer and he was a delight to work with. Every morning he was out leading everyone, even into the late 1960s. He was a tremendous example as a person and as a player. He was also type of the character who always got the dressing room going. He was very funny. His nickname was Smiler – so you could picture that in a dressing room, particularly with the characters we had. He had the banter going as soon as he walked in the front door.

'I heard so often about how he'd scored the winning goal in the Coronation Cup final and any time we went to Hampden from the 1950s right up to the '70s, Neilly would talk about it, and it kept getting further and further back every time he described it. At the finish, when we used to go out on the park to have a look at the conditions before the match, Neilly would take us over to where he'd hit his shot, and it was getting closer and closer to Johnny Bonnar's goal every time!'

From Bertie Auld through to Paul McStay and onwards into the 1990s, many Celts had the benefit on Neilly Mochan's footballing mind not to mention his sense of humour and people skills. He sadly passed away aged sixty-seven in 1994 after a brave fight against leukaemia but he will forever be remembered as an all-time Celtic great. Mochan was a great Celtic servant as were Bob Rooney who passed away in 1992, sadly on the eve of a Lions anniversary function when the whole squad gathered in a city centre venue, and Jimmy Steele who passed away aged eighty-five in 1999; three Celts who played mostly unwritten and unseen roles in the greatest ninety minutes, the greatest night and the greatest season in the history of Celtic Football Club.

INTER MILAN

INTER MILAN

If the 1950s had been dominated by Real Madrid, who won the first five European Cup tournaments between 1955 and '60, then Inter Milan could put forward a strong case for being considered the strongest European team of the 1960s. The likes of Benfica, Barcelona and even Real Madrid might dispute that, as would their city rivals, AC Milan, but with three Serie A titles, two European Cups and two Intercontinental Cups to their name, Inter's success during that decade was hard to match.

That their pre-eminence, even if not as definitive as Real's had been, came to an end in Lisbon's Estadio Nacional on May 25, 1967, is certainly apparent, and not only was it at the hands of Jock Stein's Celtic side, but their 2-1 defeat in the European Cup final also signalled the death knell of a defensive philosophy which had previously reigned supreme; Inter and Italian football might have remained mired in the notorious 'Catenaccio' system of defensive play but Celtic's victory, playing, in the words of Jock Stein, 'pure, beautiful, inventive football', saw an upsurge in an attacking style of play that would manifest itself in the emergence of Dutch football at club and international level in the early 1970s.

The pivotal moment in Inter's history came in 1960 when they appointed Helenio Herrera as manager. The Argentinian had won two league titles with Barcelona in 1959 and '60, bringing him to the attention of the Italian club, who hadn't won the Serie A since 1954. Herrera moved from the Nou Camp to the San Siro, and a year later he brought Luiz Suarez to Milan for 250million lira (£142,000), which made the Spanish striker the world's most expensive player. A former Ballon D'Or winner, Suarez would become an integral part of the side that became known as 'Grande Inter'.

In 1962/63, Inter Milan secured their first league title in nine years, finishing four points clear of Juventus, and the following season they lifted the European Cup, beating Real Madrid 3-1 in the final in Vienna, with Sandro Mazzola scoring twice in the game. And 1964 proved to be a successful year for Inter as they also became the 'world champions' when they beat Independiente of Argentina in a play-off victory at the Bernabeu Stadium in Madrid.

Inter only failed to retain their league title that season after losing a championship play-off 2-0 against Bologna, which came as a result of both sides finishing with the same points. However, in 1964/65, they were champions again, finishing three points clear of their city rivals, AC Milan, while they also won their second European Cup, beating Benfica 1-0 in the final, which was played in their own San Siro Stadium. And they also retained the Intercontinental Cup, beating Independiente again. The following season Inter won the Serie A title again, finishing four points clear of Bologna, but they were knocked out of the European Cup at the semi-final stage by eventual winners, Real Madrid. However, they entered the 1966/67 season confident of winning a third consecutive league title and determined to reclaim their European crown.

Helenio Herrera had, by this time, cemented his place as one of football's top coaches. Inter Milan's success was built on the application of the Catenaccio system, which employed a strong defensive foundation that, more often than not, included a sweeper playing behind a back four, making it seem impossible to the opposition, at times, to fashion any goalscoring chances. Complementing that rigid defensive discipline was a counter-attacking philosophy which benefited from the likes of his attacking full-backs, Tarcisio Burgnich and Giacinto Facchetti, with Suarez and Mazzola up front punishing teams on the break. Once Inter Milan were 1-0 ahead, it wasn't too often that they lost.

Their 1966/67 European Cup campaign began with a 1-0 aggregate victory over Torpedo Moscow, with Mazzola scoring the only goal of the tie in a 1-0 win in Italy. The referee that night was West German whistler, Kurt Tschenscher, who would be the man in charge at the Estadio Nacional on May 25, 1967. That set up a second round meeting with Vasas of Hungary. It took a Mario Corso goal five minutes from time to give Inter a 2-1 first-leg lead. In the return leg, two Sandro Mazzola goals gave the Italians an overall 4-1 aggregate victory to set up a rematch of the previous season's final against holders, Real Madrid.

Renato Cappellini scored the only goal of the game in Milan and he also grabbed another goal in Spain as Inter won 2-0 on the night to knock out Real and progress to the last four of the competition. While Celtic faced Dukla Prague in their semi-final, Helenio Herrera's side took on CSKA of Bulgaria. Both legs finished 1-1, which necessitated a play-off, which took place at the Stadio Renato Dall'Ara in Bologna, and Cappellini was once again the goal hero as he scored after just twelve minutes to give his side a 1-0 win and, more importantly, a place in the European Cup final for the third time, and having won the trophy on the two previous occasions, the Italians went into the game against Celtic full of confidence.

That confidence remained high despite the fact that their playmaker, Luis Suarez, was forced to miss the match through injury, though it was still a very strong Inter side which took to the field in Lisbon, and five of the team which faced Celtic that day in May would help Italy win the European Championship twelve months later. And when they took the lead after just seven minutes through Mazzola's penalty, it would have reinforced their belief that they were going to enjoy another final success. That they didn't said much for Jock Stein's side who, rather than let their heads go down, produced a performance of such attacking intent that it eventually proved too much for Inter Milan to resist, and even before Stevie Chalmers scored Celtic's winner in the eighty-fifth minute, many of the Italian players had already realised that victory was slipping out of their grasp.

Despite the obvious disappointment at having lost the European Cup final, Inter Milan's Argentinian manager, Helenio Herrera, was magnanimous in defeat, saying: 'We can have no complaints. Celtic deserved their victory. We were beaten by Celtic's force. Although we lost, the match was a victory for sport.'

Three days after losing in Lisbon, a tired Inter side played their final Serie A fixture of the campaign, losing 1-0 away to Mantova, and thus relinquishing their league title. The era of La Grande Inter was over.

Giacinto Facchetti was perhaps the prototype of the attaching full-back, and he was certainly admired by the Celtic players, including Jimmy Johnstone who was trying to persuade the Italian defender to swap jerseys after the game even as both sides walked across the Estadio Nacional pitch before the final got underway. Tall and powerful, Facchetti had the pace of a sprinter, coupled with the passing skills of a playmaker. Herrera reinvented him as a virtual wing-back a role which today may be common, but back in the 1960s was a genuine innovation.

He is certainly one of the greatest players ever to have worn the famous black and blue stripes of Inter, and he remains a revered figure amongst supporters. He spent his entire career with the Nerazzurri (the Black & Blues), making over 600 appearances for the club between 1960 and '78, while he was also capped ninety-four times by Italy. He won four Serie A titles, two European Cups, two World Club titles and an Italian Cup, while perhaps most remarkably, he was only over sent off once in his career, and on that occasion, the referee subsequently apologised, explaining that he had confused Facchetti with another player. Sadly he passed away in September 2006 at the age of sixty-four.

In May 2001, the Inter Milan legend spoke to the *Celtic View*, and recalled a conversation he had which proved to be an important one in Celtic's history.

'It was early December, back in 1965. I was playing for Italy and we had beaten Scotland 3-0 to clinch a spot at the 1966 World Cup in England. I remember the game like it was yesterday, because I scored the second goal and set up the third.

'Back then, it was customary to share a meal with your opponents after the game. Everybody was very social, despite the language barrier and we had a lovely time. After dessert, I was getting ready to go to bed when Jock Stein (then interim Scotland coach) came up to me, grabbed me by the arm and suggested we adjourn to the hotel bar. I told him that I was tired, that I needed to sleep, but he begged me to join him. I have to say, I was a little intrigued. We sat down and he began to grill me about Inter Milan. I mean, he wanted to know everything. I talked about our training sessions, about how we would stay in hotels for several days to prepare for important matches. Our coach at Inter, Helenio Herrera, insisted that we be cut off from the rest of the world and that we focus only on the upcoming match. I never felt like I was being grilled, though, in retrospect, that's exactly what he was doing. He made me feel comfortable, he was so easy to speak to, that the thought never crossed my mind.

'Stein understood what I did on the pitch, but he wanted to know more about how it was possible for us to keep our shape when I came forward. We spent several hours diagramming formations on napkins and bits of paper, but it did not stop there. I explained how the other players moved, what their duties were, how we defended set-pieces. He was particularly interested in our sweeper, Armando Picchi, probably because back then few British teams employed a sweeper system. Before I knew it, we were the only people left. Everybody else had gone to bed, but Stein was still there, asking me questions, eager to learn.

'I think in some ways, the way Celtic approached that match in 1967 was similar to the way we approached our first European final, against Real Madrid three seasons earlier. At the time, they were going for their sixth European title, they were the legendary club we'd all heard so much about: Di Stefano, Puskas, Gento, Santamaria, etc. We, on the other hand, were the young upstarts. Most of us were in our early twenties, I myself was barely twenty-two. Apart from Suarez, none of us had much experience; we had that mixture of fear and apprehension which can sometimes spur you on to achieve great things. I have a feeling Celtic felt the same way. I'm not suggesting we were as great as Real Madrid but, at the time, we were considered the benchmark in Europe. We could see the respect in their eyes, but also a fire, a determination to prove themselves against the best.

'We figured Celtic would expect us to sit back and allow them to take the initiative. Instead, Herrera ordered us to change it around. We were going to take Celtic by surprise, push up early and turn up the heat in the first fifteen minutes. Because they were young and inexperienced at this level, we figured that an early goal would demoralize them and they would throw in the towel. And, even if they didn't, few teams in history were as good as we were at defending a narrow lead.

'Well, the first part of the plan worked brilliantly. We went for the jugular straight away and, after just six minutes we were already 1-0 up as Mazzola converted a penalty. The problem was, their heads did not go down. Losing 1-0 did not demoralise them, they simply fought even harder. It was incredible. They just kept coming and coming.

'I can count on the fingers of one hand the number of times that Inter team let a lead slip away. We defended like clockwork, we were sure we could resist their increasingly desperate assaults. Instead, Tommy Gemmell equalised with seventeen minutes gone in the second-half. We were shocked. This was not supposed to be happening. Maybe that's where we lost it altogether. Celtic wasn't following the script and we weren't sure how to react. We were left with ten men after I pulled a hamstring in the second-half. Back then you were not allowed substitutions. Then Stevie Chalmers scored the winner with five minutes to go and we realised it was the end of an era.

'Eras come and go. Celtic were hungrier, they wanted it more than we did and they fully deserved to win. All of Italy was shocked. Some made excuses, pointing out that Jair and Suarez were unavailable for that game, Suarez's replacement, Stefano Bicicli, was making his first appearance of the season. But those are just excuses. We'll never know what would have happened if Luis Suarez had been fit, but it doesn't matter. Celtic deserved the crown.

'Jock Stein had figured out how to neutralise our counter-attack and I suspect it might have had something to do with the fact that he knew what we were going to do before we actually did it. Furthermore, they had an attacking full-back of their own, Gemmell; you could say he was a Scottish Facchetti. I'm not suggesting he had copied us, but I think we had definitely influenced him.'

Mario Corso was a winger for Inter Milan during the 1960s under Helenio Herrera, providing pace and attacking menace to a side whose aura of near invincibility was built largely upon their defensive attributes. He spent sixteen years with the club between 1957 and '73, and was part of all of the club's major successes during that time, both in Italy and on the European stage. Like Facchetti, he also made over 500 appearances for the club, scoring ninety-four goals. Ahead of the 2014 UEFA Europa League meeting between Celtic and Inter Milan, he recalled the '67 European Cup final clash.

'We were pretty confident going into the final and even more so after Sandro Mazzola's penalty gave us the lead, and usually, once we had taken the lead we were able to get the victory. But that night I have to admit that Celtic made the situation very difficult for us because of the way they played and at the end, they deserved to win the cup. We were very confident because when we got the first goal, we were usually able to get the result, but on that night I have to admit that we expected Celtic to play very physically and throw long balls forward but they played very good football instead.

'Before the game we knew Celtic and the way they played because our coach, Helenio Herrera, got into the details of our opponents before the game, but maybe that night he lost his notes because we didn't do so well and Celtic deserved to win.

'The Celtic players did impress me on the night, unfortunately! There was the right winger, Jimmy Johnstone, and I remember his red hair. That night he was unstoppable – he made us all crazy and, above all, a player like Facchetti suffered a lot against him. What was true was that Celtic played very well and we realised from the start of the game that we were facing a very good team, and they deserved the win for the way they played that night.

'To win the European Cup feels incredible, and if you asked the same question to the Celtic players, then they would probably give the same answer. At the time it was an amazing achievement, almost unthinkable, and it was also a great feeling for all of us when we won the European Cup for the first time in 1964. The first time is always the most special, but it was another amazing achievement to win the European Cup again the following season, especially in our own stadium and in front of our own supporters.'

GIULIANO SARTI

Inter Milan's goalkeeper had one of his best ever games for the club in the 1967 European Cup final, denying Celtic's attackers time and time again, though he could nothing about Tommy Gemmell's equaliser or Stevie Chalmers winning goal. Sarti joined Inter in 1953, having spent nine years previously at Fiorentina, where he won the European Cup-Winners' Cup, and he was an integral part of La Grande Inter, lifting all the major honours that Inter won at that time. He was also capped eight times for Italy. He left Inter in 1968 just short of his thirty-fifth birthday, joining Juventus, but after a year in Turin, he retired from the professional game.

ARMANDO PICCHI

Inter Milan's captain in 1967, Armando Picchi was deployed as a sweeper by Helenio Herrera in his Catenaccio system of defence. He began his career with his hometown team, Livorno, and after five years there, he moved to another Italian team, SPAL, based in Ferrara. In 1960 he moved to Inter Milan at the same time as Herrera took over as manager, originally joining as a right-back before his manager converted him to sweeper. He enjoyed many trophy successes with Inter, although his last game for the club ended in disappointment – it was the 1967 European Cup final against Celtic. After two years with Varese, he hung up his boots. Tragically, he died in May 1971 at the age of just thirty-five. The stadium in Livorno is named after him in his honour

TARCISIO BURGNICH

A tough and uncompromising defender, Burgnich was known as La Roccia (The Rock), and his pace and power proved perfect for Inter's defensive system. He moved to the San Siro in 1962 following spells with Udinese, Juventus and Palermo, and he would remain with Inter for the next twelve years. He was also capped sixty-six times for Italy, and scored two goals for his country, including one in the 1970 World Cup semi-final against West Germany. Burgnich went on to enjoy a twenty-year career in management, having finally hung his boots in 1977 following three seasons with Napoli.

ARISTIDE GUARNERI

Another player who converted from full-back to central defender, Guarneri managed to go through his entire career without being sent off once. His professional career began with Como, although he was only there for a year before he joined Inter in 1958, going on to enjoy a nine-year career with the club. And just like Picchi, he played his last game for La Grande Inter on May 25, 1967 against Celtic at the Estadio Nacional in Lisbon. As well as club honours, Guarneri also won the 1968 European Championships with Italy. After retiring, he moved into football management, though never at as high a level as he had done so during his playing career.

GIACINTO FACCHETTI

Regarded as one of football's first attacking full-backs, Giacinto Facchetti is one of the legendary figures in Inter Milan's history and one of the greatest ever Italian players. He spent eighteen years with the club, enjoying every high and enduring every low in Inter's history. Indeed, Inter, in recent years, following his death in 2006 at the age of sixty-four, have 'retired' his No.3 jersey. And for a defender, he had an impressive goalscoring tally, netting fifty-nine for the club. Inter was his club, and in his later years, he became president of the club, having previously occupied a number of executive positions at the San Siro.

GIANFRANCO BEDIN

The midfielder spent ten years with Inter Milan between 1964 and '74, having joined the club as a nineteen-year-old. He could be utilised in a defensive role in the middle of the park or as a box-to-box player, and his ability to read the game, as well as his skill in a man-marking role, made him an important player for Helenio Herrera. He made over 300 appearances for the club, scoring twenty-three goals, and winning three league titles, as well as the European Cup in 1965 before he left for Sampdoria in 1974. He retired in 1981 after further spells with Varese, Livorno and Rondinella. He also gained six caps for Italy.

MAURO BICICLI

Midfielder Mauro Bicicli was in his third spell with Inter Milan when he lined up against Celtic in the European Cup final. He first joined Inter back in 1953 at the age of eighteen, although he only made one appearance before he moved to Parma. From there, he joined Catania, but in 1957 he returned to the San Siro, and this time he spent six years with Inter, making nearly 150 appearances. He left the club in 1963, having helped them win the league title, joining Genoa and thus missing out on Inter's European Cup and World Club Championship successes. However, he returned to the San Siro for the third time in 1966, and spent that season with Inter, playing his final game for the club in the European Cup final. Spells at Vicenza and Brecia followed before he hung up his boots in 1969, going into management, with his first position as boss at Brecia. He passed away in August 2001 at the age of sixty-six.

MARIO CORSO

A strong and pacy winger, Mario Corso joined Inter Milan in 1957 and would remain at the club until 1973, facing Celtic in the '67 European Cup final and then, though he missed out on the 1972 semi-final clash. He had made his debut for the club at the age of sixteen in a Coppa Italia match, scoring to become Inter's youngest ever goalscorer. He garnered an impressive four league titles, two European Cups and two Intercontinental Cups during his time at the San Siro, and his ability to deliver pinpoint crosses into the box, or score from free-kicks, was used to great effect by Helenio Herrera. He spent two years with Genoa, from 1973 to '75, before he retired, his place as an Inter legend long since assured.

ANGELO DOMENGHINI

A forward who could play in a variety of attacking roles, Angelo Domenghini joined Inter Milan in 1964, swapping the blue and black of Atalanta, where he'd won the Coppa Italia the previous year, for the same colours of Inter. And his first season at the San Siro was a success as he helped his side win the Serie A title and the European Cup with a 1-0 victory over Benfica in the final. He was fast and skilful, with an eye for goal too, and those attributes were utilised by club and country – he won the European Championship with Italy in 1968 and was a World Cup runner-up two years later. He moved to Cagliari in 1969, and won the Serie A title with them in his first season. He eventually hung up his boots in 1979 at the age of thirty-eight.

SANDRO MAZZOLA

One of the greatest players that Italy has ever produced, the man who converted Inter Milan's penalty in the 1967 European Cup final, devoted his entire playing career to the Nerazzurri, playing for seventeen years, from 1960 to '77. He came from good football stock – his father, Valentino, had been a professional footballer with Torino, and he died in 1949 in the Superga Air Disaster, when the plane carrying the great Torino side of the late 1940s crashed into the mountains outside Turin. Sandro Mazzola was only six at the time. His younger brother, Ferruccio, who died in 2013, was also at Inter in the 1960s, but he would only make one appearance for the club. Sandro Mazzola could play in a number of attacking roles and was a key member of La Grande Inter, scoring well over a century of goals for the club. He also scored the first penalty in the 1972 shoot-out at Celtic Park which the Italian side won.

RENATO CAPPELLINI

A striker who began his career with Inter Milan in 1963, Cappellini's goals were crucial in that 1966/67 European Cup campaign for his side. He scored in both legs of the quarter-final victory over then holders, Real Madrid, and then, more crucially, netted the only goal of the game in the 1-0 semi-final play-off win against CSKA of Bulgaria. And it was Cappellini who was fouled by Jim Craig to give Inter a penalty just seven minutes into the European Cup final in Lisbon, a spot-kick that Sandro Mazzola converted. It was Cappellini's only European Cup final – he had missed out on the 1964 and '65 successes, and after five years with the club he left for Varese in 1968, before moving to Roma a year later.

HELENIO HERRERA

Inter Milan's Argentinian manager was one of the most influential football figures of the late 1950s and '60s, honing his skills with Barcelona between 1958 and '60 before moving to Italy and achieving great success at the San Siro, both domestically and in European competition, with the European Cup won in 1964 and retained a year later. Helenio Herrera had actually moved into football management in the mid-1940s, first enjoying success with Atletico Madrid, where he won two league titles. He would repeat that success later with Barcelona before taking it to a different level with Inter Milan between 1960 and '68.

Some of the things he introduced into football management were revolutionary at the time, believing in motivational techniques which included pep-talk phrases. Discipline was always strict under the Argentinian, while he also enforced a dietary plan that also included a diktat forbidding players from drinking and smoking. There was also the introduction of a pre-match retreat, which allowed him to work with his team without distraction for a couple of days before each game. And he is also said to have been one of the first managers to identify the importance of supporters and referring to them as 'the twelfth player'.

With Inter Milan, he employed a 'Catenaccio' system, with a five-man defence that usually had the captain, Armando Picchi, as a sweeper behind the back-four, though he did encourage the use of attacking full-backs in the shape of Giacinto Facchetti and Tarcisio Burgnich, something that Jock Stein would later employ to great effect against Inter Milan in 1967 with Jim Craig and Tommy Gemmell.

Inter Milan would be a dominant side in the 1960s under Herrera, winning three league titles in 1963, '65 and '66, and two European Cups in 1964 and '65. They also won the Intercontinental Cup on two occasions. Their third European Cup final appearance came in 1967, and the victory for Celtic, whose brand of fast, attacking play proved too much for the more defensively-minded approach of Inter, also signalled the end of La Grande Inter's era, and Helenio Herrera left the club in 1968, though he did return for the 1973/74 season. He died in November 1997 at the age of eighty-seven.

LISBOA
25 DE MAIO DE
1967
CELTIC 2-1 INTER
CELTIC FC
50° ANIVERSARIO

THE REFEREE

THE REFEREE

Kurt Tschenscher was the German referee who officiated at the 1967 European Cup final in Lisbon. In a match relatively lacking in robust, illegal challenging, he was still involved in a moment of controversy when he awarded Inter Milan a penalty just seven minutes into the game. He had adjudged Jim Craig to have fouled Renato Cappellini inside the box after the Italian forward cut across from the left-hand side. Sandro Mazzola duly converted the spot-kick.

The referee had already been in charge of an Inter game that season – their first European Cup tie of the 1966/67 campaign when they beat Torpedo Moscow 1-0 in the San Siro Stadium, and he was widely regarded as one of Europe's top referees. It was also the second consecutive European Cup final refereered by an official from West Germany, with Tschenscher's fellow countryman, Rudolf Kreitlein, having taken charge of Real Madrid's victory over Partizan Belgrade.

To mark the twenty-fifth anniversary of Celtic's Lisbon triumph, the club magazine, the *Celtic View*, interviewed Kurt Tschenscher about his memories of that 1967 final. And the West German whistler, who passed away in August 2014 at the age of eighty-five, remained resolute in his belief that he'd made the correct decision in giving Inter Milan their penalty against Celtic.

'At the time there was no doubt in my mind that the award was correct. Today (1992), I have no reason to view this decision differently. Although I had officiated at the 1962 European Cup-Winners' Cup final between Atletico Madrid and Fiorentina in Stuttgart, the match at Lisbon was the only occasion in which I was given the great honour of taking charge of the Champions Cup final. Prior to the match, I must confess to having little knowledge about Celtic. Internazionale arrived in Portugal as the team with the name and the reputation, but at the end of the final everybody wanted to know about the side from Glasgow.

'As the match progressed, Celtic took total control and their eventual victory was totally merited. For me there was no doubt the Scots were the better team and the result was the correct one. It was a great day for Scottish football as the Celtic team had become European champions, displaying all the qualities that epitomised the Scottish game.

'Having officiated at a number of matches involving British sides, I never experienced any problems with on-the-field discipline, and Celtic were no exception. They were a hard, strong and disciplined side but also a very fair side. Their fitness in the final was of a very high standard and an important factor in breaking down the resolute resistance of the Internazionale defence. After the game, all the Celtic supporters came on the field and began to cut up pieces of turf as souvenirs of their side's victory. There must be a few gardens in Scotland whose lawns are a permanent memory of the Estadio.

'In 1968, the year after Lisbon, I visited Glasgow to referee the European Cup match between Celtic and Dynamo Kyiv, and two years later officiated in the San Siro when AC Milan played Celtic in the same competition. Although it was a pleasure to again referee a match involving Celtic, I don't think I was a good omen for the team as they failed to progress in the competition after either tie!'

THE FANS

THE FANS

It was a case of planes, trains and automobiles for the Celtic supporters who decided to make the journey to Lisbon for the European Cup on May 25, 1967. Over ten thousand made the journey, most of them venturing outside Britain for the very first time, but it was a worthwhile trip as they saw their team make history with the 2-1 victory over Inter Milan. And even all these years later, the memory of that incredible time remains just as vivid, with each moment recalled with real fondness…

'I didn't sleep at all that night so excited was I about the next day's adventure. The day had arrived at last. May 25, 1967. Ever since that April afternoon when I sat straining to hear the crackling wireless transmission from Prague when we battled our way to a 0-0 draw, all I could think about was Lisbon.

I was a thirteen-year-old schoolboy from the Gorbals, and my Dad and brothers, Jimmy and John, were all members of the Sarsfield Celtic Supporters' Club whose bus left from the Tavern pub in Florence Street. A few days after the match in Prague my Dad announced that he thought that the club should charter a plane to Lisbon. We chartered the plane and had to pay a deposit of £300 for the privilege. That was a lot of money in 1967. Adverts were placed in the supporters' columns of the *Times* and *Citizen*, and the demand was instant. Supporters from Glasgow, Stirling, Perth, Wick, England and even Germany called to book their places on the flight. The sense of anticipation mounted as the great day neared…

And I can still remember how I felt when Stevie Chalmers scored the winner with five minutes remaining. I wasn't nervous, I just knew as did everyone watching that it was over. We were witnessing the greatest day in Celtic's history. A dream had come true! At the final whistle my Dad embraced me with tears in his eyes. There was only one challenge left. The six feet wide moat that stood between us and the pitch. At first we stood and drank in the scene before us as the Celtic fans charged on to the turf. Eventually, adrenalin pumping, we leaped and joined the throng.'
GORDON COWAN

'I was just eighteen when we got to the European Cup final. At the time we reached the final, I used to work with my father and we'd canvas round the doors for shoe repairs in Eastwood and Mansewood – my father ran a shoe-repair business – and we kept hearing wee flashes from the radio, and we were overjoyed when we found it that it had finished 0-0.

It cost me £29 to get there – I was only earning about £18 or £20 a week, so it cost me a week-and-a-half's wages, but both my grandfather and my father helped me pay the money. I went out with one of my friends and we flew from Glasgow Airport – it was Abbotsinch Airport back then. I lived in Pollok at the time so we got a lift into St Enoch's Square, and because it was a holiday of obligation we went to Mass first and, of course, St Andrew's Cathedral was packed full of Celtic fans who were all going to the game.

It was the first time in my life I had ever flown, and it was also my first time abroad. The atmosphere on the plane was great – it was a singsong all the way to Lisbon. I was 100 per cent confident that we were going to win because we had a great team, but I was so excited that in the second-half, when we were standing behind the goal where Celtic scored their goals, my hands locked – the five fingers closed over and I couldn't open my hands because it was intense, but when Tommy Gemmell scored, they opened up and we were all going crazy and I was fine after that because we knew we were going to win.'
JOE LYONS

'I was twenty-three at the time we reached Lisbon. I was working in London at the time so I hadn't managed to see many of the matches on the way to Lisbon that season, but after we'd reached the final I got a phone-call from my Dad asking me if I fancied going to the European Cup final. There were four of us who flew out – me, my Dad and my brothers, Tony and Jimmy.

I came back up to Dundee to meet up with my Dad and my brothers and then we flew out to Lisbon on the day of the game. When Inter got the penalty, it was disappointing to say the least, but it didn't seem to upset the team and they just kept going forward, and I felt that despite Inter leading 1-0, there was only going to be one team who would win.

When Tommy Gemmell scored, it was incredible, and Celtic kept going all-out for the winner, and after Stevie Chalmers scored, I could hardly bear the last few minutes – it was probably the longest few minutes of my Celtic-supporting life, but when the final whistle went, that was the best moment ever. And, for me, it was extra special because I was there with my Dad and my brothers to see our team win the European Cup.'
JOE CARROLL

'I was twenty-one at the time of Lisbon and it was great to get a couple of days off to go out to the European Cup final because I'd been at all the home matches that season in the campaign. Vojvodina was the hardest game for us on the road to the final, and we were on a roll that season and everyone felt there was something special about Jock Stein and the team and the way they were playing – beautiful football.

My Dad had made a promise that, if we got to the final, he'd take us, and I was despatched through to Glasgow to book our flights and get our tickets, although it was my Dad who looked after the tickets when we headed out there. It was my first time abroad and it was a great adventure for us. I'd travelled to Lisbon with a three-piece suit on and a pair of winkle-pickers, and when we arrived in Lisbon the heat was awesome.

Inter Milan were a fantastic side, and it was a bit worrying when they took the lead, but Celtic just kept pushing forward and Sarti, the Inter goalkeeper, had the most amazing game. We were all ecstatic when Tommy Gemmell scored and it seemed like the whole stadium erupted in celebration. And when Stevie Chalmers scored the winner, we knew we'd done something great but I don't think it really hit me just how special it really was until we returned to Glasgow and there were hundreds of fans at the airport waiting for the team, and they were clapping all the fans through. That's when we knew that we'd done something really special.'

TONY CARROLL

'I was thirty and working at Prestwick Airport in 1967 as a meteorologist and that's where I really got my love of Celtic because several of the guys who worked with me took me to a Celtic versus Clyde game in January 1967, and it all took off from there, and I saw the home games against Vojvodina and Dukla Prague.

I was from Edinburgh and, in my earlier days, had been a Hibernian fan, but once you get the Celtic bug and the great devotion to the club, that never leaves you, and it never has for me. The Estadio Nacional in Lisbon was an unusually shaped stadium and it's great when we've been back to Lisbon to see the stadium just as it looked in 1967. And when we won the European Cup, there was a real sense that we had achieved something special and that it would be something which would be talked about and remembered for many years.

It was a terrific feeling when the final whistle sounded, and to think that all the players came from within a thirty-mile radius of Celtic Park was tremendous. I did go on the pitch and I managed to retrieve a bit of turf, but much to my eternal regret, it has been mislaid at some point over the years so I no longer have it unfortunately.'

MIKE ROGERSON

'I was actually in the Kimberley pub in Tollcross, which is where we left from for the final, when we heard the news from Prague that we'd drawn 0-0 and we were in the European Cup final. And then we started booking the flights and everything for getting to Lisbon. There were about twenty-two of us left from the pub.

When we got off the plane, I remember there were planes everywhere – on the tarmac, the grass verges – and there were thousands of Celtic fans. We didn't really know too much about Inter Milan except what we'd read in the newspapers, but we knew they were a good team because they'd won the European Cup twice already. And when we got to Lisbon, all you heard was the Portuguese people shouting 'Celtica! Celtica!', and they took us to their hearts. Nobody was shouting for Inter Milan. I was eleven when I started going to see Celtic in 1951 with my brother, John, and then to see Celtic lift the European Cup sixteen years later was incredible.'
FRANK McFARLANE

'I was twenty at the time of Lisbon. It was a dream for Celtic to get to the European Cup final.

It was the first time I was ever on a plane, and it was unbelievable. And before we landed, there was a hat passed round for the air stewardesses. It's what we did when we were on the bus to an away game – a hat for the driver – so we did for the girls on the plane.

When we got the bus to the stadium, we took two Portuguese boys with us and my brother-in-law, Dan, was determined to get them in to see the game. We were all singing Celtic songs and one of the boys wanted to sing. There was a microphone at the front of the bus, so the boy got the microphone and kicked off his shoes and started singing *Puppet On A String* in Portuguese, and the whole bus went mad. It was a big hit in Europe after Sandie Shaw won the Eurovision Song Contest with it. When Stevie Chalmers scored the winner it was hard to believe. We made our way down to the front, ready to go on the park when the final whistle went.'
JIMMY PRENTICE

THE ROAD TO LISBON

THE ROAD TO LISBON

ZURICH

FIRST ROUND, FIRST LEG
September 28, 1966
Celtic Park • Att: 50,000

CELTIC 2
Gemmell 64, McBride 69

FC ZURICH 0

Celtic: Simpson; Gemmell, O'Neill;
Murdoch, McNeill, Clark; Johnstone,
McBride, Chalmers, Auld, Hughes.

FC Zurich: Iten; Munsch, Leimgruber;
Stierli, Neumann, Brodmann; Khun,
Martinelli, Bani, Meyer, Kunzl.

FIRST ROUND, SECOND LEG
October 5, 1966
Stadion Letzigrund • Att: 23,000

FC ZURICH 0

CELTIC 3
Gemmell 22 & 48 pen, Chalmers 38

FC Zurich: Iten; Munsch, Kyburz;
Neumann, Stierli, Leimgruber, Khun,
Bani, Kunzl, Sturmer, Kubala.

Celtic: Simpson; Gemmell, O'Neill;
Murdoch, McNeill, Clark; Johnstone,
Lennox, Chalmers, Auld, Hughes.

NANTES

SECOND ROUND, FIRST LEG
November 30, 1966
Stade Marcel Saupin • Att: 25,000

NANTES 1
Magny 16

CELTIC 3
McBride 24, Lennox 50, Chalmers 67

Nantes: Castel; le Chenadec, Budzinski;
Robin, De Michele, Kovacevik; Suaudeau,
Blanchet, Simon, Magny, Michel.

Celtic: Simpson; Gemmell, O'Neill;
Murdoch, McNeill, Clark; Johnstone,
Chalmers, McBride, Lennox, Auld.

SECOND ROUND, SECOND LEG
December 7, 1966
Celtic Park • Att: 41,000

CELTIC 3
Johnstone 13, Chalmers 56, Lennox 78

NANTES 1
Georgen 36

Celtic: Simpson; Gemmell, O'Neill;
Murdoch, McNeill, Clark; Johnstone,
Gallagher, Chalmers, Auld, Lennox.

Nantes: Georgin; Le Chenadec,
Budzinski; Robin, Grabowski,
Kovacevik; Georgen, Blanchet, Simon,
Magny, Michel.

VOJVODINA

QUARTER-FINAL, FIRST LEG
March 1, 1967
Stadion Gradskie • Att: 30,000

VOJVODINA 1
Stanic 69

CELTIC 0

Vojvodina: Pantelic; Aleksic, Radovic;
Nesticki, Brzic, Dakic, Rakic, Radosav,
Sekeres, Djordjic, Stanic.

Celtic: Simpson; Craig, Gemmell;
Murdoch, McNeill, Clark; Johnstone,
Lennox, Chalmers, Auld, Hughes.

QUARTER-FINAL, SECOND LEG
March 8, 1967
Celtic Park • Att: 75,000

CELTIC 2
Chalmers 58, McNeill 90

VOJVODINA 0

Celtic: Simpson, Craig, Gemmell;
Murdoch, McNeill, Clark; Johnstone,
Lennox, Chalmers, Gallagher, Hughes.

Vojvodina: Pantelic; Aleksic, Radovic;
Sekeres, Brzic, Nesticki; Rakic, Dakic,
Radosav, Trivic, Pusibric.

DUKLA PRAGUE

SEMI-FINAL, FIRST LEG
April 12, 1967
Celtic Park • Att: 75,000

CELTIC 3
Johnstone 27, Wallace 59 & 65

DUKLA PRAGUE 1
Stunc 44

Celtic: Simpson; Craig, Gemmell;
Murdoch, McNeill, Clark; Johnstone,
Wallace; Chalmers; Auld, Hughes.

Dukla Prague: Viktor; Cmarada, Cadek;
Taborsky, Zlocha, Geleta; Strunc, Dvorak,
Masopust, Nederost, Vacenovsky.

SEMI-FINAL, SECOND LEG
April 25, 1967
Stadion Julisce • Att: 22,000

DUKLA PRAGUE 0

CELTIC 0

Dukla Prague: Viktor; Cmarada;
Novak; Taborsky, Zlocha, Geleta;
Strunc, Pnebort, Masopust, Nederost,
Vacenovsky.

Celtic: Simpson; Craig, Gemmell;
Murdoch, McNeill, Clark; Johnstone,
Wallace; Chalmers; Auld, Hughes.

INTER MILAN

FINAL
May 25, 1967
Estadio Nacional, Lisbon, Portugal
Att: 55,000

CELTIC 2
Gemmell 62, Chalmers 85

INTERNAZIONALE MILAN 1
Mazzola 7

Celtic: Simpson; Craig, Gemmell; Murdoch, McNeill, Clark; Johnstone, Wallace, Chalmers, Auld, Lennox.

Inter Milan: Sarti; Burgnich, Facchetti; Bedin, Guarneri, Picchi; Domenghini, Cappellini, Mazzola, Bicicli, Corso.

	APPS	GOALS
Stevie Chalmers	9	5
John Clark	9	-
Tommy Gemmell	9	4
Jimmy Johnstone	9	2
Billy McNeill	9	1
Bobby Murdoch	9	-
Ronnie Simpson	9	-
Bertie Auld	8	-
Bobby Lennox	7	2
Jim Craig	5	-
John Hughes	5	-
Willie O'Neill	4	-
Willie Wallace	3	2
Charlie Gallagher	2	–
Joe McBride	2	2

ACKNOWLEDGEMENTS

ACKNOWLEDGEMENTS

The story of Celtic's 1967 European Cup triumph is one that is well-known and well-loved by supporters of all generations, a high point in the history of a unique football club. The fiftieth anniversary of that extraordinary achievement on May 25, 1967 in Lisbon's Estadio Nacional is the perfect opportunity to relive that momentous season and pay homage to the men who turned a dream into a green and white reality, and that is what this book sets out to do.

In writing the story of the 1966/67 season, which culminated in Celtic beating Inter Milan 2-1 to become the Kings of Europe, I have drawn on the archives of the club's official publication, the *Celtic View*, along with a host of reference books and player biographies and autobiographies, all of which are listed in a bibliography and, where possible, acknowledged in the course of the book. There can be no other club with such a rich literary history to call upon, and my grateful thanks go to all of those other Celtic writers whose work is always enlightening, entertaining and inspiring.

In particular, I want to thank my *Celtic View* colleague, Joe Sullivan. His Celtic knowledge is both impressive and invaluable, and he has been a great help throughout this project. And to my Celtic colleagues, Audrey Baird and Fiona Smith, who have worked tirelessly behind the scenes to help the book come to fruition.

In focusing on each of the eleven men who played in the Lisbon final, I have also used archive Celtic multi-media interviews with the players in order to tell the story 'in their own words'. This proved invaluable given that, sadly, some of them are no longer with us.

And it is to the Lisbon Lions – the squad of players who contributed to that European campaign – our legendary manager, Jock Stein, assistant, Sean Fallon, and the backroom staff, that the gratitude of every Celtic supporter continues to be directed. Their success in Lisbon back in 1967 has long been celebrated in story and song, and will continue to be so wherever and whenever Celtic supporters gather together to celebrate our beloved Hoops … a grand old team to play for and a grand old team to see.

Paul Cuddihy

September 2016

BIBLIOGRAPHY

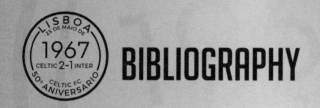

BIBLIOGRAPHY

The Lisbon Lions: A Celebration of the European Cup campaign 1967: Andy Dougan

One Afternoon In Lisbon: Kevin McCarra & Pat Woods

The Lisbon Lions: The Real Inside Story of Celtic's European Cup Triumph: Alex Gordon

Celtic In Europe: From the Sixties to Seville: Graham McColl

Jock Stein: The Celtic Years: Tom Campbell & David Potter

Jock Stein: The Definitive Biography: Archie Macpherson

Sure It's A Grand Old Team To Play For: Ronnie Simpson

A Lion Looks Back: Jim Craig

The Big Shot: Tommy Gemmell

Lion Heart: Tommy Gemmell

All The Best: Tommy Gemmell

All The Way With Celtic: Bobby Murdoch

For Celtic And Scotland: Billy McNeill

Hail Cesar!: Billy McNeill

Fire In My Boots: Jimmy Johnstone

Jinky ... Now And Then: Jimmy Johnstone

Heart of A Lion: Willie Wallace

The Winning Touch: Stevie Chalmers

A Bhoy Called Bertie: Bertie Auld

My Story: Bobby Lennox

Yogi Bare: John Hughes

Keeping In Paradise: John Fallon

Charlie Gallagher? What A Player: David Potter

Celtic View archives: 1965 – 1967

Daily Record archives: 1966/67 European Cup campaign match reports

125 Years of Competitive Matches: David Potter & Marie Rowan

The Celtic Football Companion: David Docherty

An Alphabet of the Celts: Eugene MacBride, George Sheridan, Martin O'Connor

Celtic: A Complete Record 1888-1992: Paul Lunney

The Essential History of Celtic: Graham McColl & George Sheridan